Anthropological Studies of Education

Series Editor
Amy Stambach
University of Wisconsin
Madison, WI, USA

This series examines the political, ideological, and power-laden dimensions of education from an anthropological perspective. Books in this series look at how society is defined in relation to education. It delves into the kinds of communities that are imagined through educational policies, curricula, institutions, and programming. Many books in the series use ethnography to capture diverse educational positions and experiences. The series uses concepts such as social practice, myth-making, political organization, and economic exchange to address substantive issues pertaining to education in the moment and over time.

More information about this series at
http://www.palgrave.com/gp/series/14767

Helen E. Ullrich
Editor

The Impact of Education in South Asia

Perspectives from Sri Lanka to Nepal

Editor
Helen E. Ullrich
Tulane University Medical School
New Orleans, LA, USA

Anthropological Studies of Education
ISBN 978-3-319-96606-9   ISBN 978-3-319-96607-6   (eBook)
https://doi.org/10.1007/978-3-319-96607-6

Library of Congress Control Number: 2018949320

This Palgrave Macmillan imprint is published by the registered company Springer Nature Switzerland AG
The registered company address is: Gewerbestrasse 11, 6330 Cham, Switzerland

In Memory of
Pauline M. Kolenda
Scholar, Mentor, Friend

FOREWORD

This book project started with a 2015 panel to honor the memory of Dr. Pauline Kolenda at the American Anthropological Association conference in Denver, Colorado. The four panelists, all of whom are included in this volume, amply recognized her contributions to sociology, social anthropology, and South Asian studies generally.

Students and colleagues alike have benefitted from Dr. Kolenda's methodological strengths, as well as her commitment to support and describe the plight of the powerless and marginalized members of society, especially Dalits (Scheduled Castes) and women. She strongly promoted their rights, including rights to education. She participated in one of the earliest India community studies, and she conducted research in several different South Asian regions, using both statistical and qualitative analysis methods.

It is indeed an honor to participate in the coming-together of this distinguished group of scholars. All have long experience of South Asian life, urban and rural. Three of the five larger South Asian countries are represented in this collection, including a diverse group of Indian states. These papers include histories of education: national policy changes in mid-twentieth century Nepal; a school building frenzy in Sri Lanka starting in the early 1900s; the evolution of Christian missionary schooling in a district of Tamil Nadu. These authors' close connections with multiple generations support nuanced views of personal and family life, the lives of men and women, of boys and girls, of multiple status groups. Their understandings shed a great deal of light on the ways that specific families and communities do or do not connect with schools and the educational system as a whole. Such in-depth research strategies show that small-scale studies can help us to understand large-scale trends.

Formal education poses challenges to South Asian society, as we see in these studies. But social institutions also challenge education systems. Regarding the first challenge, we see that the dramatic increases in access to primary, secondary, and higher education in all parts of the subcontinent have profoundly affected social life: gender roles, household organization, the "patrilineal/patriarchal/patrifocal" family, and even the caste system. Some of these papers argue that widespread formal education is contributing to a shift from caste to socioeconomic class as a basis of social status. As more and more people become educated, livelihood patterns change. Indigenous knowledge and skills may be eclipsed by the prestige associated with formal education. Men and women alike are finding (or seeking) new types of employment. Parents and other guardians have come to view children's education as an investment in their own long-term welfare. While arranged marriages still are the norm, "love marriages" may result from young people attending college and university together. Families are responding in a variety of new ways to their children's changed attitudes and practices.

Many of these authors talk about the social tensions produced by sending girls to school, but virtually in all places, families have overcome fear of perceived dangers to family honor, and so on, and have been sending more and more of their girls to school. In places where it was the norm, the purdah system is affected by this change. Women with education tend to feel empowered and hopeful that they can be more or less self-sufficient when facing life's inevitable crises.

The other challenge is that which society poses to the educational system itself. While most of this group of authors take a generally positive view, some strongly criticize the system. Educational institutions can reflect and reproduce society's internal divisions and discrimination patterns, rather than acting as forces for positive change. Rural, low caste, and poor people tend to receive inferior educational services. The government-run schools they usually attend may be poorly equipped, and the teachers, even if well trained, offer little more than rote learning opportunities. Humiliation is too often part of the school experience of poor children, especially for those of the lowest castes. Some types of for-profit educational institutions are not much better, though they are perceived as superior. India, in particular, may not be creating institutions that properly educate all citizens. (There is not enough detail on other South Asian countries in this volume to parallel that on India.) Even prestigious and costly primary and secondary schools depend heavily on families to support students' educational progress with extensive tutoring. Some of these reports suggest that only schools for the socially elite are working well by international standards.

This collection, then, poses some difficult questions with policy implications. What actually *is* "education" in South Asia? Does the concept extend far beyond minimal literacy and numeracy? Is the "curriculum" presented in meaningful ways? Does the educational experience work equally well for students from all walks of life? If not, why not? What could be done to improve the quality of teaching and the management of government schools and others serving children of low status families? This group of papers can help us to think creatively about these and other pressing education issues.

Pasadena, California   Suzanne Hanchett Ph.D.
                                                       Partner, Planning Alternatives
                                                                   for Change LLC

ACKNOWLEDGEMENTS

The contributors to this book have provided a panoramic perspective on the impact of education in India, Sri Lanka, and Nepal. I thank them for presenting diverse views in their interesting and well-written chapters. An edited volume owes as much to the contributors as to the editor. Indeed, each chapter has enriched my comprehension of the evolution and current status of education in different areas of the subcontinent.

I am grateful to the Palgrave Macmillan staff for their unvarying support. At the 2015 American Anthropological Association meetings in Denver, Colorado, Mireille Yanow expressed interest in publishing the papers of the panel commemorating Pauline M. Kolenda, a panel I chaired. Alexis Nelson ushered the nascent book to contract. Kyra Saniewski has promptly responded to my numerous questions and assisted me throughout the manuscript preparation. Sharon Rajkumar has stepped in when Kyra Saniewski has been unavailable. Mary Al-Sayed has also facilitated the path to publication. Amy Stambach, the editor of the Anthropological Studies of Education, has also contributed to the path toward the publication of this volume. In conclusion, I am impressed with the efficiency and accuracy of the project manager, Sridevi Purushothaman, and her production team at Springer. My experience working with the Palgrave Macmillan editorial staff has proven a welcome collaboration. I also wish to express my appreciation to the anonymous reviewers of the manuscript and to those who contributed to the transformation of the manuscript into a book.

CONTENTS

NOTES ON CONTRIBUTORS

Geoffrey L. Burkhart is Associate Professor Emeritus in the Department of Anthropology, American University, Washington DC, USA. His fieldwork in India has centered on a village in northern Tamil Nadu and in the town of Polur. He has published on issues of social structure, research with retired Danish women missionaries, and with gay men in the South Asian diaspora.

Ann Grodzins Gold is the Thomas J. Watson Professor of Religion and Professor of Anthropology at Syracuse University, USA. During the academic year 2014–15 she held fellowship awards from the Guggenheim Foundation and the National Humanities Center to support writing a book, *Shiptown: Between Rural and Urban North India* (University of Pennsylvania Press, 2017). Gold's earlier publications include numerous articles and four books: *Fruitful Journeys: The Ways of Rajasthani Pilgrims* (1988); *A Carnival of Parting: The Tales of King Bharthari and King Gopi Chand* (1992); *Listen to the Heron's Words: Reimagining Gender and Kinship in North India* (1994, co-authored with Gloria Raheja); and *In the Time of Trees and Sorrows: Nature, Power and Memory in Rajasthan* (2002, co-authored with Bhoju Ram Gujar), which in 2004 was awarded the Ananda Kentish Coomaraswamy Book Prize from the Association for Asian Studies.

Chinu Gujar lives in Bhilwara, Rajasthan; she holds B.A. and M.A. degrees in the natural sciences as well as a B.Ed.; she aspires to a career in education.

Ghumar Gujar lives in Jamoli village, Rajasthan; she holds degrees in Hindi, and has recently completed her B.Ed. as she plans to be a teacher.

Madhu Gujar is a Sales Promoter for the Himalaya Baby Care Company in Bhilwara, Rajasthan; she has B.A. and M.A. degrees in Sanskrit and Hindi literatures, as well as a B.Ed., and aims to become a teacher.

Suzanne Hanchett a social/cultural anthropologist based in the USA, has worked as an applied anthropologist in international development since 1991. Her focus, mainly on Bangladesh, has been on gender and development and on water and sanitation issues as a consultant to organizations such as UNICEF, CARE, and WaterAid. She did her dissertation research in Karnataka State, India, and has taught at Queens College (City University of New York), Bard College, and Barnard College. From 1979 to 1991 she worked as a practicing anthropologist, focusing on community development, reproductive health, teen pregnancy, and child welfare in New York City. Her publications include two books: *Coloured Rice; Symbolic Structure in Hindu Family Festivals* (1988), and *Water Culture in South Asia: Bangladesh Perspectives* (2014), as well as a number of articles in peer-reviewed journals.

Nita Kumar is Brown Family Professor of South Asian History at Claremont McKenna College, Claremont, California. Her books and articles include *Artisans of Banaras* (Princeton, 1998), *Friends, Brothers and Informants* (Berkeley, 1992); *Women as Subjects* (Virginia, 1994); *Mai: A translation* (Kali, 2001); *Lessons from Schools* (Sage, 2001), *The Politics of Gender, Community and Modernities* (Oxford, 2007); and she is working on two books called *Educating the Child: The Family-School Relationship in India* and *Education and the Rise of a New Indian Intelligentsia*. From 1990 she has also been engaged in innovative education in Varanasi, India, through both service and advocacy, working with children, teachers and families to develop curricula, fiction for children, arts materials, and teachers' training units (www.nirman.info).

Sarah LeVine was educated at Oxford and the University of Chicago and received a Ph.D., in Sanskrit, Religion & Anthropology from Harvard. As a research associate in the Harvard Graduate School of Education in Massachusetts, USA, she studied family life, the socialization of children, the impact of maternal schooling on reproductive and child health in sub Saharan Africa, Latin America, and South Asia, and religious belief and practice in the Buddhist Himalayas. She is the author and coauthor of numerous academic monographs and most recently, with Robert A. LeVine, *Do Parents Matter? Why Japanese Babies Sleep Soundly, Mexican Siblings Don't Fight, and American Parents should Just Relax* (Public Affairs 2016).

Carol C. Mukhopadhyay Professor Emerita, Anthropology, San Jose State University, USA, specializes in gender, family, sexuality, race/ethnicity, methodology and comparative education, in India and USA. Her publications include "Gender and Trump," 2017 (http://www.socialjusticejournal.org/gender-and-trump/), "Gender and Sexuality" (with T. Blumenfield), 2017, in *Perspectives* (http://www.perspectivesanthro.org/); *How Real is Race?* 2014, (with R. Henze and Y. Moses); A Feminist Cognitive Anthropology: The Case of Women and Mathematics 2004. *Ethos*; How Exportable are Western Theories of Gendered Science? 2009 in N. Kumar, *Women and Science in India*; *Women, Education and Family Structure in India* (with S. Seymour), 1994; "Sati or Shakti: Women, Culture and Politics in India." 1982. In J. O'Barr, *Perspectives on Power*. Website: www.sjsu.edu/people/carol.mukhopadhyay.

Shailaja Paik an Associate Professor of History at the University of Cincinnati, USA, is the author of *Dalit Women's Education in Modern India: Double Discrimination* (Routledge, 2014) and several articles. She is currently working on her second book that examines the politics of caste, class, gender, sexuality, art and aesthetics, community and nation in popular culture in modern Maharashtra. Her work has been funded by the National Endowment for the Humanities-American Institute of Indian Studies, Ford Foundation, Yale University, Emory University, Indian Council for Social Science Research, and the Charles Phelps Taft Center, among others.

R. Thomas Rosin Professor Emeritus of Anthropology and Linguistics, Sonoma State University, trained in anthropology at Reed College (1960, B.A.), University of Chicago, and University of California at Berkeley (1968, Ph.D.). R. Thomas Rosin has researched the village Gangwa in the context of regional variations within Rajasthan, India across forty years, with a book on land reform ("Land Reform and Agrarian Change: Study of a *Marwar* Village from *Raj* to *Swaraj*," [Jaipur: Rawat Press, 1987]), and articles on adaptation, groundwater irrigation, ethno-mathematics, architecture, the built environment, sibling-set marriage and joint family, traffic and trash. He just completed a memoir of a mid-career year of fieldwork titled "Entangled: Research and Romance in a *Rajputana* Transformed." R. Thomas Rosin is based in California, USA.

Susan C. Seymour is Jean M. Pitzer Professor Emerita of Anthropology at Pitzer College, Claremont, California. She has been doing research in India since the 1960s. Her books include *The Transformation of A Sacred Town: Bhubaneswar, India* (1980), *Women, Education, and Family Structure in India* (co-edited and authored with Carol Chapnick Mukhopadhyay, 1994), *Asian College Women's Aspirations: A Comparative Study of the Effects of Maternal Employment* (co-authored with Carolyn D. Spatta, 1995), *Women, Family, and Child Care in India: A World in Transition* (1999), and *Cora Du Bois: Anthropologist, Diplomat, Agent* (2015). She is based in California, USA.

Helen E. Ullrich in private practice and Clinical Assistant Professor in the Department of Psychiatry and Behavioral Sciences at Tulane University Medical School in New Orleans, USA, has published articles on sociolingustics, cultural anthropology, cross-cultural psychiatry, psychiatry, and the impact of education on culture. As a linguist and cross-cultural psychiatrist, she has focused on a Karnataka community and its kinship ties throughout the world. Her three books are a linguistic description of Havyaka Kannada, *Clause Structure of Northern Havyaka Kannada (Dravidian): A Tagmemic Analysis*, (1980) an edited volume, *Competition and Modernization in South Asia* (1975), and *The Women of Totagadde Broken Silence* (2017).

A. R. Vasavi a Social Anthropologist, is based in Karnataka, India. Her academic interests are in sociology of India, agrarian studies, and sociology of education. Her publications include *Harbingers of Rain: Land and Life in South India* (Oxford Univ. Press 1999), *In an Outpost of the Global Economy* (co-edited with Carol Upadhya, Routledge, 2008), *The Inner Mirror: Translations of Kannada Writings on Society and Culture* (The Book Review Press, 2009), which is also available in Kannada as *VollaGannadi: Samakalina Samaja Mathu Samskruthi Kurita Kannada Barahaghalu*. Her most recent book is *Suicides and the Predicament of Rural India* (Three Essays Collective, 2012). Kannada University, Hampi, has brought out a collection of her writings which has been translated into Kannada. She is currently working on developing an alternative learning program for rural youth.

Deborah Winslow is Program Director for Cultural Anthropology at the National Science Foundation. A cultural anthropologist, she has conducted fieldwork periodically in Sri Lanka since 1973. She has also done research in India. She is particularly interested in regional economic and religious systems; the articulation between households, communities, and regions; and the unfolding of economic and social change over the long-term. Her work has been supported by, among others, the National Institute for Mental Health, the National Science Foundation, the National Endowment for the Humanities, the American Institute for Sri Lankan Studies, and Fulbright (in India and Sri Lanka). Her publications include two edited volumes and numerous articles, book chapters, and encyclopedia articles. Deborah Winslow is based in Washington, D.C., USA.

LIST OF FIGURES

LIST OF TABLES

CHAPTER 1

Introduction: The Impact of Education in South Asia—From Sri Lanka to Nepal

Helen E. Ullrich

A grandmother in 2008 takes her newborn grandson for his inoculations while her college-educated daughter is spending the traditional three months after delivery at her mother's home. To my surprise, the grandmother accompanied only by her infant grandson insures that he receives all the requisite inoculations and vaccines including the hepatitis vaccine. Would she have had the skills to know about the appropriate inoculations and vaccines and the initiative to take her infant grandson to the physician without some education?

One generation earlier in a Karnataka village, members of a caste emphasizing education had immunized their children against pertussis, while women of a caste without an emphasis on education believed that the goddess Mariamma caused pertussis. For these women, worshipping Mariamma was the only prevention and treatment. No child of the educated caste contracted pertussis, in contrast to every child of

H. E. Ullrich (✉)
Tulane University Medical School, New Orleans, LA, USA

© The Author(s) 2019
H. E. Ullrich (ed.), *The Impact of Education in South Asia*, Anthropological Studies of Education,
https://doi.org/10.1007/978-3-319-96607-6_1

1

the uneducated caste. This is another example of the impact of women's education on the health of their families. Since the pertussis outbreak, children of all castes in this South India village have received inoculations. Moreover, education has become available to all castes in this village.

Both of these examples highlight the importance of mothers' education to disease prevention and improved child health (http://www.uniteforsight.org/women-children-course/health-promotion-women-children; http://www.prb.org/Publications/Media-Guides/2011/girls-education-fact-sheet.aspx). Studies have shown that reduced maternal and child deaths, improved child health, a later age at marriage, decreased fertility, and improved nutrition are among the benefits of education for women and girls (http://www.prb.org/Publications/Media-Guides/2011/girls-education-fact-sheet.aspx, accessed February 24, 2018). In this volume, Sarah LeVine (Chapter 2) refers to a prior study she conducted with Robert LeVine et al. (2012) on the impact of women's education and children's health.

Benefits from education also include improved income potential for women. Women with a single year of primary school have salary increments 10–20% above those with no education. Women with a secondary school education earn 15–25% more than an uneducated woman (Behreman 2006: 147; Summers 1992; Semba 2008: 322–328; Vandemoortele and Delamonica 2000; De Walque 2004; Psacharopoulos and Patrinos 2004: 111–134 all cited in http://www.prb.org/Publications/Media-Guides/2011/girls-education-fact-sheet.aspx, accessed February 24, 2018).

The purpose of this collection, which emphasizes education throughout India, Sri Lanka, and Nepal, is to examine its impact in different geographical areas and socio-cultural groups. There are similarities and differences in the different regions. In addition to the impact on women and families, education provides professional opportunities for members of all social groups. In many places, education has prompted a shift from a caste to a class structure (Fuller and Narasimhan 2014; Ullrich 2017). The move from rural to urban areas makes possible a professional identity that supersedes caste and may extend to the home and to alterations in marriage patterns. Some younger people, while respecting their elders, have their own belief systems that allow their adaptation to the recognition of talent among those of other castes and religious groups. They credit their respect of others to their education. The chapters in this book will enable the reader to determine to what extent the impact of education has been local or extends throughout the regions represented. Moreover, the tensions which differential educational opportunities pose for women and members of different castes and socioeconomic groups bring to the surface resentments as Shailaja Paik (Chapter 6) and A.R. Vasavi (Chapter 7) illustrate. Geoffrey L. Burkhart (Chapter 8) in his focus on Christians presents another path for Dalit education, a path providing opportunities and an exit from the caste system.

An important question is, whether these advantages are available to all children in the three countries covered by this collection. The answer is a qualified yes. In India, there is compulsory education from the ages of 6–14[1]; in Sri Lanka, from 5 to 13[2]; and according to the Nepal constitution, each person has the right to education in his/her native language until the secondary level.[3] Nepal, unlike India and Sri Lanka, included the right to education in its constitution. Special laws insure governmental support for the right to education in India and Sri Lanka. The contributions to this volume suggest that with the exception of Sri Lanka, the progress in education has fallen short of the goals stated in the relevant constitutions and laws.

One might think the benefits of education were most obvious to those in Nepal, as the right to education was included in its 2007 interim constitution. The Constitution of India became effective in 1950 and that of Sri Lanka, in 1978. The policy focus on education and appreciation of its broad social advantages may have occurred after the drafting of the Constitutions of India and Sri Lanka. Deborah Winslow (Chapter 12) attributes the early interest in Sri Lankan education to British colonial policy. As in Sri Lanka, during the colonial period the British introduced western education in India. During the colonial period in India, the British introduced education with the assumption that it would lead to compliant subjects. During this same period, missionaries started schools. The missionary boarding and day schools in South India, which the Church Missionary Society and the Scottish Church Society established, were especially successful. Rather than supporting colonial subjects' subordination, western education provided new vistas and awareness of opportunities, which led to activism and rebellion (Rosin, Chapter 10).

Western education was congruent with Muslim beliefs, which held that every Muslim should learn to read their religious texts. This provided a sharp contrast with Hindu religious education. Hindu

Brahmin men were traditionally designated as the guardians of Hindu religious texts. Brahmin priests often tutored boys for a set number of years for induction into the priesthood. At times, a Brahmin would host a religious school in his home for a month or more to instruct the Brahmin boys of a village. Brahmins initially became literate in order to read the sacred texts. Men of other twice-born castes had a more practical education.

Women and Shudras[4] lacked the ritual purity to learn and read sacred literature. In a 1960s' South India village, elders scolded younger women for reading during their period of menstrual taboo, as the elders believed touching books would offend Saraswati, the goddess of learning. This example of women's inherent impurity failed to discourage these women from reading, as they disagreed with their elders. Indeed, by keeping a library of these women's favorite authors in my room, I may have alleviated their boredom during their ritual pollution, as well as unwittingly provided incentive for their questioning their inferiority with respect to the gods.

Some fathers and husbands taught their wives and daughters to read. Women, among whom Rassundari Devi is an example, taught themselves to read. "Many of the women who learned to read before the 1870s have reported hiding their accomplishments from other women[5] (Forbes 2008: 58–59, reprinted from 1996)." Occasionally, Shudras also became literate. Unlike Hindus who limited formal education to men of the twice-born category, Muslim women read religious texts. "Muslim girls were expected to learn the Quran and some accounting skills, but the strict seclusion observed by upper-class families prohibited daughters from attending schools (Forbes 2008: 58, reprinted from 1996)."

Formal school education, the focus of this book, involves literacy. However, traditional education was oral. The sharing of resources among members of the same caste meant community support as to whose crops to harvest first and the allotment of irrigation water. To negotiate, market places and cattle fairs also required practical knowledge. R. Thomas Rosin (Chapter 10) describes the co-operation of Rajasthani male tenant farmers, a sharp contrast with non-Brahmins in a South India village where the women controlled the finances and co-operated with men in decision-making and practical knowledge. From this, we know that women in some tenant farming communities were able to manage the farm work, unlike secluded women who had little opportunity to obtain practical knowledge.

Nita Kumar (2007: 11, Chapter 11) presents a more negative perspective, arguing that education displaced the Indian way of thinking with

Western patterns of thinking "in a way that enslaved them." My field observations support Nita Kumar's eloquent description of plural intellectual worlds (Kumar 2007: 12). I argue in this introduction that some did overtly display the Western manner of thinking in a Western environment while covertly combining both types of thinking. The switching back and forth may have been so automatic that the individual was unaware of the contextual shifts.

The recognized benefits and impact of education have led to compulsory education in Nepal, India, and Sri Lanka. However, one wonders whether everyone benefits. School experience can reinforce early socialization in either self-confidence or inferiority. Socioeconomic or caste status can provide a basis for either support or discrimination. According to Nambissan and Srinivasa Rao (2013: 2), economic and social pressures accompanying globalization and privatization have increased rather than decreased inequalities. This trend surely influences people's experience of educational systems.

Research on those who drop out suggests that school may fail to meet students' individual needs. Family pressures to earn a living or to help with the family business also may cause dropping out. The two chapters (Shailaja Paik, Chapter 6; A.R. Vasavi, Chapter 7) focusing on Dalits argue that even with—or because of—reserved seats, they experience greater discrimination than any other caste group. Should a Dalit earn a first class with distinction (85% or higher) or a second class (45–59%) on examinations, he or she would still occupy a reserved seat and not a "merit" seat. So merit might be unrecognized, disbelieved, or ignored. Nita Kumar in Chapter 11 describes the school curriculum and further documents inequality in the school systems.

These studies of personal experience can offer new perspectives, some possibly surprising to researchers. The case studies in this book mostly show that individuals regard education as enhancing their lives, even when they are unable to achieve their stated goals or desired careers. Ann Grodzens Gold, Chinu Gujar, Ghumar Gujar, and Madhu Gujar illustrate the importance of family encouragement in educational achievements and show that the value of education involves more than securing the desired job. In their case, paternal support was crucial in their education. This suggests that the most effective challenge to the patrifocal, patriarchal belief system may originate with the patriarchs. Other chapters in this volume that suggest patriarchal challenges to the patrifocal system include Chapter 2 (Sarah LeVine), Chapter 3 (Susan C. Seymour), Chapter 4 (Carol C. Mukhopadhyay), and

Chapter 9 (Helen E. Ullrich). Carol C. Mukhopadhyay further portrays the significance of the Indian family in determining educational options for women and the cultural challenges women experience at the Indian Institutes of Technology. Sarah LeVine and Susan C. Seymour both show the transition from women's education and employment being negative to becoming positive factors in enhancing marriageability. These longitudinal studies from different areas of India, Nepal, and Sri Lanka and the focus on women's education illustrate the benefits in family income, self-confidence, societal acceptance, and perhaps most important, its impact on self-image and co-operation.

Private schools in India are known as "public schools." A Central Board of Secondary Education (CBSE) sets the syllabus and examinations for grades 1–12. Although Delhi, the capital city, is a member of the CBSE, it has its own board with its own, slightly different examinations (Fig. 1.1).

Fig. 1.1 Youth educated in a Central Board of Secondary Education (CBSE) school, earned his Master's degree and found employment in the United States

The CBSE is especially useful for children whose parents have frequent transfers to other cities and states. This centralized approach allows for a consistent education across the whole country. Parents and students both regard the CBSE schools as tough, rigorous, and providing an excellent education. In addition to this national school system, each state has its own syllabus and examinations. Otherwise, there is no standardized national government school system.

TERMS FOR EDUCATIONAL ACHIEVEMENT

To help the reader unfamiliar with the South Asian education system, an explanation of some significant terms follows:

10th grade graduation is regarded as equivalent to high school. The examination to obtain the Secondary School Leaving Certificate (SSLC) (10th standard) is equivalent to the Senior Secondary. Usually students take the examination at age 16.

Failing the 10th standard is equivalent to failing the 10th grade and failing to get the SSLC.

Higher Secondary = 11th and 12th grades: in the past, those passing this examination received the Pre-University Certificate (PUC) which is also known as Intermediate, an older term equivalent to the PUC (12th grade). Later, the PUC was divided into two categories.

First Pre-University Certificate (First PUC): the certificate received upon passing the 11th grade examinations

Second Pre-University Certificate (Second PUC): the certificate received upon passing the 12th grade examinations

College Degree: 3-year course

Bachelor of Engineering: 4-year course

Bachelor of Medicine Bachelor of Surgery (MBBS): 4-½ year course with internship

First Class: 60–100% in examination scores

First Class with Merit: 80–84% in examination scores

First Class with Distinction: 85–100% in examination scores

Second Class: 45–59% in examination scores

This edited volume began with the suggestion of my Palgrave/ Macmillan editor, Mireille Yanow, in 2015. Over lunch at the American

Anthropological Association meetings, she expressed interest in publishing an edited volume based on the panel I had organized to honor Pauline Kolenda who worked in different areas of India and with different strata of Indian society. Six of the contributors to this volume have had a close association with Pauline. This volume with chapters representing Karnataka, Maharashtra, Nepal, Odisha, Tamilnadu, Rajasthan, Sri Lanka, Nepal as well as a chapter on the Indian educational systems provides a nice complement to her research. Moreover, in this volume, the chapters are inclusive of different socioeconomic groups and religious groups including Christianity, Buddhism, and a range among Hindu castes from Brahmin to Dalit. This edited book on the state of education among various social groups in different areas of India, Sri Lanka, and Nepal is an appropriate recognition of the diversity of Pauline Kolenda's research.

NOTES

1. "The Right of Children to Free and Compulsory Education Act or Right to Education Act (RTE), is an Act of the Parliament of India enacted on 4 August 2009, which describes the modalities of the importance of free and compulsory education for children between 6 and 14 in India under Article 21a of the Indian Constitution. India became one of 135 countries to make education a fundamental right of every child when the Act came into force on 1 April 2010 (http://righttoeducation.in/, accessed February 23, 2018)." All private schools (in India public schools) were to reserve 25% of their positions for those in economic need or for Dalits. Sam Carlson, the World Bank education specialist for India, commented: "The RTE Act is the first legislation in the world that puts the responsibility of ensuring enrolment, attendance and completion on the Government. It is the parents' responsibility to send the children to schools in the US and other countries." A report released a year later revealing that 8.1 million children failed to attend school raises the question of the effectiveness of the government in enacting the RTE Act. Moreover, Dalits are the population most likely to quit school.

2. "Education is state funded and offered free of charge at all levels, including the university level. The government also provides free textbooks to school-children. Literacy rates and educational attainment levels rose steadily after Sri Lanka became an independent nation in 1948 and today the youth literacy rate stands at 97%. ... (http://www.sundaytimes.lk/160501/news/education-compulsory-for-children-between-5-and-16-years-191731.html)" Chandani Kirinde May 1, 2016 (accessed 2/24/18).

3. http://r2e.gn.apc.org/country-node/380/country-constitutional (accessed 2/25/18). The Interim Constitution of Nepal January 15, 2007.

EDUCATION
Part 3—Fundamental rights.

17 (1) Each community shall have the right to receive basic education in their mother tongue as provided for in the law.

(2) Every citizen shall have the right to receive free education from the State up to secondary level as provided for in the law.

Part 4—Directive principles and policies of the State.

26 (1) The State shall pursue a policy of raising the standard of living of the general public through the development of infrastructures such as education, ...

(7) The State shall pursue a policy of making the female population participate, to a greater extent, in the task of national development by making special provisions for their education, health and employment.

(8) The State shall make necessary arrangements to safeguard the rights and interests of children and shall ensure that they are not exploited, and shall make gradual arrangements for free education.

(9) The State shall pursue such policies in matters of education, health and social security of orphans, helpless women, the aged, the disabled and incapacitated persons as will ensure their protection and welfare.

(10) The State shall pursue a policy which will help promote the interests of the economically and socially backward groups and communities by making special provisions with regard to their education, health and employment.

33. Responsibilities of the State
The State shall have the following responsibilities:

(h) to pursue a policy of establishing the rights of all citizens to education, ...

35. State policies

(1) The State shall pursue a policy of raising the standard of living of the general public by fulfilling basic needs such as education, health, transportation, ...

(8) The State shall pursue a policy of encouraging maximum participation of women in national development by making special provision for their education, health and employment.

(10) The State shall pursue a policy which will help to uplift the economically and socially backward indigenous ethnic groups [Adivasi Janajati], Madhesis, Dalits, as well as marginalized communities, and workers and farmers living below the poverty line by making provisions for reservations in education, health, housing, food security and employment for a certain period of time.

(16) The State shall pursue a policy of creating basic infrastructure to impart technical education, training and orientation for the development of that class of people dependent on labor including farmers and laborers, to motivate their participation in the development process of the country. Constitution of Nepal January 15, 2007.

4. Shudra and Sudra are alternate terms. In my writings I have used Shudra.
5. This is similar to African-Americans slaves who were rarely taught to read. In his comments on the movie, "Black Panther" Lawrence Ware (*The New York Times: SR* 3: Sunday February 18, 2018) discusses reading comic books in private because he knew of no black person who read comic books. This portrayal resembles that of Indian women who kept their enjoyment of reading secret.

REFERENCES

Forbes, Geraldine. 2008. Education for Women. In *Women and Social Reform in Modern India a Reader*, ed. Sumit Sarkar and Tanika Sarkar. Bloomington: Indiana University Press (reprinted from Forbes, Geraldine. 1996. *Women in Modern India*. Cambridge: Cambridge University Press).

Fuller, C.J., and Haripriya Narasimhan. 2014. *Tamil Brahmins: The Making of a Middle-Class Caste*. Chicago: University of Chicago Press.

http://righttoeducation.in/. Accessed 23 Feb 2018.

http://www.prb.org/Publications/Media-Guides/2011/girls-education-fact-sheet.aspx. Accessed 24 Feb 2018.

http://www.sundaytimes.lk/160501/news/education-compulsory-for-children-between-5-and-16-years-191731.html. Chandani Kirinde May 1, 2016. Accessed 24 Feb 2018.

http://www.uniteforsight.org/women-children-course/health-promotion-women-children. Accessed 23 Feb 2018.

Kumar, Nita. 2007. *The Politics of Gender, Community, and Modernity*. Oxford: Oxford University Press.

LeVine, Robert A., Sarah LeVine, Meredith Rowe, Beatrice Schnell, and Emily Dexter. 2012. *Literacy and Mothering: How Women's Schooling Changes the Lives of the World's Children*. New York: Oxford University Press.

Nambissan, Geetha B., and S. Srinivasa Rao, eds. 2013. *Sociology of Education in India*. India: Oxford University Press.

Ullrich, Helen E. 2017. *The Women of Totagadde: Broken Silence*. New York: Palgrave Macmillan.

CHAPTER 2

Getting in, Dropping out, and Staying on: Determinants of Girls' School Attendance in Nepal

Sarah LeVine

DETERMINANTS OF GIRLS' SCHOOL ATTENDANCE IN THE KATHMANDU VALLEY OF NEPAL: 1950–2000

The gender gap in school attendance in South Asia is greater than anywhere else in the world and is as enduring a form of social inequality as poverty (King and Hill 1993; King and Sohoni 1993; Mathema 1998; UNICEF 2000). In Nepal, just as in wide areas of India, caste, frequently an indicator of economic status, is also a barrier to education (Shrestha et al. 1986; Stash and Hannum 2001) and to the quality of education received (Liechty 1996, 2001, 2003). This article, which analyzes factors determining school attendance of mothers of

An earlier version of this paper appeared in *Anthropology & Education Quarterly*, Vol. 37, 2006, 21–41.

S. LeVine (✉)
Harvard Graduate School of Education, Cambridge, MA, USA

© The Author(s) 2019
H. E. Ullrich (ed.), *The Impact of Education in South Asia*, Anthropological Studies of Education,
https://doi.org/10.1007/978-3-319-96607-6_2

11

young children, is based on data drawn from a study of the impact of women's schooling on child health and children's acquisition of literacy conducted in two communities in Lalitpur District of the Kathmandu Valley, the most developed region of Nepal, between January 1997 and June 1998 with follow-up visits in 1999 and 2000 (LeVine et al. 2001, 2004, 2012). The study, which focused on two groups of mothers, one urban and one rural, demonstrated that the literacy skills of mothers who had attended poor schools for just a few years contributed to their children's survival and health as well as to their mastery of the fundamentals of literacy (LeVine et al. 2012). The first group of mothers was composed of city-dwelling Newars, the majority of whom were Buddhists living in Patan, and the second of Hindu Bahun-Chetris or Parbatiyas (hill people), living in a semi-rural farming community six miles to the south. The women were born between 1950 and 1975 and reached primary school age between 1955 and 1980. By the time of the study, many had secondary school-going daughters. A review of the history of Western-style education in Nepal, an evaluation of the position of women in Newar and Parbatiya society, and brief descriptions of the sample and the two study locations are followed by a discussion of factors determining whether girls were sent to school in the 1950s through the 1990s, and why, in most cases against their wishes, they withdrew. The article concludes with a review of developments from 2000 to the present.

The majority of parents of the women in the study had viewed a daughter's education as a poor investment relative to a son's since, in a patrilocal society, after marriage, a son would continue to contribute to his parents' support whereas a daughter would transfer the benefits accruing from her education to her husband's family. However, by the 1990s, the proportion of school-going girls as well as boys had greatly increased; in urban areas, female employment outside the home had also risen. Thus, in contrast with their own parents, many women in the study said they wanted to educate their daughters to the same level as their sons in the belief that a daughter should have the capacity to be financially independent; furthermore, since after marriage she was likely to remain emotionally close, she might prove a more reliable source of financial support than a son. In the decades since our study, while some attitudes and behavior noted in the 1990s have become mainstream, others have endured.

THE SPREAD OF WESTERN-STYLE EDUCATION
IN LATE TWENTIETH-CENTURY NEPAL

Prior to the 1950/1951 revolution ousting of the autocratic Rana regime, which had ruled the country as dynastic prime ministers for more than a century, Nepal had minimal exposure to Western ideas. The Ranas had gone to great lengths to protect Nepal from contamination by notions of democracy that, by the end of the nineteenth century, had begun circulating south of the border in British India (Hoftun et al. 1999: 1–45; Onta 1996). Since the Ranas viewed modern education as potentially threatening to their regime, they resisted its introduction as long as they could. From the mid-1850s, their own male offspring and those of the royal family and their high caste counselors received a Western-style education from Indian and occasionally English teachers. Postsecondary education was introduced with the establishment of Tri Chandra College in 1918, but only the sons of a tiny elite, from whom the Ranas recruited the country's bureaucrats, were admitted. From the palace school, a few boys went on to university in India. When following the revolution that brought the end of Rana rule, Nepal opened its borders to foreigners and development aid in 1951; the country had no national educational system and no Ministry of Education.

In that year—in which the oldest woman in the study was born—Nepal had only 321 Western-style primary schools, 11 secondary schools, and one college with a total—overwhelmingly male—student population of about 8500 (Shrestha 1988: 82). Most schools were located in the Kathmandu Valley, as were a number of small informal schools functioning under religious auspices, a few of which admitted girls (LeVine and Gellner 2005; Ragsdale 1989: 88). Khaniya and Kiernan (1994) estimated that altogether only 0.5% of the school-age population was attending a school of any kind. The first girls' primary school in Nepal had opened at Hanuman Dhoka in Kathmandu in 1942; in addition to reading and writing in Nepali and Sanskrit, it offered instruction in knitting. A man belonging to a prominent Newar merchant family, whose sister had entered the school at age six, recalled, "The school had much difficulty in recruiting students because in those days it was widely believed that if a girl learned even seven letters of the alphabet when she grew up she would become either a prostitute or a witch." Nevertheless, the notion that daughters as well as sons should be educated in the Western style was slowly gaining acceptance in elite high-caste families.

Meanwhile, the overwhelming majority of Nepalese children were excluded from modern education by poverty, low-caste status, gender, and cultural prejudice and an extreme shortage of schools and teachers to staff them. Of the few children who did go to school, boys outnumbered girls by more than ten to one. The first national census (1952) reported literacy rates of 9.5% for men and 0.7% for women, respectively, i.e., literate males outnumbered literate females almost 1:14 (His Majesty's Government/Nepal Population Council/Central Bureau of Statistics [HMG/NPC/CBS] 1987a).

Education data for Nepal from the decades between the revolution of 1950/1951 and the People's Movement (*jan andolan*), the revolution of 1990 are uneven and often contradictory. Nevertheless, an enormously expanded and increasingly complex national educational system was emerging. Convinced that wide-based literacy was essential for the transformation of an impoverished, "backward" country into a modern society, the government, privileging Western-style education and the "three R's" over Sanskritic, Buddhist, Ghandian, or Indigenous approaches, encouraged the establishment of many thousands of primary schools and sponsored nonformal literacy courses for adults. By 1961, the literacy rate had inched up to 8.9% and by 1971 to 12.6%. However, the female literacy rate (3.4%) lagged far behind that of males (21.9%) (HMG/NPC/CBS 1987b).

In the 1970s, the government's concentration on modernization, economic development, the use of the Nepali language, and the spread of high-caste Hindu culture in order to build national unity brought with it an intensified focus on education, pronounced by the Constitution of 1962 to be the right of every citizen (Pfaff-Czernika 1997; Ragsdale 1989). The New Education Plan of 1971–1976 was intended to provide educational opportunities for boys and girls equally. However, as Edna Mitchell wrote, "Only the affluent can reasonably encourage their daughters to attend school" (1976: 172). In the case of males, however, education was gaining acceptance as the main path to social mobility. Theoretically, regardless of caste or ethnic background, it gave bright young men access to politics and positions in government service (Bista 1991: 119). Increasingly, foreign aid was earmarked for education. Between 1970 and 1980, the number of schools increased by almost 40% (HMG/NPC/CBS 1987b) and student enrollments increased even more rapidly (Stash and Hannum 2001). Census figures for 1981 indicated a literacy rate of 23.3%, which was almost double that of a decade earlier. Apart from the Kathmandu Valley and a few urban centers, however, enrollment rates in primary school of children was only 23% of children of school going age (boys: 33.9%; girls: 12.1%).[1]

In the 1980s, committed to reforming and expanding the primary school system, the government implemented the Education for Rural Development Project and the Primary Education Project under the auspices of UNESCO and the World Bank (Khaniya and Williams 2004). But by 1985, although nation-wide enrollment of school-age boys had jumped to 85%, only 29% of school-age *girls* were enrolled (Shrestha 1988: 97). Furthermore, with widespread absenteeism, and drop-out rates in Classes One and Two at 50%, only 25% of children completed the five-year primary school course (Shrestha 1988: 89). Again, UNESCO 1991 figures indicated a 45.5% repetition rate among boys in Class One, 20% in Class Two, and 18% in Class Three. Repetition rates for girls (who were attending school in much smaller numbers) were 40, 19, and 14%, respectively (Stash and Hannum 2001). In short, children took a very long time to complete primary school, if indeed they ever did.

In 1985, the government launched its nationwide Basic Needs Fulfillment Programme aimed at reducing poverty. With universal primary school enrollment by 2000 as one of its goals, school-building and (minimal) teacher training proceeded apace and parents were especially encouraged to educate their daughters (Graner 1998). Following the revolution of 1990, the government made great efforts to broaden the educational base to include children who, by virtue of residence in rural areas (where 90% of the population lived), poverty, low-caste status, and ethnicity had been largely excluded. Census figures for 1991 indicated a national literacy rate of 39.9%, up from 23.3% in 1981; but at 25%, the female literacy rate was less than half that of males (54.5%) (HMG/NPC/CBS 1995).

Drawing once again on multiple sources of foreign funding, in 1992, the government introduced the Basic and Primary Education Project, which focused on curriculum reform, provision of textbooks and instructional materials, and the Primary Education Development Project, which provided teacher training courses (Khaniya and Williams 2004). Both projects aimed at countering non-enrollment, absenteeism, and low retention of impoverished girls living in rural areas (Bhatta 2000). As an incentive, small stipends and daily snacks were offered to thousands of primary school-aged girls, and larger stipends and boarding facilities in town to rural secondary school girls (Tuladhar and Thapa 1998). A major secondary school-building program was launched and branches of the national university were established in many urban centers. At the same time that the government was making great efforts to expand educational facilities at all levels, private for-profit primary and secondary schools began springing up in towns and villages all over Nepal. Several private tertiary-level institutions were soon in operation as well. Monthly fees at private schools ranged from a few hundred to several thousand rupees (at the time, US $1 = R.70); additional expenses included uniforms, textbooks, and food. Despite an ineffective parliamentary system, widespread corruption, economic stagnation, steadily declining confidence in government at all levels, and, starting in 1996, a Maoist guerilla war, greatly improved communications—better roads, television, telephones, and in the city, the Internet—was drawing Nepal out of its geographical and cultural remoteness. As a result, there was a widespread conviction among parents in the emerging middle class that high levels of education and especially fluency in English were essential for personal economic advancement (Liechty 2003: 58). With so many parents prepared to make great financial sacrifices in order to educate their offspring in private purportedly "English-medium" schools, entrepreneurs scrambled to meet the demand. In semi-rural Godavari, ten for-profit primary schools opened between 1992 and 1997 alone. Lacking government-mandated standards, private schools varied widely in quality. Nevertheless, they syphoned off the children of wealthier families leaving government schools as the recourse of last resort to which the poorest, mainly low-caste and untouchable parents sent their children.

THE STATUS OF WOMEN IN NEWAR AND PARBATIYA SOCIETY

Newar and Parbatiya societies are patrilineal, patrilocal, and patriarchal in structure. Ideally, the family lives jointly; the patriarch lives with his wife, his sons and their wives and children in a household in which the women take turns to cook at the same hearth. Brothers separate only after the patriarch's death. Brides are brought "in" from outside the kin group and daughters are married "out" to unrelated husbands who are often total strangers before the wedding day. Although the large majority of women in this study were married in the conventional way, some had love marriages (*luv marij*)—a tendency that in recent years has markedly increased (Ahearn 2001). In general, behavior within the family is strictly regulated according to gender, generation, and whether one was born in the family or married into it. Wives are expected to be modest, obedient, patient, and sexually faithful.

Regardless of whether her marriage was arranged or she chose her husband herself, when a bride leaves her own house and goes to the "house of strangers" she finds herself in a highly ambiguous position. She is valued for her domestic labor and as the future mother of sons; and yet her current status is lower than the children who were born into that household. Her position will begin to improve only when a bride junior to herself enters the house or she bears a son. From then on, she may look forward to the day when her son marries and she comes into her own as a mother-in-law (Bennett 1983: 165–213; Gray 1995: 104; Kondos 1989: 162–191; Levy 1990: 114–116; Nepali 1965).

Reflecting her mother's continuing attachment to her natal home, during childhood every Newar and Parbatiya woman enjoys a special closeness with her mother's brothers (New: *paju*; Nep.: *mama*). In contrast with the father–child relationship, which typically is one of respect and distance, the relationship between a maternal uncle and his nephews and nieces is relaxed and affectionate. If a girl gets married in the traditional way, she receives a dowry (*stridan*) consisting of clothes, gold jewelry, and household goods (*saman*) and renounces all further claims on her father's property (Bennett and Singh 1979: 29). Nevertheless, she continues to look for emotional and monetary support from her natal home (New: *thaache*: Nep.: *maiti*), especially from her brothers who, once she becomes a mother, assume a special relationship with her children. Often it is her brothers to whom she first turns for advice and support in the event of conflict with her husband and in-laws (Bennett 1983: 247–249; Levy 1990: 113), and for financial support for her children's education, should her husband refuse or be unable to provide it.

THE TWO STUDY COMMUNITIES

The Newars of Patan (N= 86)

According to 1991 Census data, the Newars, the indigenous people of the Kathmandu Valley, make up about half the population of the Valley and 5.5% of the population of Nepal. Although they speak a Tibeto-Burman language, suggesting that their distant ancestors migrated into the Valley from the northeast, by the early Middle Ages after many centuries of contact with South Asian culture, the Newars had developed their own exceedingly complex endogamous caste-system (Riccardi 1980). Since the beginning of recorded history, they have practiced both Hinduism and Buddhism (Slusser 1982: 213). Prior to being deposed by the Nepali-speaking Parbatiya king, Prithivi Narayan Shah in 1768/1769, Newar kings, although almost always officially Hindus (*sivamargi*), were also major patrons of Buddhist institutions and festivals. Furthermore, while Buddhism is theoretically an egalitarian religion that prohibits hierarchical divisions, at least within the *sangha* (monastic community), the Newar caste system includes Buddhists as well as Hindus (Gellner 1995: 1–37).

The Patan sample was composed of Newar women belonging to three high castes (*Vajracharya, Shakya, Shrestha*) and a large middle caste made up of several intermarrying farming groups (*Maharjan, Awale, Dagol* et al. called collectively *Jyapu* in Newari). In terms of their traditional socio-religious identity, Vajracharyas and Shakyas are Buddhist domestic and temple priests (Gellner 2001: 106–133). Most Shresthas are Hindu and a majority of Jyapus identify themselves as Buddhists.

The Setting: Patan is the administrative headquarters of Lalitpur District and one of the three principal cities of the Kathmandu Valley. Although the majority of Patan residents are Newars, since the 1990 revolution, the city has grown rapidly as people from many other ethnic groups have immigrated from elsewhere. Patan now sprawls far beyond the old city boundary.

Until the latter half of the twentieth century, Buddhist Newars tended to be less open to Western ideas than Hindu Newars, especially with regard to education. This may be explained by the fact that the Hindu Newar kings employed high-caste Hindus, notably Shresthas, as their counselors and administrators, a pattern followed by the Shah kings and the Ranas. Excluded from government service, high-caste Buddhists pursued their traditional occupations for which modern education was not considered necessary. When, after the revolution of 1950–1951, Western-style education began to take hold, Shresthas joined high-caste Parbatiyas in sending their sons and daughters to school. By contrast, high-caste Buddhists were slower to recognize the advantages of Western education. Although like most urban Nepali parents, today's Buddhist Newar parents want their children to receive a modern education, they tend to have lower academic aspirations than Hindu parents (LeVine et al. 2004). Thus after a year or two of college, the sons of merchants and craftsmen may withdraw without finishing their degrees in order to enter the family business. Again, since it is generally thought that a wife should have less education than her husband, Buddhist girls tend not to go to college, or to drop out before graduation and get married. By contrast, Hindu girls are more likely to graduate from college, seek employment, marry later than Buddhist girls, and continue working after marriage.

The Bahun-Chetris of Godavari (N= 81)

The Godavari sample was drawn from two Parbatiya high castes, *Brahman/Bahun,* and *Chetri* who, with minor discrepancies, share a single cultural heritage (Bennett 1983: 4).[2]

The Setting: Godavari is on the southern edge of the Kathmandu Valley. In the village center, there are government offices, a few large houses belonging to locally prominent people, some small stores and tea-shops, and many huddled shacks occupied by quarry laborers, most of whom are landless low-caste and untouchable Parbatiyas and tribal people from the surrounding hills. The majority of Godavari residents, however, are Parbatiya farmers belonging to the Bahun and Chetri castes who live on their own land in storied brick houses of traditional design at some distance from the village center.

In a period of high inflation and rising school costs, farming no longer generates sufficient surplus to support a family. Thus almost all men under age 50 are obliged to seek employment off the land. A few work locally but most are employed in the city. Until they retire in middle age, they have little time for agricultural tasks. The bottom lands of Godavari are so fertile and well-irrigated that they produce three crops a year. Aside from plowing, which is carried out by men with teams of oxen, women are responsible for planting, weeding, harvesting, and animal husbandry. Other than a few study women in Godavari and Patan who took care of the family store, none was employed outside the home.

1950s–1980s: Who Went to School?

Historically, female school attendance in the Kathmandu Valley has been higher than in other regions of Nepal, and yet as of 1991, only 32% of *adult women* in Lalitpur District had any schooling (Nepal Fertility, Family Planning and Health Status Survey 1991). However, census data for the same year indicated that *girls* were going to school in large numbers. The ratio of girls to boys in primary school was 1:1.2, and in secondary school it was 1:1.4 (HMG/NPC/CBS 1993). At the time of our study, virtually all primary school-age children of both sexes in Patan and Godavari were enrolled in school, most upper caste boys and girls in fee-paying schools, children from lower castes in free government schools; a smaller proportion of girls than of boys were enrolled in secondary school, however. Given the rapid rate at which education had expanded, it was easy to forget that as recently as the 1970s, few parents in either community believed that the advantages—to the girl or to themselves—of sending a daughter to school outweighed the loss of her domestic labor and the dangers of exposure to a world outside the home.

The Study

Data were collected from 167 mothers of young children who were enrolled in kindergarten and Class One. Since our focus was on school-based literacy skills, we over-sampled women who had been to school in order to achieve a relatively equal distribution across levels of school attainment. Thus the sample did not precisely reflect levels of adult female schooling in the district. All the women in the study belonged to six high and middle castes because significant numbers of schooled women could only be found in those particular castes. 108 women (64.6%) had attended school for between 1 and 16 years; the remaining 59 women (35.3%) were unschooled. 91 (54.4%) of their husbands had been to school, of whom 44 had attended and 24 had completed secondary school. Only 15 (8.9%) women reported that their own mothers had attended school. Data regarding school experience were generated by the following:

1. Preliminary open-ended interviews conducted with 20 married women 20–50 years of age, all of whom were mothers and had some schooling. Topics included their school experiences, parents' and siblings' schooling, and educational goals for their children.
2. A survey questionnaire based on the preliminary interviews was submitted to 167 different women. This included questions such as, "Who paid your school expenses?"; "Who encouraged you to continue your schooling?"; "Why did you stop going to school when you did?"; and "How far is the furthest that any of your brothers/sisters went to school?"

BARRIERS TO EDUCATION: GENDER, GEOGRAPHY, AND POVERTY

Ministry of Education 2001 figures indicate that nationwide girls made up 44.5% of students enrolled in primary school, and 42% of students enrolled in secondary school. But in the years when the women in the study were of school-going age, gender was by far the most important factor preventing girls from attending school.

Despite having grown up in urban neighborhoods close to schools, many Newar women had no schooling. Some Vajracharya and Shakya women from well-to-do families reported they were kept out of school because priests, craftsmen, and merchants—i.e., their potential husbands—did not want educated wives. They recalled parental fears that Western education could "spoil" their chances of making a good marriage. Thus they had cloistered childhoods, rarely going out except, closely chaperoned, on festival days. By contrast, most Jyapu (farming) women reported that by age six, they were taking food to family members who were working in the fields; by age ten, many were working in the fields themselves. Their future was on the land and the surest way to attract a good husband was to become known as a good worker, the characteristic most desired in a farmer's wife. A girl needed to know how to add, subtract and divide, and handle money; but she didn't need to go to school to learn that, and as a farmer, she didn't need know how to read and write.

Riva, a Chetri woman in her twenties, grew up on the outskirts of Kathmandu within easy walking distance of a government school. "My brothers all studied," she recalled, "but my parents never thought of sending me to school because there was so much work to be done at home. Besides, they didn't think it was necessary to send a girl. 'All you'll do is get married,' they said, 'so what's the point of you studying?'" After they reached adulthood, Riva's brothers would marry and bring their wives to work in the parental home while they themselves went out to work and contribute their earnings to the household. But Riva was going to marry "out." In the unlikely event that she was employed outside the home after she married, her husband's family would claim her wages. When Riva was 14, her parents arranged her marriage to a Godavari boy a few years older than she who was apprenticed to an automobile mechanic in Kathmandu. His family was looking for a wife for him who, in addition to being a good worker, was a little more sophisticated than the average village girl.

"I was very young when I left my home," said Riva, "and for the first five years, I was the only daughter-in-law. So I had a lot of work to do. I'm lucky—my mother-in-law is a good person—really, she's my best friend. Though it was very hard at the beginning, I've been happy here. Still, I think girls should have as much education as boys. They need it in order to protect themselves. My daughters aren't going to be like me, working in the fields all day for nothing! They should get office jobs and earn their own money...."

Riva spent her childhood doing domestic chores with little time for play. Her daughters, by contrast, did little house or agricultural work. In their case, the work of childhood was going to the private school in a nearby town whose fees their father, Arun, could only just afford; when they got home in the afternoon, they diligently completed their assignments and then went out to play. Riva, who never went to school herself, had nevertheless had her "consciousness raised" (Tamang 1997); she'd absorbed what Stacy Pigg (1992) has called "the ideology of modernization." Education is the main route to social mobility and the affluent life which Riva glimpsed on the flickering images of the family's black-and-white TV. She never had a chance to live such a life but she was determined her daughters would.

Riva's neighbor, Sanu was a Brahmin woman in her thirties. "My father went off to work in India," she told me, "and we didn't hear from him again. We never knew if he'd died or simply disappeared. There wasn't a school in our village—the closest one was three hours' walk away." Sanu's mother managed to scrape together the money needed to cover Sanu's brother's school expenses. "But when I asked to go as well, my mother said the school was too far and the path wasn't safe for a girl. Anyway, she needed my help at home, so I never went."

Enabling Factors: Family Status, Financial Support, and Birth Order

Some high-caste Western-oriented Hindu fathers who had attended secondary school in Rana times, and in a few cases Tri Chandra College or even an Indian university, viewed education as the essential bridge between the caste-based society of their youth and the class-based society of a rapidly modernizing Nepal. In their view, sending a daughter to school was necessary for two main reasons: First, like her brothers, she had a constitutional right to education; and second, even though she might never work outside the house herself, education prepared her for marriage to a man in government service, which, until the 1990s, was considered the most prestigious career. Thus girls from elite families growing up in the 1950s through the 1980s took paternal support for education as a given. By contrast, women from more traditional backgrounds frequently reported that encouragement came from their unschooled mother and money to cover expenses from their mother's brother.

In Patan in the 1970s, many people still believed that schooling made a girl "go to the bad." Once having learned to assert herself in the classroom, and—supposedly—to flaunt her body in the street on the way to school, she would no longer be fit for marriage and would be claimed by the hotels and bars of the city center (Liechty 2001). "My father died and after that his brother was head of our family," Sushila, a Newar woman recalled. "My father had agreed to my going to school along with my brothers, but my uncle, who was a goldsmith, didn't like us going to school. He said my brothers didn't need book learning to be goldsmiths, and to be a wife and mother I didn't need it either. So he took all of us out of school. Luckily for my brothers, our paju (mother's brother) took them to live with him and they continued going to school from his house. They wanted to be engineers, not goldsmiths, and both *did* become engineers eventually. As for me, I wanted to be a nurse but I was married off...."

Another Newar woman named Sujan from a prosperous merchant family had completed two years of college. She remembered her illiterate mother impressing upon her the need for education. "She'd say, 'After you get married, the only way to avoid asking your brothers for help is by earning your own money'. In her own case, being uneducated, she'd had to ask her brothers for money on several occasions, causing trouble between herself and her sisters-in-law." At the time she was interviewed, Sujan was busy taking care of two young sons, but when the younger one entered school she planned to start her own business. Her brothers were all doing well in business and she was confident that she had similar talent. Even though at marriage Newar and Parbatiya women renounced all claims to their father's property, they retained the right to financial support from their relatives, especially from their brothers. Thus Sujan planned to ask her brothers for seed money for a business that would make her financially independent. "After all, I'm from the same family," she said fiercely.

Sometimes older siblings paid the school expenses and in other respects took on a parental role. A Shakya teacher named Chandra reported that if it had been up to her parents she would not have gone to school. But her oldest sister who had been married at age five and had never gone to school herself, returned to her natal home after her husband brought in a second wife. "I was about six at that time," Chandra recalled, "and my sister kept telling me, 'To protect yourself, you have to get educated!' She earned a meager living as a seamstress and yet somehow she managed to pay my school expenses." Throughout her childhood, Chandra looked to her sister, an unschooled but determined woman, as her role model. "Really, she was more of a mother to me than my actual mother."

Position in the sibling order could be crucial. Maya Devi, the mother of two boys, had a degree in economics and worked for an international aid organization. "I'm the youngest of six siblings and you might say I was lucky," she said. Although she was from a farming family of limited means, her father, who had very little schooling himself, wanted all his children to get some education, daughters as well as sons.

"Each child in turn went to school just a little longer. My father had a low-level job in a government office so he couldn't afford to send most of his children beyond primary school. But by the time I finished primary school my oldest brother was already employed and helping my parents financially. So they were able to pay my secondary school expenses and after that, I went on to college and then I got a job".

Some girls benefited from having no brothers. Subha, a Brahmin, who grew up in an elite family in Patan, recalled, "Because my father only had daughters, he was happy to educate us as far as we wanted to go." A propertied government official, Her father knew that maintenance of his own elite status in large part depended on his daughters marrying high-status men, which, in the 1970s, meant *highly-educated* men; furthermore, their chances of finding highly educated husbands would be enhanced if they too were well-educated.

For girls who attended coeducational schools, the onset of menarche was an especially dreaded event. Subha recalled, "My older sister Mridula stopped going to school right when she got her first period. She was terrified that next time she'd get blood on her skirt and the boys, who, because she'd been absent from class for some days, guessed what had happened, would tease her mercilessly. So she didn't take her exams and didn't get her School Leaving Certificate. She just stayed at home until, after about two years, she received a good proposal and got married."

Despite seeing many of her female classmates drop out of school not long after getting their period, Subha stuck it out. "I suppose I was bolder. In any event, I kept on studying. And once I'd finished secondary school I went to Padma Kanya, the girl's college." With a grin, she continues, "My father would never have considered sending me to a co-educational college. He was frightened I'd fall in love with a boy of a different caste and elope with him. In those days, parents dreaded inter-caste marriage and most still do. I couldn't say I particularly *enjoyed* studying, but my father wanted me to keep on until a good marriage proposal came... I was twenty-one when one finally arrived." By then, Subha added ruefully, "even though I'd been studying just to pass the time, I had my Intermediate Certificate. It was only after I got married that I appreciated, in retrospect, the opportunities I'd been given... My younger sister was a more serious student. She completed her BA before she got married and later she finished her MA. There were only a few years between us three sisters, but because attitudes and expectations as far as education and marriage were concerned were changing fast, we each had quite different experiences."

Like Subha, Prabha had no brothers. Her Brahmin father was also in government service but because he owned little property he knew that when he retired he and his wife would be looking to their daughters to supplement his small pension. Thus he focused his resources on the girls' schooling. Prabha was only 22 when he died; but she already had a master's degree and a job with good prospects which enabled her to help her mother educate her three younger sisters.

A Jyapu woman named Sujata who never went to school recalled, "A lot of our neighbors disapproved of educating girls. They'd say, 'Those girls are being treated as if they were boys!' What they really meant was that, unlike most of us who only left the house to go the fields, a girl who went to school was out on the street twice a day, which meant she had the chance to behave badly [to have sexual encounters]. If a boy behaved badly, parents didn't need to worry. But if a *girl* behaved badly, her name—and her family's reputation [*ijjat*]—would be ruined, and no decent man would want to marry her. Still, there *were* some Jyapu girls in my neighborhood who went to school," Sujata continued. "Their families were better-off than mine, and besides, they didn't have any brothers so their parents thought that by paying for their education they were helping themselves."

The schools that the women in the study attended varied in structure and condition, quality of teachers, teacher-pupil ratio, and equipment. In rural areas, the construction costs of government schools were usually borne by the community. Built of crumbling brick, both government schools in Godavari had irons roofs, glassless windows, and packed earth floors; students sat on mats or on the floor itself and no latrines. Urban schools were more substantial. For example, the two-storied Nag Bahal school in Patan, which several of the women in the study had attended, dated from Rana times. The walls were of plastered brick painted red with a white trim and the floors were tiled; students sat at desks and teachers wrote on blackboards. In both urban and rural areas, classes had up to 80 students of whom boys far outnumbered girls. Although by 1990 ten percent of the national budget was devoted to education, only about forty percent of teachers had any training and fewer still received supervision; textbooks were out-of-date and in rural areas mightn't be delivered until late in the academic year (Khaniya and Williams 2004). Gutschow (1987) reported that the majority of teachers whom she interviewed in Kathmandu in the 1980s—when some of the Newar women in our study would have been at school across the Bagmati River in Patan—admitted they viewed girls as less intelligent than boys and, therefore, called on them less often. The fact that few women in the study could remember being close to any particular teacher reflects the paucity of female teachers. Despite great efforts to increase their number, in 1996, only one-fifth of teachers were women (Tuladhar and Thapa 1998).

Why Did Girls Drop Out?

Domestic Responsibilities, Lack of Economic Benefit to Parents, and Marriage

A large proportion of Nepali girls who went to school before the 1990s only studied for a year or two. As the headmaster of the government school in Godavari explained, "Parents didn't want their daughters to know too much or to get too clever. Once a girl knew her letters and could count to 100, they'd take her out."

Many women reported that they had left school without learning to read. More than a quarter were pulled out because they were needed at home: a new baby had been born; an older sister, who had been taking care of younger siblings, had got married; or someone in the household had become chronically ill. Although money could be found to pay a son's school fees, when it came to daughter's continuing in school, parents often pleaded poverty.

A Chetri woman who grew up in a village reported, "I wanted to go to secondary school but there wasn't one in our place. My parents sent my brothers to a boarding school in town, but when it was my turn to go they told me they couldn't afford to send me, the hostel was too expensive. If I'd studied longer, my life would be a lot different now. Maybe I wouldn't have a job but at least I'd be able to help my children with their homework. As it is, when they ask me questions and I don't know the answers because I didn't study that long myself, I feel terrible."

Meanwhile, a secondary school graduate in Godavari saw the downside to education, admitting that it made the repetitiveness of her daily life tedious and her mother-in-law's demands hard to bear. "Perhaps I'd be better off if I'd never set foot inside a school," she said bitterly. For her part, her mother-in-law confided her regret at choosing an educated wife for her businessman son. "A girl with a year or two of primary school would have been easier to deal with," she told me. "And a girl from the hills who'd never been to school at all would have been even better!"

The reason most often given for dropping out of school was the arrival of a "good" marriage proposal from a civil servant, or a young man whose family had a large piece of land, or a thriving curio shop or a cloth business. Wishing to do as well as possible for their daughters, parents felt they couldn't pass them up. A quarter of the schooled women recalled being "married off" before they began menstruating. About half made it to the end of secondary school and a few made it to college. For whatever reason they dropped out, few ever resumed their education. A Shrestha woman reported that when, at seventeen she had just graduated from secondary school and was looking forward to college, she was shocked when she learned that her father had arranged her marriage. "I'd guessed this might happen," she admitted, "But even so, I was extremely upset. I'd been hoping to get my degree."

By the 1980s, in elite circles, a college education had begun to carry weight in marriage negotiations. Rather than a sign that a young woman had "gone to the bad," it was seen as an indicator of high social status. But too often, once the new bride settled into her husband's home, she discovered her in-laws wouldn't permit her to work.

"My father-in-law was only thinking about *ijjat* [prestige]," a Chetri woman complained. "Yes, it's prestigious to have an educated daughter-in-law. But if I were to work in an office, it would be a source of shame because people would think, why is he letting his daughter-in-law spend her days with men who aren't relatives? It was assumed to be because he can't meet household expenses himself and needs her salary."

Determinants of Girls' School Attendance in Nepal in the Twenty-First Century

Until late in the twentieth century, the Kathmandu Valley, historically the most developed region of Nepal, was its undisputed educational leader. As schooling has spread throughout the country, attitudes and behavior both enabling and barring girls from education noted in in our study are to be found in many areas.

Contrary to expectation, widespread conflict during the Maoist insurgency (1996–2006) had no negative affect on school attendance for girls (Valenti 2011, 2013). Indeed, given their egalitarian ideology, Maoists actively challenged traditional gender roles. Not only were a third of their combatants female but they also insisted that parents send their daughters to school. While the abduction of girls as well as boys was commonplace, in general after a short period of indoctrination abductees were released to parents who were ordered to enroll them in school. And yet, while today primary school enrollment is close to gender parity throughout Nepal, class repetition and drop-out rates remain high for boys and higher still for girls. Just as they did in Kathmandu a generation ago (Gutschow 1987), girls attending coeducational schools face prejudice from their teachers. Jennifer Rothchild (2006) found that in the hill country of Eastern Nepal, teachers, the great majority of whom were male, paid much more attention to boys. As future heads of household, they believed they were sharper, more assertive, and more promising. Thus they called on, praised, and criticized boys more than girls whom they deemed shy, passive, "soft," and naturally suited to care giving roles. Whereas a boy needed education in preparation for adulthood in the workplace, for a girl, education was preparation for motherhood and running a household. Were she to venture into the workforce, it should be as a nurse or teacher of young children. Meanwhile, Rothchild noted, at home, parents still expected daughters to perform more domestic chores than sons; therefore, having less time for homework, daughters were more likely than their brothers to fail examinations. And if an extra hand was needed at home, parents were far more likely to pull a daughter than a son out of school.

While attendance at a government primary school involves quite minimal expenditure, secondary education, whether in a government or a private school, requires money for fees, books, uniforms, contributions to the building fund and transportation. Of children who finish primary school, boys are still more likely to go on to secondary school than girls (Neupane 2017). An increase in (largely male) labor migration to India, the Gulf States, and elsewhere and the rise in remittances received from abroad permit many parents to educate children beyond primary school, an expense that used to be beyond their means. Here again, they are more likely to use remittance money to support a son's schooling than a daughter's, and to send a son to a private school while keeping a daughter in a lower-cost, over-crowded, and academically inferior government school (Vogel and Korinek 2012). Simply put, the conviction that a son's education is a better investment than a daughter's endures. Unlike his sister who will soon "go to another house" taking the benefits of her education with her, so long as his parents live, a son is responsible for their welfare.

Even though a daughter's help at home may be crucial, when asked why she dropped out of school, as in the past, today's parents seem to take her contribution to the household economy as a given and rarely mention it. "We needed to get her married," is still the most frequent reason (Sekine and Hodgkin 2017). At all but the most Westernized level of society, arranging a daughter's marriage to a young man belonging to the same caste and from a similar background continues to be seen as parents' most important responsibility. Under Nepal law (2006), the legal age of marriage is 18 with parental permission and 20 years of age without it. But since marriage is regarded as a family matter, the government does nothing to enforce the law. Regardless of the age at which it occurs, marriage is seldom officially registered. Reflecting poverty and low level of education as well as religious beliefs and cultural practices, many parents regard "getting a daughter married off" (sometimes before the onset of menarche), thereby handing over guardianship to another family, as the best way both of protecting her from sexual assault and pregnancy outside marriage and of defending their own honor (Sah 2008; Timsina 2011; Pandey 2016a). At the same time, adolescent marriage puts a physically immature girl at risk during pregnancy and delivery, and neonatal or under-five mortality for her child (Pandey 2016b; Male and Wodon 2016).

Child marriage remains normative for girls belonging to untouchable castes (Dalits), the poorest and least educated group in Nepal, and also for Madeshi girls living in the Terai, the lowland area along the Indian border, home to almost half the population of Nepal lives (Sah 2008; Pandey 2016b). In the case of Dalits, early marriage lowers *stridan,* dowry; in the case of Madeshis who commonly intermarry with Indians, it reduces wedding expenses too. Among higher caste and *janajati* (ethnic minority) Hill communities, primary school attendance (Class 1–5) appears to protect girls younger than 15 from being withdrawn from school for marriage. During secondary school (Class 6–10), however, withdrawals steadily increase (Raj et al. 2014; Sekine and Hodgkin 2017). Parents who have no sons may keep a daughter in school in the hope that education will lead to employment in adulthood and financial support in their old age; similarly, a widowed mother with some measure of economic independence may encourage her daughters as well as her sons to stay in school as long as possible (Self 2014; Hatlebaak and Gurung 2014). Nonetheless, the Nepal Demographic and Health Survey of 2011 reported that one-third of girls aged 15–19 were already married; and of them, sixty percent were pregnant or had at least one child. By age 20, 78% of girls were married.

The likelihood of a bride continuing her studies after marriage depends on caste and the economic and educational level of her parents and in-laws, and also because even in an elite family, she will be obliged to withdraw once she has a child, on contraceptive use (Rivera et al. 2015). As in the past, a traditional head of household still insists that the new bride devote her time to domestic chores in her husband's home. The more Westernized the household head, however, the more open he is to her continuing her education. Again, mothers and mothers-in-law who attended secondary school or college themselves are likely to support academic aspirations and to stand up to male kin on their daughter or daughter-in-law's behalf. A girl who delays marriage long enough to finish a college degree, gains some experience in salaried work and marries a man of similar education and outlook has options. Seen as an economic asset, her in-laws may encourage her to continue working. But regardless of education, a young wife who wasn't employed before she got married is unlikely to be allowed to work.

DISCUSSION

Between the 1950s and 1980s, when the women in this study were growing up in the Kathmandu Valley, schools were rare in rural areas; thus, except for girls who lived in town, going to school was unusual. While caste and socioeconomic status were also determining factors in who went to school, gender was centrally important. However, all but the poorest parents soon wanted primary schooling for sons, whose economic support they expected to rely on in old age; many did their utmost to educate at least one son further. But except in elite urban families, a daughter's education was still a low priority. Whereas almost two-thirds of the schooled women in the study who had brothers reported that at least one brother had completed secondary school and almost half had a brother with two years or more of college, less than one-third of the women themselves had attended secondary school and less than one-fifth had attended college. Academic ability had little bearing on whether girls continued studying or dropped out. Only seven women reported that the decision to terminate their studies was their own. The others said bitterly that, given the choice, they would have continued their studies. Regardless of academic talent, many had been pulled out of school to work in the house and on the family farm, or, in the case of Jyapu girls, to work as domestic servants or laborers on construction sites. Their parents, to whom they gave their wages, had sometimes used the money to pay their brothers' school expenses. Since arranging a daughter's marriage was the primary parental responsibility, girls who went to school were often withdrawn after only a few years to get married. Believing that the longer a girl stayed at home, the more difficult her adjustment in her husband's home was likely to be, many parents got their daughters married before puberty.

Since the women in our study grew up, however, primary school attendance has become normative for girls throughout Nepal. As children with many siblings, today's mothers may have spent virtually all their time outside of school on domestic chores. Schooling is expensive in both time and money. Yet, with contraception widely available, the birth rate has fallen dramatically. Rather than five or six children, a woman with only two or three sees post-primary education as both possible and essential for daughters as well as sons. In a society rapidly restructuring itself along class lines instead of caste, employment, albeit as a store clerk or a nursery school teacher, is regarded as the most important status marker.

In many parts of the developing world, parents, who in the recent past would have only looked to sons, are looking to daughters for financial help before and after marriage and into old age (Kiluva-Ndinda 2000). Similarly, even Nepali parents who have sons recognize that investing in the education of a daughter who, typically, after marriage remains emotionally close, may well be a better long-term strategy than investing in the education of a son whose affection and resources they would have to compete for with his wife.

NOTES

1. From 1981 to the present, the education system consists of five years of primary, two years of senior primary, and three years of secondary school, culminating in the School Leaving Certificate (SLC). Government primary schools are tuition-free; while students are required to purchase supplies, uniforms are no longer required.
2. Compared with the Newar caste system, whose (simplified) form includes more than 30 castes grouped in six levels in a hierarchy of purity/impurity, that of the Parbatiyas is quite simple. It consists of three "clean" high castes whose "twice-born" adult males wear the sacred thread, Brahmin/Bahun, Thakuri, and Chetri, and a number of "unclean" occupational castes from whom members of "clean" castes may not accept drinking water.

REFERENCES

Ahearn, Laura M. 2001. *Invitations to Love: Literacy, Love Letters, and Social Change in Nepal*. Ann Arbor: University of Michigan Press.
Bennett, Lynn. 1983. *Dangerous Wives and Sacred Sisters*. New York: Columbia University Press.
Bennett, Lynn, and Shilu Singh. 1979. *Tradition and Change in the Legal Status of Nepalese Women*. The Status of Women in Nepal, Part 2. Kathmandu: CEDA, Tribhuvan University.
Bhatta, Pramod. 2000. Community Mobilization in Primary Education. *Studies in Nepali History and Society* 5 (2): 201–216.
Bista, Dor Bahadur. 1991. *Fatalism and Development: Nepal's Struggle for Modernization*. Calcutta: Orient Longman.
Gellner, David N. 1995. Introduction. In *Contested Hierarchies: A Collaborative Ethnography of Caste Among the Newars of the Kathmandu Valley*, ed. David N. Gellner and Declan Quigley, 1–37. Oxford, UK: Clarendon Press.

Gellner, David N. 2001. Monkhood and Priesthood in Newar Buddhism. In *The Anthropology of Buddhism: Weberian Themes*, 106–133. New Delhi: Oxford University Press.

Graner, Elvira. 1998. Geography of Education in Nepal. *Contributions to Nepalese Studies* 25 (2): 191–213.

Gray, John N. 1995. *Householder's World: Purity, Power and Dominance in a Nepali Village*. Delhi: Oxford University Press.

Gutschow, Kim I. 1987. What the Construction of Gender Roles in the Education System Reveals About Social Change in Nepal. Honors thesis in Social Studies, Harvard University.

Hatlebaak, Magnus, and Yogendra B. Gurung. 2014. IDEAS Working Papers Series, St. Louis.

His Majesty's Government/Nepal Population Council/Central Bureau of Statistics (HMG/NPC/CBS). 1987a. *Population Monograph of Nepal*. Kathmandu: Government Printing Office.

His Majesty's Government/Nepal Population Council/Central Bureau of Statistics (HMG/NPC/CBS). 1987b. *Statistical Yearbook, 1987*. Kathmandu: Government Printing Office.

His Majesty's Government/Nepal Population Council/Central Bureau of Statistics (HMG/NPC/CBS). 1993. *Population Census, 1991*. Kathmandu: Government Printing Office.

His Majesty's Government/Nepal Population Council/Central Bureau of Statistics (HMG/NPC/CBS). 1995. *Population Monograph of Nepal*. Kathmandu: Government Printing Office.

Hoftun, Martin, William Raeper, and John Whelpton. 1999. *People, Politics and Ideology: Democracy and Social Change in Nepal*. Kathmandu: Mandala Book Point.

Khaniya, Tirth R., and M.A. Kiernan. 1994. Nepal Systems of Education. In *International Encyclopedia of Education*, ed. Torsten Husen and T. Neville Postlethwaite, 4062. Tarrytown, NY: Elsevier Science.

Khaniya, Tirth R., and James H. Williams. 2004. Necessary but Not Sufficient: Challenges to (Implicit) Theories of Educational Change: Reform in Nepal's Primary Education System. *International Journal of Educational Development* 24 (3): 315–328.

Kiluva-Ndinda, Mutuni Mumba. 2000. *Women's Agency and Educational Policy: The Experience of Women in Kilume, Kenya*. Albany: State University of New York Press.

King, Elizabeth, and Anne M. Hill. 1993. *Education in Developing Countries*. Baltimore, MD: Johns Hopkins University Press.

King, Elizabeth, and Kuckreja Sohoni. 1993. Women in India. In *Women in the Third World: An Encyclopedia of Contemporary Issues*, ed. Nelly Stromquist and Karen Monkman, 572–582. New York: Garland.

Kondos, Vivien. 1989. Subjection and the Domicile: Some Problematic Issues Relating to High Caste Nepalese Women. In *Societies from the Inside Out*, ed. John N. Gray and David J. Mearns, 162–191. New Delhi: Sage.

LeVine, Robert A., Sarah E. LeVine, and Beatrice Schnell. 2001. "Improve the Women": Mass Schooling, Female Literacy, and Worldwide Social Change. *Harvard Education Review* 71 (1): 1–50.

LeVine, Robert A., Sarah E. LeVine, Meredith Rowe, and Beatrice Schnell. 2004. Maternal Literacy and Health Behavior: A Nepalese Case Study. *Social Science and Medicine* 58: 863–877.

LeVine, Robert A., Sarah LeVine, Meredith Rowe, Beatrice Schnell, and Emily Dexter. 2012. *Literacy and Mothering: How Women's Schooling Changes the Lives of the World's Children*. New York: Oxford University Press.

LeVine, Sarah, and David N. Gellner. 2005. *Rebuilding Buddhism: The Theravada Movement in Twentieth Century Nepal*. Cambridge, MA: Harvard University Press.

Levy, Robert, with K. Rajopadhyaya. 1990. *Mesocosm: Hinduism and the Organization of a Traditional Hindu City in Nepal*. Berkeley: University of California Press.

Liechty, Mark. 1996. Paying for Modernity: Women and the Discourse of Freedom in Kathmandu. *Studies in Nepali History and Society* 1 (1): 201–230.

Liechty, Mark. 2001. Consumer Transgressions: Notes on the History of Restaurants and Prostitution in Kathmandu. *Studies in Nepali History and Society* 6 (1): 57–102.

Liechty, Mark. 2003. *Suitably Modern: Making Middle-Class Culture in a New Consumer Society*. Princeton, NJ: Princeton University Press.

Male, Chata, and Quentin Wodon. 2016. Basic Profile of Early Childbirth in Nepal, Health, Nutrition and Poplution Knowledge Brief. World Bank, Washington, DC.

Mathema, Madhuri. 1998. Women in South Asia: Pakistan, Bangladesh and Nepal. In *Women in the Third World: An Encyclopedia of Contemporary Issues*, ed. Nelly Stromquist and Karen Monkman, 583–592. New York: Garland.

Mitchell, Edna. 1976. The New Educational Plan in Nepal: Balancing Conflicting Values for the National Survey. In *The Anthropological Study of Education*, ed. Craig J. Calhoun and Francis A.J. Ianni, 156–172. The Hague: Mouton Publishers.

Neupane, Pramila. 2017. *International Education Studies* 10 (2): 68–83.

Nepali, G.S. 1965. *The Newars*. Bombay: United Asia Publications.

Onta, Pratyoush. 1996. Creating a Brave Nation in British India: The Rhetoric of Jati Improvement, the Rediscovery of Bhanubhakta and the Writing of Bir History. *Studies in Nepali History and Society* 1 (1): 37–76.

Pandey, Shanta. 2016a. Mothers' Risk for Experiencing Neonatal and Under-Five Child Deaths in Nepal: The Role of Empowerment. *Global Social Welfare* 4 (3): 105–115.

Pandey, Shanta. 2016b. Persistent Nature of Child Marriage Even When It Is Illegal: The Case of Nepal. *Child and Youth Services Review* 73: 242–247.

Pfaff-Czernika, Joanna. 1997. Vestiges and Visions: Cultural Change in the Process of Nation-Building in Nepal. In *Nationalism and Ethnicity in a Hindu Kingdom: The Politics of Culture in Nepal*, ed. David N. Gellner, Joanna Paff-Czarnecka, and John Whelpton, 419–470. Amsterdam: Harwood Academic Publishers.

Pigg, Stacy Leigh. 1992. Inventing Social Categories Through Place: Social Representations and Development in Nepal. *Comparative Studies of Society and History* 34 (3): 491–513.

Ragsdale, Tod A. 1989. *Once a Hermit Kingdom: Ethnicity, Education and National Integration in Nepal*. Kathmandu: Ratna Pustak Bhandar.

Raj, Anita, Lotus McDougal, Jay G. Silverman, and Melanie L.A. Rusch. 2014. Cross-Sectional Time Series Analysis of Associations Between Education and Girl Child Marriage in Bangladesh, India, Nepal and Pakistan, 1991–2011. *PLOS One* 9 (9): e106210.

Riccardi, Theodor. 1980. Buddhism in Ancient and Medieval Nepal. In *Studies in the History of Buddhism*, ed. A.K. Narain, 265–282. Delhi: B.R. Publishing.

Rivera, Aguilar, Ana Milena, and Rafael Cortez. 2015. *Family Planning: The Hidden Need of Married Adolescents in Nepal*. Washington, DC: World Bank Group.

Rothchild, Jennifer. 2006. *Gender Trouble Makers: Education and Empowerment in Nepal*. New York and London: Routledge.

Sah, Nepali. 2008. How Useful Are the Demographic Surveys in Explaining the Determinants of Early Marriage of Girls in the Terai of Nepal? *Journal of Population Research* 25 (2): 207–222.

Sekine, Kazutaka, and Marian Ellen Hodgkin. 2017. Effect of Child Marriage on Girls' School Dropout in Nepal: Analysis of Data from the Multiple Indicator Cluster Survey 2014. UNICEF Nepal, Kathmandu.

Self, Sharmistha. 2014. Explaining the Ambiguous Impact of Mother's Autonomy on Daughters' Welfare in Patriarchal Societies. *Canadian Journal of Development Studies* 35 (4): 579–589.

Shrestha, Gajendra Man, Sri Ram Lamichhane, Bijaya Kumar Thapa, Roshan Citrikar, Michael Useem, and John Comings. 1986. Determinants of Educational Participation in Nepal. *Comparative Education Review* 30 (4): 508–522.

Shrestha, K.N. 1988. *On Primary Education in Nepal*. Kathmandu, Nepal: UNICEF.

Slusser, Mary Shepherd. 1982. *Nepal Mandala: A Cultural History of the Kathmandu Valley*, 2 vols. Princeton, NJ: Princeton University Press.

Stash, Sharon, and Emily Hannum. 2001. Who Goes to School? Educational Stratification by Gender, Caste, and Ethnicity in Nepal. *Comparative Education Review* 45 (3): 354–378.

Tamang, Seira. 1997. Questioning Netribad. *Studies in Nepali History and Society* 2 (2): 24–27.

Timsina, G. 2011. Educational Participation of Girls in Nepal: An Ethnographic Study of Girls' Education in a Rural Village. Christ Church University, UK, ProQuest Dissertations Publishing.

Tuladhar, Sumon K., and Bijaya K. Thapa. 1998. Mainstreaming Gender Perspectives into the Education System of Nepal. Paper presented in the Gender Sensitization Workshop (UNICEF), Pulchowk, Lalitpur.

UNICEF. 2000. *The State of the World's Children 2004.* New York: UNICEF House.

Valenti, Christine. 2011. What Did the Maoists Ever Do for Us? Education and Marriage of Women Exposed to Civil Conflict in Nepal. HiCN Working Paper No. 105.

Valenti, Christine. 2013. Education and Civil Conflict in Nepal. *World Bank Economic Review* 28 (2): 354–383.

Vogel, Ann, and Kim Korinek. 2012. Passing By the Girls? Remittances Allocation for Educational Expenditures and Social Inequality in Nepal's Households 2003–2004. *International Migration Review* 46 (1): 61–100.

CHAPTER 3

"Going Out to School": The Impact of Girls' Education on Family and Gender Systems in Bhubaneswar, India

Susan C. Seymour

Bhubaneswar, Odisha, has provided a microcosm for examining rapid change in India, in particular, change associated with the availability of schools—schools of all kinds and of all levels, from nursery schools to post-graduate universities.[1] Following independence from Great Britain in 1947, Bhubaneswar was selected to become the capital city of the newly organized state of Odisha. A new planned town was built next door to an ancient Hindu temple town. What had been a population of some 10,000 persons living in caste-based neighborhoods nestled together around temples and a sacred water tank, by 1965–1967 when I began doing fieldwork there, had jumped to 50,000. When I last returned in 2012, the population had expanded to 1.5 million. The sheer increase in population and commensurate establishment of schools suggest change, but change in India is like a moving tapestry—many long-term beliefs and practices are still woven into the fabric while new threads are added.

S. C. Seymour (✉)
Pitzer College, Claremont, CA, USA
e-mail: susan_seymour@pitzer.edu

© The Author(s) 2019
H. E. Ullrich (ed.), *The Impact of Education in South Asia*, Anthropological Studies of Education,
https://doi.org/10.1007/978-3-319-96607-6_3

1965–1967 RESEARCH

In 1961, Cora Du Bois, Zemurray Professor of Anthropology at Harvard University, selected Bhubaneswar as a site to examine rapid sociocultural change in post-World War II, post-independence India. It was planned as a twelve-year project with both American and Indian graduate students, representing different disciplines, studying the impact of Bhubaneswar's new capital city (the New Capital) upon the old temple town (the Old Town) and surrounding villages (Seymour 1980). My part of that project was to compare families and childrearing practices in the two parts of town. To do this, I selected a stratified sample of households from the Old Town and the New Capital, using caste as a diagnostic criterion in the Old Town and father's status in the government bureaucracy in the New Capital. After some months of meeting people, explaining my research goals in my newly acquired Oriya, and asking permission to observe their most intimate lives, I had a sample of 24 households—twelve from each side of town, with 130 children under the age of ten (Table 3.1). I have remained in touch with most of these families over the course of some fifty years.

In the Old Town, families ranged from high-level Brahmin priests at the top of the caste hierarchy to low-caste Washerman and Bauris, an outcaste group of laborers. In between were a set of clean Shudra castes—Carpenters, Barbers, and Milkherders. My New Capital sample of families ranged from top-level government officials to mid-level ones and peons at the bottom of the new class hierarchy. Haris, unclean Sweepers who lived in a special colony provided for them on the edge of town, constituted the lowest level. Caste and class status overlapped in the New Capital. The New Capital had been intentionally designed as a set of intersecting boulevards that created rectangular housing "units," which mixed people by the housing they were assigned—larger houses and Western-style yards on the exterior, with smaller houses and yards on

Table 3.1 Total number and sex of sample children (1965–1967)

Old Town			New Capital		
Status	M	F	M	F	Total
Upper	23	12	7	11	53
Middle	12	8	10	10	40
Lower	12	15	5	5	37
Total	47	35	22	26	130

the interior of each quadrangle. It provided a very different lifestyle from the caste-based neighborhoods of the Old Town where mud and brick houses shared walls and were accessed by narrow lanes that could not accommodate automobiles. My house was located in a neighborhood of private homes that, together with extensive paddy fields, separated the old and new parts of Bhubaneswar.

My objective was to do systematic observations of caretaker-child interactions[2] in each family over the course of two years and to learn as much as I could about how families operated—who performed what tasks, who ate with whom, who slept where, what rituals were observed, who was attending school, etc. My initial research predated feminist anthropology that, in the 1970s, made the study of gender central to the discipline, but in Bhubaneswar, I was deeply immersed in a gender system that varied by caste and class and Old Town–New Capital residence. Gender and family structure provided the context for understanding what was happening with children and determined who attended which schools.

With respect to household structure, there were significant differences between each side of town. In the Old Town, almost universally, people lived in what Carol Mukhopadhyay and I (1994) have called the "patrifocal family"—joint (lineal and collateral) households with fathers and sons, or sets of brothers, residing together with their children and wives, who married in from the outside. These patrifocal families were characterized by gender and age hierarchies as well as by gender differentiated roles and gender segregation. Adult women observed purdah. Ideally, the oldest male was the household head whose wife oversaw the domestic work of the family. Formal authority resided with men, although women exercised power over younger women and children, including adult sons. The patrifocal gender system of low-status Old Town families was more relaxed because women in these families worked outside the home and helped support the family financially. As workers, they could not observe purdah, and in the home, men and women helped one another rather than observing sexual segregation.

By contrast, New Capital families were in transition. Although the patrifocal joint family remained the cultural ideal, it could not be realized in a context where people had recently changed residence to participate in the new state government. Not all extended kin could move together, so households were centered on a married couple and their children, with extended kin visiting for extensive periods. There were a number of grandmothers and servants available to help with childcare, and rural relatives provided supplies of rice and other goods. They formed "supplemented nuclear" families whose core was a single married couple rather than a hierarchy of related men. New Capital women did not have to observe purdah, but they did not go outside their immediate neighborhoods unaccompanied by men. Men in both sides of town, for instance, did all the food shopping, leaving me as the only woman to visit the farmers market.

Going out to school was a new phenomenon for girls and for many boys in this part of Odisha, at the time one of India's most "backward" states.[3] I use the Indian expression "going out" because it implies there were conflicts in allowing girls to attend school when women lived secluded lives. To stray far from home was considered dangerous for girls. But schools were available everywhere, and girls' schools and colleges had been established for families that were protective of their daughters and wanted them to avoid contact with boys.

In the 1960s, determining who was attending school and why had not been one of my research objectives, but the evidence was in front of me.[4] Despite the availability of government support for low caste children to attend school, most of them were not in school—not because their parents were uninterested but because, as I would observe, children in poor families were needed at home to care for younger siblings and help with housework and other chores. One New Capital Sweeper father regularly apologized to me for not having his older son in school. "Bapu should be in school," he would say and then add, "But we need him at home to help with childcare." Bapu had a younger brother and an infant sister. His father, mother, and paternal grandmother all worked as Sweepers (janitors) in the New Capital, so Bapu was needed at home during the day to care for his younger siblings. By contrast, one Old Town Washerman father was sending all of his children, including a daughter, to school, an unusual phenomenon that I will address later.

In the 1960s, all middle and upper-status children from both parts of town were attending primary and secondary schools—a new phenomenon for many families. Until Bhubaneswar became a capital city and the educational center for Odisha, schools had not been available for Old Town residents and villagers. Now they were. As part of India's new status as an independent country, developing a literate public was viewed as essential. The federal government offered special incentives to get girls and low-caste children in school. All but the poorest families took advantage of these incentives. When I asked parents about their aspirations for sons' and daughters' education, most responded that they wanted their sons to go as far as possible—so they might qualify for "good" government jobs. Some Old Town families wanted to educate some of their sons for these new kinds of jobs while orienting others to traditional occupations such as serving as temple priests or carpenters. They wanted a foot in both worlds. Educational decisions were *family* decisions, and schooling was an economic investment for the family, *not* an opportunity for individuals to pursue their own interests.

No one, in the 1960s, had high expectations for their daughters' education. Girls were to receive some schooling so that they would be literate and suitably attractive to grooms' families at the time of marriage. (Arranged marriages were paramount.) One New Capital father told me how important it was that his wife was literate and could speak a little English so that she could answer the telephone for him. Such remarks symbolized the general attitude toward girls' education—some but not too much. Furthermore, *going out to school* beyond early childhood might endanger a girl's and her family's social reputation in a society that still believed in secluding women and carefully guarding their sexual purity—one of the principles of the patrifocal family and accompanying ideology (Mukhopadhyay and Seymour 1994).

EDUCATIONAL CHANGE: 1965–1989

Two years of research did not provide enough time to observe significant change, but it did provide a baseline for examining change over a longer period of time. When I returned to Bhubaneswar a decade later, in the mid-1970s, I was surprised to learn that all middle and upper-status Old Town and New Capital girls, as well as boys, were still in school. And many parents proudly told me how well their daughters were doing academically, some outperforming their brothers. The Washerman father, whom I mentioned earlier, also had his daughter and sons still in school, as did one very poor Bauri family whose oldest son was still in school. They had selected one child to go to school while the others helped with childcare and other tasks at home.

A new educational philosophy, especially about girls' schooling, had evolved during the 1960s and 1970s as Bhubaneswar became an established center of education. Unlike in some parts of India, where schools for women had been established over a century ago (Chanana 1994; Karlekar 1991, 1994), in Odisha that had not occurred. Whereas in nearby West Bengal, an educated female elite had emerged by the time of independence, it was about to happen in 1960's–1970's Bhubaneswar.

When I returned to Bhubaneswar in 1987, many families—New Capital ones more so than Old Town ones—were in crisis. All they wanted to talk about was marriage—the challenge of arranging marriages for their now older and highly educated daughters. In the patrifocal family model, grooms need to be older and more educated than brides, so the search for suitable men to marry their daughters became more complicated for many families who had allowed their daughters to become highly educated. In addition, a highly educated girl was often perceived as too old and potentially too independent-minded to make a good, accommodating wife and daughter-in-law.

How educated were these girls? In middle- and upper-status Old Town families they had, on average, completed 11.4 years of schooling as compared with their mostly illiterate mothers (Table 3.2). This meant that most had matriculated (passed the secondary school exams) and that a few had completed college. In one very conservative Brahmin family, a daughter had been pulled out of school after only a few years and married at age twelve. In a different Brahmin household, however, two daughters had been allowed to complete Master's degrees before marriage.

As one Old Town father put it, in talking with me about schooling:

Girls don't get the same educational attention as boys. I try to keep an open mind, but a 'Matriculation' or 'Intermediate' is enough. Then they are ready to marry.

This father, a Cow-herder by caste but a man with some formal education, had eight children—five sons and three daughters. Although he

Table 3.2 Mean number of years of school completed: a mother–daughter comparison by status and Old Town–New Capital residence

Status	Old Town		New Capital	
	Mothers (N=26)	Daughters (N=33)	Mothers (N=12)	Daughters (N=25)
Upper/middle	1.3	11.4	9.7	16.0
Lower	0.5	1.4	0.0	3.5

and his wife kept cows and sold milk, he had enough schooling—some secondary school—to qualify for a government job. His sons, by contrast, had all completed an Intermediate[5] or a Master's degree, while one daughter had matriculated and two had completed Intermediates. This was a high level of education compared with their illiterate mother— enough to help attract suitable suitors for marriage but not too much to make arranging a marriage difficult.

In 1989, when I interviewed these girls and their mother, Mrs. Gauda[6] reported:

> We had to concentrate on our sons' education both because of expenses and because of dangers. It's a jungle out there, and we live in an isolated house. I had to go with a lantern to meet my son every evening when he came home from college. I have always had to think about my children's safety.

Like her husband, Mrs. Gauda emphasized the importance of a son's education over that of a daughter's when there were limited resources, but she also identified another area of concern, that of danger. Sending a girl off to school, especially to a college not in the immediate area (all the colleges are in the New Capital), is considered a major social risk by many Old Town families. The Gauda's third daughter, who was not yet married, participated in this interview. I turned to twenty-five-year-old Ritu and asked her whether she would have liked to complete college. Ritu responded:

> No. I was not interested in continuing beyond the Intermediate. My father was supportive, but there was too much housework, it was difficult to study at home, and there were problems with safe transportation back and forth to school.

While Ritu also identified safety as a factor, she introduced two other factors relevant to having discontinued her education. First, she was needed at home to help with the housework. At the time, the Gaudas had just one daughter-in-law to assist Mrs. Gauda with work within the home as well as feeding and milking a herd of cows while her husband was off at work. Second, Ritu was not that interested in her studies and found it difficult to concentrate on them at home where there was other work to be done. She felt ready for marriage, and her marriage was arranged while I was in Bhubaneswar and able to observe the process.

As Mr. Gauda's earlier statement implies, education and marriage are closely connected in the minds of most Old Town families (Mukhopadhyay and Seymour 1994). Parents determine where and for how long their children will attend school and when and whom they will marry. These are important parental responsibilities because of the narrow range of years during which girls are considered marriageable. Previously, that narrow age range was linked to puberty, but today to be attractive to a suitable bridegroom, as Mr. Gauda indicated, a middle- or upper-status girl should have matriculated or completed an Intermediate level of education. Too little or too much schooling can be a problem in arranging marriages, but to remain unmarried is still not considered a viable alternative for most women in Bhubaneswar.

In the New Capital, all the middle- and upper-status girls in my sample families had received even higher levels of education. On average, they had completed 16 years of schooling, which meant most had completed at least a bachelor's degree. Fourteen had completed M.A.s in the arts and "pure" sciences,[7] one had an M.Sc. in computer science, two held medical degrees, and one was completing a Ph.D. in the social sciences. They had, in other words, become highly educated elite, far surpassing their mothers' levels of education (Table 3.2). Now arranging their marriages had become problematic.

In one middle-status New Capital home, by 1987 the issue of marriage had reached crisis proportions. Only one of seven eligible daughters was married. By 1989, only one more had married, and this was accomplished more by chance than through planning. Their father, Mr. Tripathy, had grown old and somewhat senile and was of little help, leaving his wife and two younger sons with the responsibility of trying to find suitable grooms for their highly educated and potentially too old daughters/sisters. As one daughter put it:

> Now there are no suitors available. We're too educated and there's a scarcity of educated boys in Odisha. We would like to meet more educated men, but there's no way to do it. Furthermore, they must be of Brahmin caste.

Not only were comparably educated suitors of the right caste and background scarce in Bhubaneswar and surrounding areas, but also young men and their families reportedly complained that the Tripathy daughters were too old and independent—that is, they had graduate degrees and were pursuing careers. These young women had another disadvantage as well. With so many daughters, their parents could not afford large dowries, but their daughters' earning potential was, at the time, not considered a suitable substitute. As one of the daughters expressed it, "Candidates come to our house but do not choose us. It is our fate, our fortune." At other times, however, she was less fatalistic and bitterly complained that "men just want less educated wives whom they can dominate; we are not supposed to out-achieve our husbands." She articulated one of the principles of patrifocal family structure and ideology—that a wife should be less educated than her husband and subordinate to him and his family.

My mother, who had accompanied me on the 1987 trip to Bhubaneswar, tried to console Mrs. Tripathy and the girls, pointing out that they were all beautiful and talented. Mrs. Tripathy poignantly responded by saying that she now wished she had had only a few children as my mother did. (I was translating this conversation back and forth because my mother knew no Oriya, and Mrs. Tripathy's English was very limited.) Her pride in her daughters' accomplishments no longer seemed to compensate for the marriage crisis she confronted. She took very seriously her parental duty of getting her children—especially, her daughters—well settled. And she was hurt by gossip that she and her husband were delaying their daughters' marriages in order to let them work and support their parents. It is sons, *not* daughters, who are supposed to help support their parents and extended kin, and the Tripathy made sure that their daughters' earnings were set aside for their futures. As one daughter explained:

> We are working and getting money, but we do not use it to live on. We live on our father's pension and our brothers' contributions. Nonetheless, people gossip and say our parents want their daughters' incomes.[8]

These conversations with families in 1987 triggered my return to Bhubaneswar in 1989 for a longer period to focus on women, the changes they were encountering, and the impact of these changes on family structure and gender ideology.[9] My goal was to interview three generations of women in as many households as possible—mothers, daughters, and paternal and/or maternal grandmothers. And I found that after so many years of knowing and trusting me, women were eager to talk (Seymour 1999).

Educational Change and Its Impact on Gender and Family Systems

As has already been made clear, the availability of schools in Bhubaneswar had had a major impact on all of my middle- and upper-status families but a minimal impact on lower-status ones. There were, however, three exceptions. One Old Town Bauri family sent one of their sons to school, and he became a low-level government clerk in the New Capital. One low-status New Capital family sent both its son and daughter to primary school. The father was literate and wanted his children to have some formal schooling. Their daughter, however, was pulled out after she had completed five years of school and married to an older man, a villager who resided outside of Bhubaneswar. As a little girl, I had asked Sopna how much schooling she would have. She responded, "I don't know, but my brother will go to college and become a government clerk." As a girl, she had no role models for any alternative to early marriage and childbearing, but she could fantasize about options for boys. Her brother Dipu, as it turned out, completed only ten years of school and became a bicycle repairman in the New Capital.

The most aspiring of my low-status families was one of two Old Town Washerman households in my sample. They lived side-by-side in a Washerman caste enclave. Both were large, extended-patrifocal families with sets of brothers, their wives, and children residing together. One family invested in their children's education and the other did not. By 1989, one had prospered financially and the other was impoverished. The question was, "why?"

I knew part of the answer. Mr. Sethi, the oldest brother in his family, had vision and was an entrepreneur. As the New Capital was being built, he began to solicit wash from families moving into town instead of limiting himself to his Old Town clientele. In fact, that is how I came to know him. He arrived at my doorstep one day in 1965 and asked if I needed wash to be done. Within the first decade of my knowing him, he was sending his youngest brother and all six of his children to school and had established a "laundromat" in the New Capital—a place where he and his middle brother could wash and iron sheets, towels, and clothes while his youngest brother got a college education and became a clerk in the New Capital. All contributed economically to the joint family's welfare. While his daughter Reena did not receive as much education as her five brothers, she did matriculate and at age twenty-two was married to an agricultural engineer in government service. Her oldest brother Rabi completed a bachelor's degree and by 1989 was a government clerk in the New Capital married to a woman with an Intermediate degree who also worked in the New Capital. In one generation, they, and some of their siblings, had shifted from people considered polluting because they handled others' dirty laundry to having New Capital employment and New Capital homes.

In 1989, I asked Mr. Sethi about these considerable changes. (Unfortunately, his wife and mother had died and I could not interview them, but I did interview the oldest son and his wife.) Mr. Sethi attributed the differences between his family and his Washerman neighbors to his participation as a revolutionary in the fight for India's independence from Great Britain and his service in the army during World War II. He explained that he had gained a broad experience by traveling around the country and working with people of different backgrounds and caste statuses. At the end of the war, however, he returned home to a fatherless household. His father had died and he had had to assume responsibility for his mother and younger brothers, but he had returned with the capacity to envision change. The New Capital, with its expanding population, provided him the opportunity to extend his laundry services to a new set of people while sending his children to school.

Old Town middle- and upper-status families generally handled girls' education more conservatively than New Capital ones. With one exception, they stopped schooling before daughters became difficult to marry. Nonetheless, Old Town girls did not marry as young as their mothers had married—as children or young adolescents. The age of marriage for Old Town daughters was 18–20 years. The exception was a joint Brahmin family with a widowed mother, Mrs. Mahapatra, who had three daughters. She reported:

> My ultimate aim in life was to make my children educated. My father had prevented me from studying when I wanted to continue. I don't hold this as a grudge against him and my children. I wanted them to get an education. I got them educated and then married. I brought them up differently than I was ... *With an education women can manage themselves.* Also, the cost of living is high. If both men and women are employed, they can manage better.

These were radical ideas at the time, and two of this mother's daughters completed master's degrees before marriage—one in science and one in education. Both are employed with children. The third daughter was less educationally gifted and lives a more traditional married life in the Old Town.

One of the striking factors that emerged in my interviews was the desire that many mothers and grandmothers had for their own education, which had been denied them. As a consequence, they had played supporting roles in encouraging their daughters' educational and employment ambitions. Mrs. Mahapatra had even expressed a revolutionary idea for the time—that daughters *should be able to support themselves and/or contribute financially to their household.* Her perspective was probably affected by the fact that she had been widowed at an early age. She and her husband lived with her brothers, her husband acting as head of that household after her father's death. After losing her husband, she had become financially dependent upon her brothers and did not want to see her daughters in this kind of situation.

Other Old Town mothers and numerous New Capital mothers and grandmothers expressed similar views about having wanted more education. For instance, one New Capital middle-status grandmother spoke as follows:

> I only attended school a few days. I saw the teacher cane a child and never went back. I was self-taught at home. I was always interested in higher studies and was able to teach my children in Oriya up to matriculation. I am literate in Oriya. I opposed my husband marrying our daughters and urged him to allow them to get highly educated first—to complete their studies. I was always interested in my daughters studying music and dance [that their father opposed]. I myself was interested in philosophy and aesthetics. Now [in my old age—late seventies] I enjoy reading from the *Gita* and the *Ramayana* [sacred Hindu texts].

Her two daughters, one the mother of children in my sample, had completed master's degrees and were employed outside the home in addition to being married and bearing children.

In another household, a maternal grandmother, who was visiting her daughter (a mother in my sample) and four granddaughters, discussed with me the impact of educational change. Grandmother reported,

> My marriage was arranged when I was seven and consummated at twelve. I wanted to be more educated, to learn more music. [She sings well.] I did not want to marry. My parents cooperated with me, but my grandparents objected. I wanted only two children, a son and a daughter, but I had thirteen. She [pointing to Mrs. Tripathy, the mother in my sample] was the first. I had wanted to be like my brother and sister-in-law, who are musicians and have traveled to the United States.

There was regret in this grandmother's voice as she reported her girlhood dreams. Now, she is a widow and dependent upon her various children.

Mrs. Tripathy then spoke, saying, "In my time, what I wanted could not be. Some of my friends went on; some became doctors. Our family was very conservative." Thus, despite her own and her mother's educational aspirations, she was allowed only six years of school and then married at fifteen to a widower with two children. She proceeded to bear nine children. Her daughters, however, had accomplished what had been impossible for her and her mother. They all have master's degrees, or other professional degrees, and are both married and employed.

Another upper-status New Capital mother offered the following:

> My mother was very much eager to read me more, but I was not interested at all ... I had lost my father when four years old. My older sister studied and became a doctor. My brother became an engineer ... But things have changed. Girls should have an education. *It gives them a choice. They can be economically independent.*

This mother's three daughters are all highly educated, married, and employed. Two have master's degrees and one a Ph.D.

The idea of a woman being economically independent was a radical one in the 1980s, but several mothers and grandmothers were thinking about it. And for three women in my original sample of children, it has been significant. All three left unhappy marriages and were able to do so because they had jobs and their own incomes. They did not go off and live alone but rather moved in with natal family. Nonetheless, they could support themselves and contribute to their extended family's welfare and that of their children. Their examples illustrate a radical break with traditional patrifocal ideas of family structure and gender ideology.

Having supportive in-laws for these highly educated and employed daughters was another theme that emerged from my interviews. In instances where mothers-in-law treated these highly educated daughters-in-law in the traditional manner—expecting them to do most of the cooking and housework on top of their work outside the home, observe rules of sexual segregation, etc.—led to serious disruption of families in both sides of town. Such circumstances forced a son to have to choose between his parents and his wife—a circumstance that in several instances led to the break-up of joint or extended families.

In a different case, an Old Town upper-status son, with a rudimentary education, moved out of his joint household with his conservative parents so that his children (two sons and one daughter) could attend good schools. He wanted his wife to be able to walk his children to school, but his parents would not allow her to leave the house. They made her observe purdah. Once they had their own house in a nearby neighborhood, his wife could attend to the children's education and their home became the center for tutorial sessions for theirs and others' children. Many families who could afford it hired tutors to help children with their studies at home and to prepare for national examinations.

Some Conclusions

The exposure of both men and women to formal schooling, especially to higher education, and to new kinds of employment has had a significant impact on family structure and gender systems in Bhubaneswar. Outwardly, family structure has remained reasonably stable but, inwardly, it has become increasingly flexible to meet changing employment conditions and women's aspirations. Joint households have continued to exist in the Old Town, breaking into separate households when becoming too large, but in three instances sons have set up separate households in order to avoid the authority of their parents over their wives and children. In one case, the son—with the marriage of his sons and the birth of grandchildren—is now head of his own joint family. In the New Capital, households continue to be flexible in structure, with extended kin coming and going. Two, however, have become fully joint with several sons, their wives and children, living together with a widowed parent. The ideal of the joint family lives on and is realized under certain circumstances.

While the ideal of the joint or extended family is alive and well, the "patrifocal" aspect of it is changing. Gender hierarchies and the restrictions on women have been loosened. Few women remain secluded behind mud walls, and both men and women go to the markets these days— something unheard of in the 1960s and 1970s. Also, a more conjugal relationship between husband and wife has emerged in both sides of town.

Longitudinal research has enabled me to monitor both change and continuity over the past 50 years. "Love" marriages have become the most recent threat to the stability of the patrifocal family.[10] During my 2012 visit to Bhubaneswar, one of my New Capital "grandsons" was about to marry an Eastern European woman whom he had met while working in the computer industry in Bangalore. Family members, who had gathered for the wedding ceremony, feared that such a bride would

pull their grandson away from them, not just geographically but culturally—that she would not understand and support her husband's economic responsibilities to his natal family. Yet in another New Capital
family, a "granddaughter" had entered into a love marriage with a
lower-caste but wealthy man whom she had met working in Mumbai.
Perhaps, because she was a daughter, not a son, her family seemed not
only accepting of this union but pleased with it.

Arranged marriages, nonetheless, remain predominant. In fact, during
my 2012 visit to Bhubaneswar, one Old Town Brahmin family was about
to celebrate their daughter's marriage to an Odishan residing and working in South Africa in information technology. Soon this young woman
would be whisked away from the protective confines of her joint family
in the Old Town—not to her in-laws' home but to a new international
life abroad, alone with her new husband.

NOTES

1. Between 1950 and 1965, two universities, three colleges, and a special
   college of education, serving the eastern region of India, were opened.
   The process of adding institutions of higher education in Bhubaneswar
   has continued. For instance, in 2008, the government of India established a prestigious Indian Institute of Technology (IIT) campus there.
2. This observational system was based on the methodology used in the Six
   Cultures Project (B. Whiting and W.M. Whiting 1975).
3. In the 1960s, Odisha (then known as Orissa) ranked as one of India's
   poorest and most backward states as measured by education, industrial
   production, urbanization, rice yield per acre, miles of road and railroad,
   and per capita income (*Technological Economic Survey of Orissa* 1962).
4. Alan Sable (1977), part of the Harvard-Bhubaneswar project, studied the
   town's school system.
5. An "Intermediate" refers to completion of the intermediary two years
   between secondary school and college, which is usually a three-year
   course of study leading to a B.A., B.Sc., etc., degree.
6. I have changed all peoples' names so as to protect their identities and privacy.
7. As Mukhopadhyay (1994) explains, the "pure" sciences are such fields as
   physics, chemistry, and biology, and they rank below the more applied
   sciences such as engineering and computer science. They are considered
   "safer" for girls to pursue.
8. All the Tripathy daughters did eventually marry, as was the case for all the
   other highly educated girls in my sample.

9. My 1989 research was supported by a Senior Scholar Fulbright Fellowship which enabled my family and me to return to Bhubaneswar for a six-month period.
10. There had been two love marriages in my original sample of children. Two young New Capital men, while studying or working abroad, married Western women, and their parents were shocked and dismayed. Another New Capital family made sure that their three sons, all of whom came to the United States to study and have remained, were married to suitable Odisha women before leaving India.

REFERENCES

Chanana, Karuna. 1994. Social Change or Social Reform: Women, Education, and Family in Pre-independence India. In *Women, Education, and Family Structure in India*, ed. Carol Chapnik Mukhopadhyay and Susan Seymour. Boulder: Westview Press.

Karlekar, Malavika. 1991. *Voices from Within: Early Personal Narratives of Bengali Women*. New Delhi: Oxford University Press.

Karlekar, Malavika. 1994. Women's Nature and Access to Education. In *Women, Education, and Family Structure in India*, ed. Carol Chapnik Mukhopadhyay and Susan Seymour. Boulder: Westview Press.

Mukhopadhyay, Carol Chapnik. 1994. Family Structure and Indian Women's Participation in Science and Engineering. In *Women, Education, and Family Structure in India*, ed. Carol Chapnik Mukhopadhyay and Susan Seymour, 103–132. Boulder: Westview Press.

Mukhopadhyay, Carol Chapnik, and Susan Seymour. 1994. Introduction and Theoretical Overview. In *Women, Education, and Family Structure in India*, ed. Carol Chapnik Mukhopadhyay and Susan Seymour, 1–33. Boulder: Westview Press.

Sable, Alan. 1977. *Paths Through the Labyrinth: Educational Selection and Allocation in an Indian State Capital*. New Delhi: Chand and Company.

Seymour, Susan (ed.). 1980. *The Transformation of a Sacred Town: Bhubaneswar, India*. Boulder: Westview Press.

Seymour, Susan. 1999. *Women, Family, and Child Care in India: A World in Transition*. New York: Cambridge University Press.

Techno-economic Survey of Orissa 1962. New Delhi: National Council of Applied Economic Research.

Whiting, Beatrice B., and John W.M. Whiting. 1975. *Children of Six Cultures: A Psycho-cultural Analysis*. Cambridge: Harvard University Press.

CHAPTER 4

Family Matters: Understanding Educational Choices and Gendered Science in India

Carol C. Mukhopadhyay

INTRODUCTION AND OVERVIEW

I have long been interested in how families "matter," and more specifically, how family structures, processes, and ideologies affect both internal gender-family dynamics (Mukhopadhyay 1980, 1984) and broader phenomena, such as women's career choices or political participation (Mukhopadhyay and Bald 1981). In an early comparative article on the U.S. and India, I argued that family organization and other social structural factors were the primary limitations on Indian women attaining political leadership positions, rather than essentialist gender beliefs about women and

---

The title of this chapter comes from a paper I presented honoring Pauline Kolenda for her contributions to anthropology, especially her pioneering work on Indian families, variations in family formations, and linkages to other phenomenon, including gender dynamics, dowry, widow remarriage (Mukhopadhyay 2015).

C. C. Mukhopadhyay (✉)
Department of Anthropology, San Jose State University, San Jose, CA, USA
e-mail: carol.mukhopadhyay@sjsu.edu

© The Author(s) 2019
H. E. Ullrich (ed.), *The Impact of Education in South Asia*, Anthropological Studies of Education,
https://doi.org/10.1007/978-3-319-96607-6_4

authority as in the U.S. where there still has never been a female "head of state" (Mukhopadhyay 1982, 2017a; Mukhopadhyay and Blumenfield 2017).

This chapter, however, focuses on the significance of the Indian family in decisions about education in India, especially in the education of girls,[1] and more specifically, in girls' pursuit of science and engineering degrees. Few anthropologists or educational researchers, even today, have done comparative educational research on India and the United States, especially on the scientific gender gap.

To help fill this gap, I embarked in 1988 on what I initially saw as a "small" project in India to study women's science-related academic decision processes and to evaluate the applicability of US theories of gendered science to the India context (Mukhopadhyay 2001, 2009). Although my initial fieldwork was "ethnographic," the setting and key informants were anthropologically atypical. I worked almost exclusively with urban, English-speaking, educated elites, whether they were my "expert consultants"[2] or college students from overwhelmingly elite (caste, class) urban backgrounds. My primary fieldwork site was an educationally elite engineering and science institution, IIT Madras, in Chennai, Tamil Nadu with briefer visits at similar institutions. My key student informants were for the most part from urban, highly-educated, and education-oriented, South Indian Brahmin or other "forward caste"[3] Hindu families.

I did visit and meet with individuals at less prestigious institutions, including regional government colleges, non-elite private colleges, and municipal primary and secondary schools. I also visited one government school in a village several hours outside Bangalore. Whenever possible, I talked with "ordinary" (English-speaking) people on busses, in post-offices, in trains, and in more informal settings as opportunities arose.

Information and Scholarly Exchange Component: More important, my research incorporated a significant "information-sharing and scholarly exchange component" with eventual visits to 8 Indian cities, over 30 education-oriented institutions, attendance at two research-relevant all-India conferences, and intensive interactions with over 60 "expert consultants." These are individuals in research institutions, governmental agencies, and key engineering-science-oriented universities whose position and experience gave them expert knowledge on gender-science-education issues (Mukhopadhyay 2001). This component not only yielded extensive national and state-wide educational statistics, available at that time only in India, in printed publications which

I hand-carried back to the U.S. I also gained access to scholars and to scholarly, often unpublished, gender-related reports, dissertations and theses, such as at The Indian Council of Social Science Research (ICCSR) library, the National Council for Educational Research and Training (NCERT) Women's Studies Unit, The Center for Women's Development Research (CWDR), The Indian Association of Women's Studies, and the Indian Institute of Political Economy in Pune (Maharashtra). In Bombay/Mumbai, I visited SNDT University, the oldest all-women university in India, and explored its unique Research Centre for Women's Studies. I spoke at length with director Dr. Maitreyi Krishna Raj, a pioneer on Indian gendered science, and with affiliated scholars. This led to more institutional visits, unpublished research, and contacts with Indian scholars and scientists.[4]

Through these materials and extensive discussions with expert consultants, I was introduced not only to the complex Indian educational system but also to how much influence families have on educational decisions and the role Indian cultural models of gender, family, and schooling play in girls' education. We also explored factors affecting girls' educational pursuits and achievements throughout India, across varied settings, regions, "castes," and classes. This gave me a much broader picture of the social-economic context and educational decision-making processes underlying the all-India and state educational statistical data I was obtaining. It also guided how I approached the more intensive ethnographic phase of my research.

The Ethnographic Phase: A student-focused ethnographic research phase involved over two months on-campus residence at Indian Institute of Technology (IIT), Madras, with shorter stays at the Indian Institute of Science, Bangalore (IISc) and Cochin University of Science and Technology (CUSAT) in, Kochi, Kerala. In addition to participation-observation and informal conversations with a wide range of students, administrators, faculty, and staff, I used structured interview and focus group formats to explore key research topics. I also collected 20 in-depth academic career histories. Nineteen were from science and engineering students (16 females, 3 males) and one from a female non-science "Arts" student.

Methodology: Methodologically, I drew upon cognitive anthropology, especially cultural models and ethnographic decision-modeling approaches (Gladwin 1989; Kronenfeld et al. 2011; Quinn 2005). Cultural models are shared, deeply embedded, and internalized complex cognitive structures (cultural schema) we use in everyday reasoning, for thinking, feeling, and acting, creating meaning (Strauss and Quinn 1997). They are revealed through language, in extensive analysis of ordinary discourse, particularly recurring metaphors, key words, and patterns of reasoning. One strategy for tapping cultural models is to analyze individual narratives of decision processes, such as occupational or academic choices.

My research assumption was that people employ internal, individualized versions of cultural models in making decisions. I approached the scientific "gender-gap" as the outcome of cumulative decisions made by and for students. I used ethnosemantic and more naturalistic interviewing techniques to identify key academic decision points, alternatives and choice criteria. I also probed the broader circumstances surrounding each decision, and explored key terms, phrases, and categories in informant narratives. This allowed further entry into cultural models of family, gender, schooling, science, and success. These interviews (2–18 hours in length, mostly tape-recorded and later transcribed) also provided insights into women's (and men's) subjective and varied experiences, complex family, gender, and marriage (including dowry) issues in academic choices, economic considerations, and other factors affecting girls' academic paths.

Going Beyond the Ethnographic Phase: In 1989–1990, I expanded the study to pre-college students, as this is where science-related choices occur and academic paths diverge. I also wanted a more diverse sample, including non-science students, and students from a broader range of socioeconomic backgrounds, school-types, academic achievement levels, and regions.

From the knowledge gained during the ethnographic and expert consultant phases, I constructed a "culturally meaningful" and "culturally relevant" student background and academic decision-related questionnaire (hereafter, the SAQ). The SAQ elicited information on student academic choices, achievement, family backgrounds, and sources of academic assistance, and attitudes on culturally significant issues such as arranged marriage, dowry, employment after marriage, natal family obligations, and religious orthodoxy. A narrative response segment elicited student "folk explanations" for gender-differentiated activities and student "mental images" of three science-related occupations. I also used four survey-type math and science attitude questionnaires originally developed in the US and England (Fennema and Sherman 1976; Kelly 1985; Smail and Kelly 1984). These questionnaires were administered, with the help of research assistants, to 6th, 9th, and 11th grade students at 12 linguistically, regionally, and socio-economically diverse urban schools in four major Indian cities (Madras-Chennai, Delhi, Bangalore, and Hyderabad).[5] The resulting database contains nearly 5000 questionnaires from over 1600 students (Table 4.1).

A subsequent phase, partially supported by NSF,[6] used the SAQ data base to evaluate and refine my ethnographically-derived theory of the scientific gender gap. First, I constructed a simplified decision model of science-related academic choices that emphasized academic and economic barriers to entering science and tested it using pre-college 9th and 11th grade SAQ data. Tests included conventional ethnographic decision model testing procedures and more indirect, statistical tests (Gladwin 1989). Second, I identified conditions which lead some women to enter science and tested the expanded theory using bivariate and multivariate, logistic regression modeling. Finally, I contrasted Indian and Euro-American cultural models of causality, of science, mathematics, gender, and personhood using SAQ narrative vignettes and responses on the Western-based math and science attitudes questionnaires.[7]

FAMILY REALLY MATTERS IN INDIAN EDUCATIONAL DECISIONS

Educational decisions in the United States are generally conceptualized as being "individual" student decisions, guided by individual interests, aptitudes, and goals, what I have characterized as a "school as self-discovery and self-realization" cultural model (Mukhopadhyay 2004a). In India, however, I quickly discovered that educational decisions, like marriage decisions, are usually family matters rather than simply the concern of an individual student. Family really matters in understanding Indian educational decisions and outcomes, including historical gender disparities at all levels of the educational system, as well as the gender gap in science and engineering degrees.

In the sections that follow, I describe how Indian cultural models of family, gender, and schooling interact with macrostructural features of Indian society (educational, socioeconomic, occupational) to frame the academic decision process in ways that contribute to a gender (and class) stratified scientific community. But my research also reveals increasingly complex and powerful pressures **for** girls' schooling and identifies some individual student and family circumstances which are leading more and more girls to pursue science and engineering.

Table 4.1 Pre-college data base[a]

City	School[b]	Grade	Section type	Language	School type	#SAQ	#Math	#Science Image	#Science Curiosity	#Science Activities
Delhi	1-C	6		English	Private	41		42		43
		9		English		43	38	41		
		11	Science	English		44	37	38		
		11	Commerce	English		36	33	33		
		11	Arts	English		41				
Delhi	2-C	6		Hindi	Central	35		37		
		9		Hindi	Govt	39	39	35	37	
		11	Science	Hindi	Kendriya Vidyalaya (KV)	40	36	36		
		11	Commerce	Hindi		28	31	30		
		11	Arts	English		44				
Delhi	3-B	6		Hindi	Municipal Boys	28		24		26
		9		Hindi		34	23	25		
		11	Science	Hindi		12	19	17		
		11	Commerce	Hindi		32	23	38		
Delhi	3-G	6		Hindi	Municipal Girls	27		31		26
		9		Hindi		36	33	19		
		11	Science	Hindi		19	19	30		
		11	Commerce	Hindi		28	30	30		
Bangalore	1-C	6		English	Central	36		34	34	34
		9		English	Govt (KV)	34	42	42		
		11	Science	English		39	40	40		
		11	Arts	English		36	31	31		
Bangalore	2-G	11	Science	English	Private	63	31	31		
		11	Commerce	English	Girls	63	51	51		
		11	Arts	English		44	42	42		

(continued)

Table 4.1 (continued)

City	School^b	Grade	Section type	Language	School type	#SAQ	#Math	#Science Image	#Science Curiosity	#Science Activities
Bangalore	1-G	6		Kannada	Municipal	31		43	43	43
		9		English	Girls	35	34	34		
		9		Kannada		35	32	32		
		11	Science	Kannada		37	33	33		
		11	Science	English		50	17	17		
		11	Arts	Kannada		41	31	31		
		11	Arts	English		34	29	29		
Madras	1-C	6		English	Central	0	0	49	48	50
		9		English	Govt	37	36	36	36	36
		11	Science	English		28	34	34	32	34
		11	Arts	English		18	0	0	0	0
Madras	1-C	6		English	Private			40	37	37
		9		English		27	27	28	28	28
Hyderabad	1-C	6		English	Private	42				
		9		English		33				
Hyderabad	1-C	6		English	Central	29	43	46	29	29
		9		English	Govt	39	37	37		
		11	Science	English		37	37	37		
		11	Science	English		37	38	38		
		11	Commerce	English		35	38	38		
		11	Arts	English		39	39	39		
Hyderabad	1-C	6		English	Private	29		29	29	29
		9		English		9		27	27	27
		11	Science	English		25	25		25	25

(continued)

Table 4.1 (continued)

City	School[b]	Grade	Section type	Language	School type	#SAQ	#Math	#Science Image	#Science Curiosity	#Science Activities
# of Student questionnaires by type										
Total # of questionnaires: 5019										
# Schools 12			Sections 49	#11th grade streams:	Science-12 Arts-8 Commerce-6	1649	1091	1407	405	467

[a] In the expanded pre-college level study, I tried to sample schools from different regions and languages of India, especially North and South; within each city, different types of schools (central government-Kendriya Vidyalaya, municipal, and private) and both single-sex and coeducational schools. Within each school, I tried to include English and non-English medium sections, and, most important, at the 11th grade level, sections of each of the major "streams": science, arts, and commerce

[b] The names of schools within a single city have been replaced here with a distinct number. The letter refers to the type of school: C coeducational school, G All-girls school, B all-boys school

[c] These remaining five columns show the number of students at each school who completed each of the questionnaires. I prioritized which questionnaires should be given first, if not all could be administered. Highest priority went to the SAQ, Student Background and Academic Decision Questionnaire, which I had developed based on my ethnographic data. The other four questionnaires were developed elsewhere and adapted for use in India. "Math" refers to the Fenemma-Sherman Math Attitudes Survey (Fennema and Sherman 1976). The remaining three survey-type closed choice questionnaires are: Image of Science, Science Attitudes, and Science Activities, originally developed in England (Kelly 1985; Smail and Kelly 1984)

Understanding India's Gender Gap in Science-Engineering

Despite significant advances in Indian women's education since Independence (Mukhapadhyay and Seymour 1994: 1–33), and especially in the past several decades (Government of India 2016a, b),[8] all-India nationwide statistics continue to show that women are less likely to pursue science-related degrees than are their male counterparts. In 1986, Indian women were barely 30% of students enrolled in Bachelor of Science (BSc) programs, but 37.9% of students pursuing "Arts" degrees (social sciences and humanities) and 43.9% of those seeking a Bachelor of Education (Government of India 1987a, b). By the late 1990s, despite anecdotal reports of dramatic increases in women's entry into the sciences, these figures had not altered substantially. Women still constituted about one-third of science students (33.3%) while they were relatively over-represented in Arts (40.0%) and Education (43.2%) students (Government of India 1995: 17–19).[9]

The most recent all-India data show a dramatic rise in education for both boys and girls.[10] Yet college degree enrollments exhibit familiar patterns. In 2014–2015, 33% of females were enrolled in Bachelor of Arts degrees vs. 24.6% of males. And twice as many females as males were pursuing B.Education degrees (2.85% vs. 1.37%). However, slightly more girls than boys were enrolled in B.Science degrees—12.2% of females vs. 11.44% of males (Government of India 2016a: 6).

The Indian science gender gap is most dramatic in Engineering and Technology fields. In 1985–1986, women were just 6% of those enrolled in bachelor's degree engineering courses and less than 10% of students at the Polytechnic Institutes. By 1994–1995, even with enormous enrollment gains, women were less than 15% of Engineering and Polytechnic students. In 2004, the situation had improved somewhat, although a substantial gap remained, according to participants at a NISTAD conference in India (Kumar 2009). The most recent data show that while more girls are pursuing engineering and technology degrees, a significant gender gap remains. For 2014–2015, only 3.78% of females were in B.Technology programs (vs. 8.68% males) while 3.7% females were in B.Engineering programs (vs. 7.61% males). Far more males than females are currently enrolled in "diploma" programs, which may cover subjects like computers and electronics taught at polytechnic institutes (Government of India 2016a: 4–7, 8).

The gender gap seems most persistent and significant at the most prestigious engineering and science institutions, such as the Indian Institutes of Technology (Mukhopadhyay 1994; Parikh and Sukhatme 1992). IIT data which I hand-collected in 1988 and 1996 showed women constituted fewer than 6% of students admitted to IIT undergraduate engineering programs. The percentage increased slightly by 2004, reaching nearly 10% at some IIT campuses, such as IIT, Madras (Malaithy 2004, personal communication). The most recent IIT statistics, now available on-line, show little improvement despite the dramatic increase in the number of IITs in recent years. Women's percentage of B.Tech students fluctuated from 8.8% in 2014, to 9% in 2015, dropping to 8.0% (2016) and reaching 9.2% in 2017 (Pandey 2017).[11]

WHY SHOULD THIS BE THE CASE?

One major cause, historically, has been overall disparities in girls' and boys' education, at every level of schooling, but particularly in the crucial secondary and higher secondary school phases: that is, 9th through 12th grades.[12] By the time one reaches the post-secondary level, where one can pursue science and engineering degrees, the proportion of girls is already significantly less than boys.[13] So the first reason for the scientific gender gap is a pipeline issue... fewer girls, overall, than boys make it to college. But why should such gender disparities exist in the first place?

In 1994, Susan Seymour and I, in the introduction and theoretical overview to our volume, *Women, Education and Family Structure in India*, proposed a framework for understanding the gender gap in schooling. We first argued that Indian educational decisions were family decisions, which had broader family, social, economic, and status impacts and involved a substantial investment of resources. We posited an ongoing tension between macro-structurally generated pressures that increase the desirability of education for women and microstructural pressures that constrain women's education. At the microstructural level, we suggested three major factors contributing to overall Indian gender disparities in educational enrollments (1) the emphasis on educational decisions as family decisions, guided by collective family concerns and goals; (2) gender-differentiated family obligations that produce gender-differentiated educational expectations and goals for sons vs. daughters and can lead to family educational investments which advantage sons over daughters; and (3) family concerns with female chastity, marriageability, and family honor that make the education of daughters potentially socially problematic.

These three factors are derived from one long-standing and widespread Indian cultural model of family which Seymour and I have termed "patrifocal family structure and ideology" or, simply, "patrifocality" (Mukhopadhyay and Seymour 1994: 1–33). Among its characteristics are the expression of individual goals within a broader collective set of family goals centered on family welfare; structural features (patrilineality, patrilocal residence) which reinforce the centrality of sons and the peripheral status of daughters; gender-differentiated family responsibilities and activities; regulation of female sexuality (to maintain the purity of the patriline) through arranged marriages and restricted male–female interactions; and female standards of behavior which emphasize "homely" traits such as obedience, self-sacrifice, adaptability, nurturance, restraint, and other behaviors considered conducive to family harmony.

While other cultural models of family exist in India (Kolenda 1987; Pai 1998, 2002), this is perhaps the most prominent and one to which most Indians have been exposed. As such, it provides a significant culturally rooted, conceptual and cognitive framework for thinking about and making educational decisions.

Beginning in the late nineteenth and twentieth century, and continuing after Independence, education in India was heavily promoted and became increasingly linked to and a vehicle for expressing, maintaining, and improving one's family status (Papanek 1989; Mukhopadhyay and Seymour 1994). Given the long-term family responsibilities of sons vs. daughters (and the family sexual division of labor), it is not surprising that families have tended to view investing in boys' education differently than girls'. Because sons, in this traditional patrifocal cultural model, have the primary obligation to care for natal families, investments in a son's education generally benefit the family directly. In contrast, daughters are expected to marry, "leave" the family and acquire obligations toward their husband's family. Thus a daughter's education, after marriage, primarily benefits her in-laws rather than her natal family.

The patrifocal family model assumes that a family's primary obligation to daughters is to see they "marry well" (are "well-settled") and uphold family honor. Education has in the past often been viewed as posing "social dangers" to unmarried girls, which is exposing them to situations that could harm their "reputation" as a potential bride, wife and daughter-in-law, thus threatening their marriage prospects.

Schooling, especially at secondary and college levels, requires going "outside the family" into the "male" world of public spaces. Historically, education was also seen as potentially "spoiling a girl's character," cultivating traits and values, such as independence, autonomy, out-spokenness, which could undermine patrifocal family values and roles.

Within the context of the patrifocal family model, then, educational decisions, whether for sons or daughters, are framed by their projected impact on the collective family welfare. They involve family resources, status, and marriage considerations, and (like marriage) are too important to leave in the hands of individual students. Indeed, the education-oriented families in my sample viewed decisions about students' education as major family obligations, demanding careful research and broad consultation with family (including extended family) members.

Macrostructural pressures for education, including women's education, come from the post-Independence emphasis on literacy, formal education, and science and technology, as keys to Indian national development. Educational degrees, such as being a "matriculate" (completing Secondary School—10th year) opened up new economic opportunities as well as enhancing family status. College degrees, particularly in science and engineering, were even more valuable, on both the prestige and career opportunity fronts. These factors helped fuel an enormous expansion of the Indian educational system and the rise in literacy, school attendance, and college degrees. It produced an academic hierarchy of subjects and degrees, with competition for "seats" in high-ranked fields, namely, science and engineering—at high-ranked educational institutions. Such degrees provide access to jobs "with scope"—that is, careers with financial and career advancement potential as well as opportunities to study or work "abroad."

The accompanying demand for grooms with good "academic qualifications" is linked to the rise and spread of dowry/groom price since Independence, despite its prohibition.[14] Potential bridegrooms with applied science degrees are especially "qualified" academically and hence, desirable. The association of dowry with academic qualifications is one more motivation for families to invest in sons' education, especially in science and engineering, and to help them succeed academically, within family economic circumstances and the boys' academic potential. Not only will this bring occupational opportunities (and prestige) which benefit the entire family, but also it increases a boy's marriageability and the potential for a dowry which, at minimum, can offset the expenses of the groom's education.

But modern education has not benefited everyone equally and may have exacerbated traditional class and caste disparities (Chitnis 1989). Until recently, many poor children never attended school. Among those that did, there was a high attrition rate for **both** sexes after elementary school (Seymour 1999). Only a small fraction of students' families had the financial resources to send them to college. These trends, however, have been more pronounced for girls and their school attrition rates, until 2010, were considerably higher at **each** educational stage than for boys (Government of India 1987a, 1995).

Within the framework of a patrifocal family cultural model (differential obligations of sons and daughters; the potential social dangers of educating females) and given the limited economic resources of most Indian families, many families have found it more worthwhile to devote resources to the education of sons than to daughters. Thus, while daughters received some education, sons have tended to receive more and, when economically feasible, a higher quality education in subjects leading to more competitive fields.

SCIENCE AND ENGINEERING AS COSTLY ALTERNATIVES FOR GIRLS

Pursuing science degrees, I argue, compared to obtaining degrees in other fields, such as Arts or Commerce, significantly exacerbates the gendered educational impact of patrifocal family models that I have just described. Obtaining a science degree, especially at a reputable institution, has traditionally been significantly more competitive, and hence more costly and difficult, than pursuing a non-science degree. Among other things, it requires studying science at the pre-college level. Science "streams" tend to be the most desirable and competitive of the streams available in the secondary school "academic track" (vs. Arts, Commerce). One must have sufficient "marks" (test scores) in key "subjects" (e.g., math, physics, chemistry, biology) to gain admission to such streams, assuming they exist. In urban areas, there may be several secondary schools, both public and private, with admission to the most highly "ranked" extremely difficult, overall, but particularly in the science stream. Attending a private secondary school may require substantial fees or putatively voluntary financial "contributions" to the school, in lieu of or along with sufficient "marks".

Studying science, then, even in an urban area, demands a larger investment of family resources than pursuing other streams. For rural students, there may not be a nearby secondary school or it may not offer science stream subjects. So pursuing science may require residence at a secondary school hostel (dormitory) outside the village.

Science seats are limited and require academic success, early on, so one can take the science "streams" and "subject" prerequisites, ideally at "good" schools—those which best prepare students for exams leading to the equally limited number of science seats available at colleges, especially at high-ranked colleges. My relatively well-off expert consultants lamented the growth of expensive, highly competitive, academically oriented schools in major urban centers, starting with elementary schools that sometimes required entrance exams for first-graders! Nevertheless, they felt compelled to give their children every possible advantage in the race for academic success. They also freed their children from family chores and provided academic help, paid tutors, and "tutorial" courses. Many of my IIT women engineering students had attended private, often Christian, academically rigorous, English-language secondary schools. And virtually, all came from highly educated, science-oriented, urban families.

The increased value of boys' education in science and engineering focuses family resources even more on boys than girls, and when scare, leaves less for daughters than if sons were pursuing commerce or arts. Even if girls remain in school, and do pursue a science stream, it may be at a less expensive municipal school, without tutorials, and without release from household obligations.

Marriage Risks: Science, for girls, can also pose marriage risks. In the past, science was unavailable at all-girls' schools and even today often requires attending co-educational institutions (Vasantha 1996; Wotipka 2001). As noted earlier, for village girls, it may first require living away from home in a town which has a secondary school with a science stream, and perhaps staying in a girls' hostel, if one can be found or staying with relatives in town. Further education, regardless of degree, will again require living away from home and finding a suitably socially "safe" residential arrangement.

Pursuing *applied* science degrees, especially engineering, and especially at the prestigious and highly competitive Indian Institutes of Technology (IITs) implies immersion in a virtually all male environment, unsupervised, close contact with unrelated males, and on-campus residence. Similar conditions often exist in science and engineering workplaces and represent challenges to both women and their male colleagues.[15] Some employers use these reasons to refuse to hire women, further discouraging girls and their families from pursuing science and engineering.

Both my expert consultants and my student informants viewed the male-dominated social context of science and engineering as a major barrier to women's participation. Same-sex girls' schools are still preferred by many families, especially more conservative, religious families. Yet science streams are often lacking at all-girls' schools, especially in rural areas, since they require greater expenditures of already scarce funds. Girls selecting science at "higher secondary" levels must either go "outside" to a girls' school in some other locale or risk the social dangers of attending a local coeducational school, filled with "rough" and "rowdy" boys.

In urban areas where schools with science streams are plentiful and girls can live at home, incursions into predominantly male public spaces remain socially problematic. My female informants described family concerns about the "dangers" of a daughter traveling across town, especially "alone" and at "odd" hours (e.g., after dark). Girls described the "comments," the "pinching and that sort of thing, quite common in busses, in streets, and in market places when it's crowded" and which "of course, prohibits us from going into crowded places." The associated "dangers" and "risks" were not primarily physical, at least not in the more "conservative" and "safe" South, according to my, mainly, Southern Indian student informants at IIT, CUSAT and IIScience. They viewed the "north" and northern college campuses as more dangerous for girls. Girls told me stories they'd heard about the dangers, even physical and sexual assault, female students faced at campuses like IIT Kanpur. Several said their families would never have allowed them to attend school there![16]

For my informants and consultants, at least during my fieldwork, most discussions about the "dangers" they could encounter referred primarily to social and reputational risks centered around issues of sexuality… as interpreted through a patrifocal and patriarchal lens. On crowded busses, for example, my female students said they were afraid of "creating a scene" should they resist an attempted "pinch", especially since some passengers might say it was the girl who "tempted that person." I was told that even if something "serious" happens, "your parents will ask you to keep quiet because it'll not be good for your future…..if you're not married…" Unless a girl's family can afford alternative ways of transporting her to school,[17] she must either confront the reputational risks associated with traveling "outside" or attend a closer coeducational school. Or, she may "go for" an arts (or commerce) degree at a nearby all-girls' school lacking a science stream.

The social dangers associated with the predominantly male social environment of science and engineering persist at the college level and in careers. Residence in a student "hostel" may be mandatory, with the only choice being whether it is on a coeducational or on an all-female campus. And at the time of my research, while girls could study "pure" science at women's colleges that was not the case for engineering.

The absence of "suitable housing" for girls (i.e., socially appropriate all-girls hostels) was a major concern of families and constituted a significant constraint on women studying and thus entering engineering. At CUSAT, a graduate institution, the girls' hostel I visited was at double the occupancy for which it was originally designed (168 girls in 80 single-occupancy rooms). In contrast, 350 boys were accommodated in 308 rooms.[18] But although crowded, the girls' hostel was at least in a socially "safe" space, located close to the administration building, at the opposite end of the campus from the boys' hostels. Girls had to be in the hostel by 7 p.m. unless they needed to be at the laboratory, for which they could stay out "till ten." Barring a special program or campus-wide movie, after 7 p.m. the campus (including "student cafe") was virtually an all-male world. Both the local city, Kochi, and the campus have expanded significantly in recent years. When I returned in 2008, both were nearly unrecognizable. Yet the need for socially appropriate and safe housing for women students remains.[19]

At IIT Madras, the girls' hostel was located near the campus library, far from the boys' hostel, and separated from the main road by a long, tree-shaded path. It was already significantly over-crowded and another hostel was under construction. The new hostel was next door thus preserving the all-girls residential compound.

IIT hostel girls would "wander about" in the evening, going to labs, library, and even the campus canteen. The campus was actually a residential community (staff, faculty, students) complete with post office, bank and walled, guarded campus entrances. Nevertheless, women graduate students said they experienced social discomfort when going alone for a "coffee" in the student canteen. The campus swimming pool was frequented virtually only by males. There were women-only swimming hours, but even then, my female informants told me they were not comfortable going swimming in the pool.

Girls' were a distinct minority on campus and were aware of potential social dangers in such an environment, including rumors of social impropriety that sometimes circulated. Several described initial loneliness in class because they felt it would be socially inappropriate for them to initiate conversations with male classmates. Some male students reported similar concerns about approaching their female classmates. One freshman, the only girl in her Mechanical Engineering class, said not a single male student spoke with her in class the entire semester! Yet class assignments, as well as note and textbook sharing, sometimes required girls to visit the boys hostel, presenting a dilemma. Most girls eventually managed to overcome their discomfort. However, some women students stayed away from class "industrial tours" because of the social inappropriateness of traveling in all-male, or virtually all-male company, and because there were no "suitable accommodations" (i.e., for an unmarried girl).

For families, the social dangers (and financial costs) of a girl's engineering education are minimized by sending her to a local college, even if she is eligible for a more distant, higher-ranked institution. My ethnographic and SAQ data indicate girls are more likely than boys to enroll in or anticipate enrolling in local colleges rather than in all-India engineering and technical institutions, such as the IITs. This was a recurring theme in my expert consultant interviews and in girls' academic life histories. Several of my key IIT Madras hostel-dwelling women informants were from Madras, others had nearby relatives in the city, and all but one were from Tamil Nadu or a neighboring state. Virtually, all the CUSAT hostel students I interviewed were from Kerala, usually from Kochi or nearby cities, and mentioned geographic proximity as one factor in their decision about which college to attend.

Leaving college and pursuing a career can exacerbate the social dangers. One stereotype of engineering, especially civil engineering, according to my informants, involves "fieldwork," often a rough "camp," full of "rowdy" male laborers from a variety of castes and classes. Problems of "suitable accommodations" are compounded by having to eat and travel with "all sorts" of people "at all hours", a "strenuous" and "dangerous" situation, particularly for an unmarried woman. Female engineering students tended to steer away from certain "branches" like civil and mechanical engineering, partially because of these stereotypes. In contrast, electrical and computer engineering, associated with less socially problematic contexts and social interactions, were viewed as more desirable. Nevertheless, even though most of my students anticipated employment in engineering "desk jobs", both the reality and stereotype of engineering assumes late night shifts, "posting" to different parts of India, and immersion in a mostly male, often working-class male social context—formidable dangers for marriage-conscious, middle-class families of girls.

Other risks relate to the theme that "education spoils a girl's character". Verbal assertiveness, independent thinking, and leadership were encouraged in CUSAT's graduate management studies program. Some girls from all-women's colleges seemed shocked at the behavioral expectations. In the words of one CUSAT student, "It's totally different in a girls' college...But here, everybody's so aggressive. And unless you are ready to fight it out, nobody's going to stand back and let you go and give you a chance." Women engineering students recounted, sometimes with laughter, their embarrassment at the atypical female behavior required for "practicals", such as donning overalls and learning to do "smithy" (blacksmith) work. "Shouting" was considered useful for "controlling laborers." Some IIT girls mentioned discomfort at participating in sports and other extra-curricular activities that entailed exerting authority over male peers. Yet my informants seemed to have adjusted remarkably well and welcomed, even celebrated, these educational side-effects. From the perspective of many families, however, cultivating such traits could constitute a future marriage risk.

Educational "hypergamy" is an additional issue. Girls are expected to marry up educationally, perhaps consistent with the higher rank husbands should have over wives. Relatives and parents believe that the higher the "academic qualifications" of a potential bride, the higher the academic qualifications of potential grooms. Rank is not just based on the degree but on the subject. Since science is generally ranked above arts, a girl with a bachelor's degree in arts is at relatively little risk. Science degrees, especially applied science degrees, are more problematic.

But the rank difference in marriage arrangements can be slight. One female Ph.D. chemistry student told me that her future spouse (selected by her family) had an "M-Tech" or master's degree in technology. Her family, who had arranged the marriage, considered his degree appropriate, rank-wise, because hers was only in "pure science" while his was a more prestigious applied engineering degree.

Patrifocal family cultural models, then, have a different and greater educational impact on daughters than on sons, at every educational choice point and level, but are greatest when substantial family investments are required and when the perceived social dangers for daughters are highest. Economic considerations play a major role in the educational paths selected for boys as well as girls, but within the same family, limit girls more than boys.

Families assess the marriage impact of education for boys as well as girls. In the case of boys, however, academic success and science and engineering degrees facilitate a "good marriage". In contrast to boys, girls' academic success and science degrees can make their marriages more difficult to arrange because: (1) the supply of higher academically ranked males is smaller (2) the desirability and groomprice/dowry costs associated with academically high-ranked males is enormous and (3) rather than recovering their science education costs, girls marriages will require greater expenditures than if they pursued a commerce or arts degree.[20]

Despite these constraints, girls' educational participation has grown steadily, in science, and in engineering as well as medicine. This reflects increasingly strong countervailing pressures **for** daughters' education generally, and science education specifically. Education can **enhance** a girl's marriage prospects. Historical arguments for girls' education emphasized cultivating attributes consistent with patrifocal cultural models (Chanana 1994). Educated wives were portrayed as better able to supervise the education of children (especially sons), to interact more comfortably in the world of their spouses, and to serve as companions and helpmates for their husbands. Better-educated husbands demanded better-educated wives, motivating some rural families to educate their daughters at least to some degree.

These arguments for women's education continue to carry weight, particularly among the middle-class, educated and education-oriented families best positioned to consider science and engineering degrees for either sons or daughters. As more boys acquire more education, especially in science and engineering, it is possible for more girls to do the same. From a marriage perspective, this does not threaten educational hypergamy (girls marrying up). It may facilitate a growing tendency towards educational endogamy (marrying within the same field), advantageous for those who, like several of my informants, planned to set up small electronics or IT firms with (future, not yet selected) spouses. Coeducational science-engineering colleges also offer opportunities for girls (and boys) to find a personally and socially-economically suitable spouse, making at least some families more accepting of such "love marriages".

Traditional advantages of education are augmented by the growing value of a girl's earning capacity. With more jobs available in "respectable" settings (e.g. government offices, educational and research institutions, multinational companies), and family living costs rising, an "earning" daughter-in-law can be an asset. As with boys, science degrees, especially in highly ranked fields, provide access to "good jobs" with "scope" and opportunities abroad for the girl, her future spouse and in-laws. Virtually all my college science students expected to be employed after marriage. Several students said this would be explicitly agreed upon in their arranged marriage negotiations. In the pre-college SAQ sample, female 9th and 11th grade science-choosers were more likely than non-science choosers to expect to contribute to their spousal household income after marriage.

Education is not only an asset in the marriage market. My female science students and their families placed great emphasis on their becoming "financially independent", beyond being an "earning wife". Among other things, it reduced the pressure on girls to marry, allowing the girl, and more often, her family, more time to find a "suitable" spouse. Indeed some key informants in their mid-twenties, with research stipends and good job possibilities, seemed comfortable with **never** marrying, partially because they would not be economic burdens on their families. Their parents, however, felt a moral obligation to see them "well-settled"—i.e. married.

Education, apart from marriage issues, can independently benefit a girl's natal family, before and after marriage. Science and engineering degrees have always been linked to job opportunities. But the advantages have expanded tremendously with 1990s "liberalization" policies, the growth of the IT industry in India, and India's emergence as a global "outsourcing" site for multinational corporations. Technology parks and small Indian-owned IT businesses have been springing up all-over India, especially in the last two decades, some established by returning Indian engineers who received graduate degrees abroad, including in the United States.

This expansion of science-technology fields has further fueled the demand for training and degrees in these areas along with producing educational institutions, both public and private, to satisfy this demand. Girls as well as boys are seeking such degrees (Government of India 2016a, b).

The potential earnings of girls, at least prior to marriage, can, like those of boys, compensate families for the additional costs associated with pursuing a science education. They can also be used for the education of other family members, such as younger siblings. One female IIT PhD science student's father had initially refused to allow her to attend graduate school, even though she was an outstanding student. Her family had limited financial resources and since they lived in a rural area, attending graduate school would also require residing in a hostel. She eventually convinced him her degree would improve both her job and her marriage prospects. Most important, she would receive a substantial stipend as a graduate student at an IIT, a portion of which could be used for her brother's engineering education.

Earnings can be used to reduce or offset dowry demands. Dowry in India remains alive and well, some would say even thriving, even though it is illegal (Pai 2002; Ullrich 1994). One expert consultant suggested that some families send their daughters for technically-oriented degrees because they feel a girl's earning power can reduce the chance of her "dowry death." Dowry was a subject of heated discussion among my student informants with girls being uniformly opposed while boys were more likely to express ambivalence, partially because of family pressures and concern for their female siblings. My female informants generally expected their future earning power to reduce or substitute for dowry. In a focus group of young women computer science students at CUSAT, all insisted their families would "absolutely refuse" any dowry demands and did not anticipate problems in doing so. Whether boys' families view dowry in a similar light is less certain (Seymour 1999).

Daughters' earnings can also provide additional "old-age" insurance for parents. A surprisingly high percentage of both 9th and 11th grade female science-choosers expect to be at least partially financially responsible for their parents. Most girls in my CUSAT graduate computer science and management studies sample expected to contribute to their natal family finances, even after marriage, and even if they have male siblings. As Indian families are becoming smaller, especially among the urban, middle-class, more will end up with only daughters. In such circumstances, decisions about daughters' education may involve the same considerations as those for sons.[21]

There are other benefits of girls' pursuing science. The potential social risks of girls entering engineering and science may be balanced by the prestige such an accomplishment brings the girl and her family, particularly among education-oriented families.[22] I was constantly impressed by the value my informants and other Indians I met placed on educational achievement, for girls as well as boys. Of course, I was interacting mainly with a skewed sample of Indians, people who were education-oriented in a way that went far beyond the pragmatic benefits of formal degrees. Yet SAQ responses indicate that educational achievement is highly valued by many Indian families, including those from non-educational-elite backgrounds. These data, along with discussions with my informants, suggest that being an exceptionally "brilliant", interested and motivated student is an additional condition which allows some girls, especially those from educationally-oriented, middle-class or economically elite families to pursue science, especially in highly ranked fields and institutions.[23]

The prestige associated with opportunities abroad may also be sufficient to overcome the traditional social dangers of an unmarried girl traveling and living alone.[24] This includes going abroad, as in the case of one of my key informants whose family allowed her to accept a prestigious post-doctoral award in the United States.

A girl's educational accomplishment, by itself, can also have ancillary benefits, such as arranging marriages of other family members, both male and female, to high-status, education-oriented families, including to Indians living abroad. There appears to be a growing body of Indian-born women science-engineering degree holders who have recently married Indians working in "Silicon Valley" (and perhaps elsewhere in the US). If they can't obtain work permits, they may still attend local universities, often for advanced technical degrees (e.g. computer science).[25]

Within India, "respectable" science-related jobs have been rapidly increasing. An advanced science degree from a prestigious institution can pave the way to a socially safe career as a college professor at a women's college or at a university. A socially riskier but more prestigious option is a research position at a national laboratory (Subrahmanyan 1998). With a medical degree, a woman doctor can set up a medical practice at home, specialize in a woman's field like gynecology or obstetrics, and essentially be immersed in an all-female occupational setting. Moreover, as IT jobs expand, and as more women obtain these jobs, they form a critical mass of women which facilitates even more women entering field such as IT or medicine.

Families have always been more likely to allow or encourage "brilliant" daughters to pursue science than average students. Both my ethnographic data and the survey SAQ results show that female science-choosers have a strong interest in and aptitude for mathematics and science—in some cases more than their male counterparts. Some families may even allow them to delay their marriage or arrange for them to continue their studies after marriage, as was the case with several of my student informants. My ethnographic data also suggest that families without sons, or without academically competent sons, may be more likely to encourage daughters to pursue science.

For increasing numbers of families, then, the benefits of girls' science degrees outweigh the potential social costs, especially if one avoids highly ranked fields in highly male-dominated and hence socially dangerous educational and work contexts. Engineering, especially electrical and computer science oriented degrees, is becoming more appealing along with other degrees and diplomas that provide access to jobs in the growing IT sector. This is apparent in recent educational statistics, in ethnographic accounts (Seymour 1999) and in the science-oriented academic and occupational preferences of students in my pre-college SAQ sample. Girls are exhibiting a hierarchy of academic preferences similar to their male counterparts. Not only are they selecting science (vs. arts, commerce) at the pre-college and college level; within science, they are selecting more job-oriented applied sciences (engineering, medicine) over "pure" science degrees. And among the applied sciences, more girls are considering engineering-computer science as a viable alternative to a medical degree.

These trends are most evident among the class of families who can afford college education for both sons and daughters. Once again, gender and class intersect in complex ways. SAQ data reveal that 9th and 11th grade science-choosers of **both** genders come from "elite" families—i.e. family educational, income, and occupational levels are statistically significantly higher than for non-science choosers or for the sample as a whole (Mukhopadhyay 2001). Academically, those who choose science have much higher grades in all subjects and attend higher-ranked schools then the sample as a whole. In statistical analyses, these variables are the most consistent predictors of science-related outcomes, for both sexes, and they are highly inter-correlated. Class, then, somewhat compensates for gender-related barriers among female science-choosers. However, female science-choosers are **even more** socio-economically and academically elite than their male counterparts, and the gap between female science-choosers and non-science choosers is greater than the gap that exists between male science and non-science choosers.

CONCLUSION

I have presented an analysis which focuses on the role of family, and specifically, a "patrifocal" cultural model of family, in shaping educational decisions and outcomes for girls, overall, and especially in science and engineering. At the same time, I do not wish to reify cultural models, generally, nor the patrifocal prototype I have described. Cultural models are mediating structures—not determinants of behavior. The patrifocal family model is itself a "model", an attempt to conceptualize a multi-component, flexible, adaptable, context sensitive, and dynamic framing process that families (and anthropologists) can use creatively to think about and make (or comprehend) educational decisions.

Equally important, this chapter conceptualizes patrifocality as far more than simply an "oppressive family structure." Girls are not "powerless victims" of patrifocality. While patrifocality can and has historically limited girls' educational opportunities, especially among poorer and more conservative families, it can also facilitate girls' educational pursuits and successes both before and after marriage. The most recent educational statistics, and the virtual disappearance of the gender gap in school going rates, at primary, secondary, higher secondary, college and post-graduate levels shows that this is happening generally, even though gender disparities at IITs and in engineering continue. Whether these gains carry-over to the occupational sphere is yet to be seen although available research (Kumar 2009) suggests that the workplace is an even harder "nut to crack".

NOTES

1. Indian informants conventionally refer to "girls" and "boys" when talking about college students. I follow this convention here.
2. I developed the term "expert consultants" to differentiate this set of informants from the more typical anthropological informant who is a "native" but not a local expert on the topic being investigated. See later sections and Mukhopadhyay (2001) for a fuller description.
3. India has a complex system of tracking and, in some cases, providing "reserved seats" at educational institutions for particular communities, so-called "backward castes" and tribal groups. An entire vocabulary has arisen in relationship to this, including the term "Forward Castes" or Other Forward Castes (OFC) for some non-Brahmin communities.
4. For a more detailed description of the methodological approaches and challenges in carrying out this research, see Mukhopadhyay (2017b).

The Joys...and Perils....of Cross-Cultural, Comparative Educational Research: A Case Study from India. Sage Research Methods Cases Part 2. http://dx.doi.org/10.4135/9781526420794.

5. Questionnaires were administered to representative sections at various schools. Different versions of the SAQ were created for 6th, 9th and 11th "standard" students, in 3 languages: English, Hindi, and Kannada. Members of all classes were expected to complete the SAQ; other questionnaires were prioritized and administered selectively and when conditions permitted.

6. National Science Foundation (Award #9511725). Additional support came from San Jose State University, especially the College of Social Science and the Department of Anthropology.

7. For a detailed description of the SAQ data and testing phase results, see Mukhopadhyay (2001).

8. The period between 2001 and 2010 has shown particularly rapid advances in school-going, overall, and a decrease in the gender gap. The Ministry of Human Resources (MHR) has created what they call a "Gender Parity Index" (GPI), the ratio of the number of female students enrolled at primary, secondary and tertiary levels of education to the corresponding number of male students in each level. During the period from 2005–2006 to 2014–2015, they note "substantial progress has been achieved towards gender parity in education..." (Educational Statistics at a Glance, Government of India, 2016a, p. A2. Source: http://mhrd.gov.in/statist Accessed 3 Apr 2018). For other related data see Government of India (2016b). http://mospi.nic.in/publication/women-and-men-india-2016, Accessed 3 Jan 2018.

9. Despite growing computerization, it is only recently that updated educational statistics have been accessible on-line. There is generally a 5–10 year lag between collection and publication dates. However, data presented at a 2004 conference on Gender and Science in New Delhi as well as conversations with Indian scientists at the conference indicate the trends I describe for the 1990s persist. This is true for all-India as well as for specific institutions, such as the IITs.

10. Government of India data show that the gender gap in school attendance at the primary school level had disappeared by 2010. At the Secondary Level, the ratio of girls to boys was 0.88 in 2010–2011 but had reached 1.00 by 2014–2015. Girls' enrollments in higher education still lagged somewhat but had reached 0.86 in 2010–2011 and 0.92 by 2014–2015 (Government of India 2016a, see Part 1, Tables 6a–6D, pp. 4–7).

11. On-line IIT sources provide overall enrollment data, by numbers, for individual campuses but no all-IIT data nor percentages for each campus. Additionally, the enrollment data includes non-B.Tech, non-engineering

students, primarily graduate students pursuing M.Sc. or Ph.D. degrees in one of the "sciences", such as Math, Physics, or Chemistry. My own IIT research and data collection, at IIT Madras and elsewhere, suggests that a significant portion of women students in these figures, perhaps at least half, are enrolled in pure science graduate degree programs rather than in the B.Tech engineering program. This may explain why some preliminary calculations I did, using this "raw" data, were higher than the recent 8–9% women IIT engineering student estimates.

12. The number of years of schooling at the pre-college level has fluctuated over time and in different regions and types of systems in India. For many years, some students were on a 11 year pre-college system; some bachelor degree programs were only 3 years; there were also 2 year "intermediate" college-type degrees for the 11th–12th year of schooling (a 10+2+3 system). IIT, however, always had a 4 year bachelor's degree. In recent decades, more uniformity has been achieved, including a 12 year pre-college system.

13. See educational statistics in Mukhopadhyay and Seymour (1994), Introduction and Theoretical Overview.

14. There has long been discussion as to whether contemporary material exchanges from bride to groom's family should be labeled "groomprice" rather than dowry (Billig 1992; Kolenda 2001).

15. A 2004 conference I attended at NISTADS in New Delhi on Women in Science included several papers on workplace issues. See Mukhopadhyay (2004b). See also articles in Kumar (2009).

16. Apart from the horrendous Delhi rape case, there are other indications that Delhi and probably other parts of India, as well, have become more physically dangerous for women. I have certainly been told that by Indians on my last 2 visits.

17. My informants mentioned autorickshaws, taxis, or private cars. More recently, some families, if they can afford it, may buy a girl a scooter so she can avoid public transportation (Helen Ullrich, personal communication).

18. CUSAT ethnographic and interview notes, 1987.

19. Personal communication, Sarada Rajeevan Sridevi, CUSAT, 2008, 2015.

20. There are also age issues that accompany higher degrees. I was told that the ideal marriage age was 20–24. A common strategy was for families to arrange their daughter's marriage to coincide with graduation, even during final exams.

21. The educational impacts of changing demographics are fascinating to contemplate.

22. See for example Sylvia Vatuk's chapter in Mukhopadhyay and Seymour (1994).

23. Recent educational statistics from 2010 on the percentage of students passing Class X (Matriculation) and Class XII (Higher Secondary) exams

show that higher percentages of girls passed both exams than did boys, and the gap was greater for Class XII than Class X girls (Government of India 2016a, Table 11: Examination Results). Mean Achievement scores for Class X in 2015 on Math, Science, Social Studies were the same for girls and boys, with girls scoring slightly higher in English (Government of India 2016a, Table 14: Subject-wise Mean Achievement Score of Students at National level).

24. My original study preceded (but anticipated) the huge demand for Indian technical labor abroad in the mid-1990s and certainly increased the pressures FOR girls entering science and other lucrative fields.

25. These impressions come both from my residing in "greater" Silicon Valley and my teaching at San Jose State which has a significant population of Indians and Indian "wives". My colleague Dr. Tulsi Patel (Delhi University) and I have discussed this at length.

REFERENCES

Billig, Michael S. 1992. The Marriage Squeeze and the Rise of Groomprice in India's Kerala State. *Journal of Comparative Family Studies* 23 (2): 197–216.

Chanana, Karuna. 1994. Social Change or Social Reform: Women, Education, and Family in Pre-independence India. In *Women, Education and Family Structure in India*, ed. Carol C. Mukhopadhyay and S. Seymour, 37–58. Boulder, CO: Westview Press.

Chitnis, Suma B. 1989. India. In *International Handbook of Women's Education*, ed. Gail P. Kelly, 135–162. New York: Greenwood Press.

Fennema, E., and J. Sherman. 1976. Fennema-Sherman Mathematics Attitudes Scales. *JSAS Catalog of Selected Documents in Psychology* 6: 31 (Ms. 1225).

Gladwin, C.H. 1989. *Ethnographic Decision Tree Modeling*. Newbury Park, CA: Sage.

Government of India. 1987a. *A Handbook of Educational and Allied Statistics.* New Delhi: Ministry of Human Resource Development.

Government of India. 1987b. *Selected Educational Statistics 1985–1986.* New Delhi: Ministry of Human Resource Development.

Government of India. 1995. *A Handbook of Educational and Allied Statistics,* 17–19. New Delhi: Ministry of Human Resource Development.

Government of India. 2016a. *Educational Statistics at a Glance.* New Delhi: Ministry of Human Resources Development, Department of School Education and Literacy. http://mhrd.gov.in/statist. Accessed 3 Mar 2018.

Government of India. 2016b. *Women and Men in India-2016.* New Delhi: Ministry of Statistics and Programme Implementation. http://mospi.nic.in/publication/women-and-men-india-2016. Accessed 3 Jan 2018.

Kelly, Allison. 1985. The Construction of Masculine Science. *British Journal of Sociology of Education* 6 (2): 133–154.

Kolenda, Pauline (ed.). 1987. *Regional Differences in Family Structure in India.* Jaipur: Rawat Publications.

Kolenda, Pauline. 2001. Dowry. Paper Presented at Center for South Asia Studies Annual Meeting, Berkeley, CA.

Kronenfeld, D.K., et al. (eds.). 2011. *A Companion to Cognitive Anthropology.* New York: Wiley-Blackwell.

Kumar, Neelam (ed.). 2009. *Women and Science in India: A Reader.* Delhi: Oxford U Press.

Mukhopadhyay, Carol C. 1980. The Sexual Division of Labor in the Family. PhD dissertation, UC Riverside.

Mukhopadhyay, Carol C. 1982. Sati or Shakti: Women, Culture and Politics in India. In *Perspectives on Power: Women in Asia, Africa and Latin America,* ed. Jean O'Barr, 11–26. Durham: Center for International Studies, Duke University.

Mukhopadhyay, Carol C. 1984. Testing a Decision Model of the Sexual Division of Labor. *Human Organization* 43: 227–242.

Mukhopadhyay, Carol C. 1994. Family Structure and Indian Women's Participation in Science and Engineering. In *Women, Education and Family Structure in India,* ed. C. Mukhopadhyay and S. Seymour, 103–132. Boulder: Westview Press.

Mukhopadhyay, Carol C. 2001. *The Cultural Context of Gendered Science: The Case of India.* NSF Final Report Award #99511725. Available at: www.sjsu. edu/people/carol.mukhopadhyy.

Mukhopadhyay, Carol C. 2004a. A Feminist Cognitive Anthropology: The Case of Women and Mathematics. *Ethos* 32 (4): 458–492.

Mukhopadhyay, Carol C. 2004b. Preliminary Summary of Conference Themes and Potential Policy Recommendations. International Conference on "Women in science: Is the Glass Ceiling Disappearing?", Organized by NISTADS, National Institute of Science and Technology Development Studies, Cosponsored by the Department of Science and Technology.

Mukhopadhyay, Carol C. 2009. How Exportable Are Western Theories of Gendered Science? A Cautionary Word. In *Women and Science in India: A Reader,* ed. Neelam Kumar, 137–177. Delhi: Oxford University Press.

Mukhopadhyay, Carol C. 2015. Family Matters: Honoring Pauline Kolenda. Presented at Panel: Pauline's Pearls: The Contributions of Pauline Kolenda. American Anthropological Association Annual Meetings, 2015, Denver, CO.

Mukhopadhyay, Carol C. 2017a. Gender and Trump. *Social Justice Blog,* January 19. http://www.socialjusticejournal.org/gender-and-trump.

Mukhopadhyay, Carol C. 2017b. *The Joys…and Perils….of Cross-Cultural, Comparative Educational Research: A Case Study from India.* Sage Research Methods Cases Part 2. http://dx.doi.org/10.4135/9781526420794.

Mukhopadhyay, Carol C., and Suresht Bald. 1981. Women, Politics and Development: The Indian Case. In *Women and Politics in 20th Century Africa and Asia: Studies in Third World Societies*, Publication #16, 91–122.

Mukhopadhyay, C., and S. Seymour. 1994. Introduction and Theoretical Overview. In *Women, Education and Family Structure in India*, ed. Carol C. Mukhopadhyay and S. Seymour, 1–33. Boulder, CO: Westview Press.

Mukhopadhyay, Carol C., and Tami Blumenfield. 2017. Gender and Sexuality. In *Perspectives: An Open Invitation to Cultural Anthropology*, ed. Nina Brown, Laura Gonzalez, Tad McIlwraith, Philip Stein, and Jeanne Thompson. Society for Anthropology in Community Colleges [SACC]. Available at: http://www.perspectivesanthro.org/.

Pai, Seeta. 1998. Female Autonomy in India and Its Linkages with Female Education and Family Structures: A Critical Review. Qualifying Paper, Harvard Graduate School of Education.

Pai, Seeta A. 2002. Family, Childbirth, Marriage, and Schooling Among Nair Women in Kerala, India: Portraits in Cultural Change. Doctoral thesis, Harvard Graduate School of Education.

Pandey, Neelam. 2017. IIT Admissions: Number of Women Joining Engineering Goes Up in 2017. *The Hindustan Times*, July 15. http://www.hindustantimes.com/india-news/improving-sex-ratio-in-iits-more-women-take-admission-in-2017/story-2EKeUwqbqG6ibB0Tf5EftL.html. Accessed 3-2-2018.

Papanek, Hannah. 1989. Family Status-Production Work: Women's Contribution to Social Mobility and Class Differentiation. In *Gender and the Household Domain: Social and Cultural Dimensions*, ed. M. Krishnaraj and K. Chanana, 97–115. New Delhi, India: Sage.

Parikh, P.P. and S.P. Sukhatme. 1992. *Women Engineers in India: A Study on the Participation of Women in Engineering Courses and in the Engineering Profession*. Sponsored by Department of Science and Technology. Bombay: Indian Institute of Technology.

Quinn, Naomi (ed.). 2005. *Finding Culture in Talk: A Collection of Methods*. New York: Palgrave-Macmillan.

Seymour, Susan. 1999. *Women, Family, and Child Care in India: A World in Transition*. Cambridge: Cambridge University Press.

Smail, Barbara, and Alison Kelly. 1984. Sex Differences in Science and Technology Among 11-Year-Old Schoolchildren. *Research in Science and Technological Education*. I: Cognitive 2 (1): 61–76. II: Affective. *Research in Science and Technological Education* 2 (2): 87–106.

Strauss, Claudia, and Naomi Quinn. 1997. *A Cognitive Theory of Cultural Meaning*. Cambridge: Cambridge University Press.

Subrahmanyan, Lalita. 1998. *Women Scientists in the Third World: The Indian Experience*. New Delhi: Sage.

Ullrich, Helen. 1994. Asset and Liability: The Role of Female Education in Changing Marriage Patterns Among Havik Brahmins. In *Women, Education and Family Structure in India*, ed. Carol C. Mukhopadhyay and Susan Seymour, 187–212. Boulder: Westview Press.

Vasantha, A. 1996. Participation of Boys and Girls in Mathematics and Science at Secondary School Level in India. In *Mathematics as a Barrier to the Learning of Science and Technology by Girls*, ed. Ved Goel and Leone Burton. Report of a Conference, Ahmedabad, India. London: Commonwealth Secretariat.

Vatuk, Sylvia. 1994. Schooling for What? The Cultural and Social Context of Women's Education in a South Indian Muslim Family. In *Women, Education and Family Structure in India*, ed. Carol C. Mukhopadhyay and Susan Seymour, 135–164. Boulder, CO: Westview Press.

Wotipka, Christine Min. 2001. Feminist Theoretical Critiques of the International Discourse on Women in Science and Engineering Higher Education: The Cases of UNESCO, UNICEF, and the World Bank. Paper presented at Annual Meeting of the Comparative and International Education Society.

CHAPTER 5

Rural Women's Education: Process and Promise

Ann Grodzins Gold, Chinu Gujar, Ghumar Gujar
and Madhu Gujar

In this chapter, we offer an experiential account of higher education and its ongoing challenges and rewards for a first generation of college-going women in a provincial area of Rajasthan. To acknowledge the complexities of co-authorship as transparently as possible, our essay's parts are individually voiced.

COLLABORATION

Ann

While engaged in doctoral research on Hindu pilgrimage in 1980, I first met Bhoju Ram Gujar, and employed him sporadically as a research assistant. Since then, for over 35 years now, I have continued to work

A. G. Gold (✉)
Syracuse University, Syracuse, NY, USA

C. Gujar · G. Gujar · M. Gujar
Rajasthan, India

© The Author(s) 2019   83
H. E. Ullrich (ed.), *The Impact of Education*
in South Asia, Anthropological Studies of Education,
https://doi.org/10.1007/978-3-319-96607-6_5

with Bhoju on multiple projects. During this period, my relationship with Bhoju and his growing family developed along multiple pathways: friendship, kinship, collaborative research, co-authorship. Bhoju and I have written and published a number of reflections on our many-faceted, long-term, ever-deepening association (Gujar and Gold 1992; Gold and Gujar 2002: 30–52; Gold 2017: 29–36, 77–80). In 2010–2011, Bhoju's two older daughters, Madhu and Chinu, also assisted me in my field-work, and they too participated in producing a published account of how we worked together (Gold et al. 2014). Madhu, Chinu, and Ghumar (the youngest sister) and I composed this chapter specifically for this volume. It differs significantly from earlier co-authored reflections on collaborative research.

This chapter aims to present experiences emerging from, and with ongoing impact upon, my co-authors' daily lives. These lives in the larger picture have little to do with me or my anthropologizing, but much to do with dramatic changes for women that have permeated rural Rajasthan. While I can and do draw on our earlier collaborative work, and our long-term and comfortable relationships, I am acutely conscious of venturing into a new level of shared authority in which my own voice can only be subsidiary.

Together with these articulate young women, first-generation educated daughters, I aim to present reflections on aspiration intertwined with reality. Village-born, town-educated, with their in-laws' homes rooted in rural spaces, my co-authors' residences have shifted more than once. Making their separate ways in truly uncharted waters, these young women have moved between urban centers and village natal and marital homes. As we write this chapter, the oldest of my co-authors is 30, and the youngest is 24. Readers should keep well in mind that these histories are unfinished and still rich in potential.

I initially present distilled backgrounds and contexts for our collaboration, and provide a prose chronology of each young woman's educational career as gleaned from limited conversations on a brief visit in February 2017. The chapter's central substance follows: a translation of Hindi responses by Madhu, Chinu, and Ghumar to questions I posed. They will have the last word. I anticipate that their particular educational histories and views on the transformative potency of education might inform broader understandings of how women's status, independence, self-esteem, family roles, and more have changed and will continue to change (Fig. 5.1).

Fig. 5.1 The authors, clockwise from top left: after wedding, preceding ritual departures, 2011; back home, married but still studying, 2011; we visit Ghumar at her marital home, 2015

Background

I have seen and interacted with Madhu, Chinu, and Ghumar as babies, small children, teens, brides, and grown women. As the mother of three sons and no daughters, I have been emotionally engaged in these young women's lives. For an author photo on the back of my co-authored book about rural women's songs and stories (Raheja and Gold 1994) I posed with Madhu and Chinu sitting on my lap when they were little girls. In a published article about fieldwork with rural women, incidents surrounding Ghumar's birth and naming comprise the article's true heart, if not exactly its subject—which was the possibilities or impossibilities of feminist anthropology (Gold 2001). In January 2011, I attended their triple wedding, to which I devoted an entire chapter of my most recent monograph (Gold 2017: 211–246).

As an anthropologist of gender and contemporary life in South Asia, I have been fascinated by Bhoju's daughters' passages through life stages of infancy, childhood, student, bride, wife and in two cases mother. Their accommodations to the many kinds of demands, pressures, and difficulties inherent in these stages have frequently awed me, especially their perseverance and good humor. All three are deeply attached to one another, to their parents and brothers, to their goals of securing salaried jobs. They help each other whenever possible.

In one short piece about girls' education, composed in the late nineties, I offered a translation of a song, likely disseminated by the government, intended to deliver a message promoting social change. Madhu and her friends performed this song at a school assembly in Ghatiyali village when they were perhaps in fifth grade. Here are a few lines extracted from it:

> Don't get me married when I'm young,
> Let me study, let me study!
> Many literate sisters go to work at jobs, but
> The illiterate sit, their veils pulled down,
> In their homes, darkness and shadow.
> Let me bring the new light! (Gold 2002: 93)

These lyrics explicitly link literacy and jobs, using metaphors of darkness and light. The song pejoratively contrasts the plights of uneducated women living in purdah with those of literate women with salaried positions.

An almost casual observation about class and gender roles found its way into my recent book. Most of Bhoju's family was living at that time in a largely middle-class suburb called Santosh Nagar, on the outskirts of an old market town, the *qasbā* of Jahazpur.

> I vividly remember an early interview with a Brahmin girl who was just Madhu's age and lived right next door in Santosh Nagar. This young woman was from a family with many generations rooted in the qasba [walled market town]. Her mother and several aunts were all teachers. She had female role models in the women who surrounded her, among whom she grew up. This contrasts strikingly with the Gujar girls and their Mina and Jat contemporaries, whose mothers were largely non-literate. The interview provided me with a kind of fieldwork epiphany: What a leap Bhoju's family was taking with these educated daughters! And how

different for Gujars than it is for Brahmins. I suspect both these realizations would yield a justly deserved "duh" from any member of Bhoju's family (not to mention many of my readers): "You mean you just figured that out?" But knowing something is different from getting it, viscerally. (Gold 2017: 244)

Much has been written about the thwarted aspirations of educated young men in the late twentieth and early twenty-first centuries in India. Alienation from farm work and labor, lack of job opportunities to match their qualifications, engagement in local politics, susceptibility to participation in communal violence—all these are examined and identified as facets of their plight. Such men may feel useless (*bekār*) or unutilized (*phāltū*), or describe themselves as having nothing to do but "timepass" (Jeffrey 2010; Jeffrey et al. 2008). Far less ink has thus far been spilled on the plight of educated, unemployed or under-employed women.[1] Obvious explanations could seem to make the latter a non-subject. In a society where well-defined gender roles remain largely intact, prevailing assumptions are that a woman will be a wife, and will do housework. If she has a job, and her in-laws approve, that job may be the capstone of her qualifications as a wife, but rarely would it supersede domestic duties.[2] Except for the highly educated elite, no woman is considered too educated to do housework in the same way that a man may be considered, or consider himself, too educated to do farming or other physical labor.[3] Our contribution intends to exemplify the subtler, less visible ramifications of educated women reaching towards unobtainable, or less than ideal, employment, keeping in mind that there is never a dearth of work expected of women.

THREE EDUCATIONAL HISTORIES: A BRIEF SYNOPSIS

Madhu Gujar was born in 1987, the first child of Bhoju and his wife Bali. Bhoju was the only son of Sukhdev and Raji Gujar; he has one elder sister.[4] Madhu's birth, several years after Bhoju and Bali were married, brought the whole family much happiness. Bhoju's father had been in the British army in colonial times, and was minimally literate. Bhoju himself had pursued his education through a B.Ed. and become a Government teacher, eventually achieving the rank and responsibilities of headmaster. However, there were no literate women in the immediate family.

Madhu attended grade school in Ghatiyali. As we typed up the record of her schooling, and in later conversations, she told me that initially she had little motivation to excel in school; some teachers including a notorious "Madam" or female teacher, would beat the children painfully. Madhu saw her girl cousins and neighbors playing carefree, while she had to fear beatings, study for exams, at times be forbidden to play with her neighborhood age-mates. Especially in her earlier years, Madhu would have preferred to graze sheep and buffalo like her cousins Kali and Kamalesh. In 2001 she finished 8th grade at the Girls Government Middle School with a first division pass; two years later she completed her studies through tenth grade at the Government Secondary School, with a second division pass.

At that point, Madhu had reached a critical juncture for all Ghatiyali youth, but especially girls. She had either to leave her studies, or travel by bus to the larger town of Sawar (7 km from Ghatiyali) in order to complete Senior Secondary School. Boys might have the option of traveling to Sawar by bicycle or motorbike, but conventions of modesty prevented girls from using those modes of transport, while the public bus put them at risk of harassment. Few village girls braved this challenge, and Madhu was the sole Gujar girl at this time.[5] Her father encouraged her. Madhu is petite—small-boned and slender. Around this era of her life, I vividly recollect her telling me with shining eyes and a firm voice that she feared nothing. I believed her.

In Sawar Madhu selected as her three major topics: Hindi, Sanskrit and Political Science. She received a first division pass in eleventh grade, and a second division pass for twelfth (the difference between 64 and 57.38%). Around this time Bhoju decided it made sense for him to rent rooms in the subdistrict headquarters of Jahazpur, for the sake of his children's education, and also to reduce his own daily commute by motorcycle to his rural posting. Initially Bhoju kept only Madhu and Monu, the elder of his two sons, with him in those rather cramped rooms. Later he purchased a house in the suburb of Santosh Nagar, where eventually his other children would come to live.

At this time Madhu began college at Dave Mahavidyalaya, an almost all-girls college temporarily housed in the spacious and underutilized *Khādī Bhaṇḍār* (government-sponsored warehouse for homespun cloth) on the outskirts of Jahazpur. Many village-born young women enrolled there, as they embarked on a collective adventure in higher education. As are most local colleges, this one was affiliated with an urban university, in this case Maharshi Dayanand Saraswati University (hereafter MDSU) in Ajmer. Here Madhu completed her B.A. in 2008, focused on Hindi, Sanskrit and Political Science. From 2009–2010, Madhu worked towards a B.Ed. certificate from Vardhman Teachers Training College, in Tonk, and earned a first division pass keeping her major subjects in Hindi and Sanskrit with the third as Civics (in place of Political Science).

In January of 2011 Madhu along with her two younger sisters was married. Madhu's husband, Amit Gujar, from the village of Thavala, was also pursuing higher education. For the sake of academic goals, Madhu did not immediately go to live in her in-laws' home, her *sasurāl*. Rather she returned to her father's Jahazpur residence shortly after her wedding and continued her studies—working towards a master's degree in Hindi from the Government College of Devli, also administered by MDSU, Ajmer. Madhu's Master's degree, for which she received a second division pass, was focused on Tulsidas, author of the much-loved sixteenth-century Hindi version of the Ramayana epic.

After this, Madhu prepared and sat for two competitive exams to qualify for government teaching positions, but she did not score high enough marks to be successful. When she took the second of these exams, she was only a few days away from delivering a baby. After the birth of her son, while residing in her in-laws' home in 2013 and 2014, Madhu taught at a private school in the nearby village of Nasirda. She found the work unsatisfying, the school (both children and staff) undisciplined, and the pay inadequate (Fig. 5.2).

Madhu gave up this work, and was pleased to join her husband in the district capital of Bhilwara where he had found a clerical job with Saras Dairy. For several years in Bhilwara she was housewife and mother. Most recently, after her son started school, Madhu entered the business world, employed in the marketing department for Himalaya Baby Care products. She is successful in this job but, as she describes in the following pages, to become a Sanskrit teacher remains her primary goal.

Chinu was born almost five years after her sister. Like Madhu she studied through tenth grade in Ghatiyali, her home village. In her early teens, she was not keen on her studies, for several reasons she elaborated as I photographed her diplomas. Chinu explained that at this time, Madhu was in Jahazpur and her younger sister Ghumar had never taken to housework. Chinu, therefore, did all the housework, which much diminished her study time. With her educated father away from home most of the time, and her unschooled mother not understanding the

Fig. 5.2 Author Madhu Gujar as a young married woman, left to right: in Bhilwara city, standing between her husband Amit and her sister Chinu, with son Nandu and, far left, cousin Dev Raj, 2017; in the kitchen in Thavala, her rural marital home, 2014

importance of study, she herself had the thought that she would "fail and be free." Again, there loomed in the school a punitive teacher, whose beatings the students feared so much they would have preferred not to attend. Chinu's 10th grade pass in Ghatiyali, in 2008, was a second division "by grace"—an Indian English term that means a promising student who has barely missed a pass is awarded enough points to make up the difference.

At this point Chinu's educational history took a more fortunate turn. Bhoju brought her also to live in Jahazpur where Madhu and even Monu shared the housework burden. Moreover, chores in suburban Jahazpur were less arduous than in rural Ghatiyali. While attending Jahazpur's Higher Secondary School Chinu encountered a teacher, Banna Lal Gujar, who took pains with his students and who inspired her. His untimely death which took place while I was living in Jahazpur was a great shock and sorrow to the family and community. By the time Chinu reached her 12th year of high school, she distinguished herself with a first division pass. Taking a different path from her elder sister, she specialized in agricultural sciences. Chinu continued to study science in her college—the Rajeev Gandhi Mahavidhalaya in Amarvasi, on the highway outside the town of Devli. As was Madhu's college, this too is a local affiliate of MDSU, Ajmer (Fig. 5.3).

Along with her two sisters, Chinu was married in January of 2011. However, unlike the others, she postponed cohabitation with her husband for over six years, and single-mindedly continued to pursue higher education and her dreams of a salaried job. For several years Chinu shared housing and cooking with other female students in the town of Kekari, obtaining several additional degrees. In 2012, she earned a B.Sc. in Biology, with a first division pass of 71%; in 2013 she earned a B.Ed. in Biological Sciences, with a First Division Pass of 70%. I highlight these numbers as the only scores among all three young women's records where the percentage is above the mid-sixties.

Fig. 5.3 Author Chinu Gujar: portrait, 2011

Chinu remained in Kekari to pursue her Masters in Science, specializing now in Zoology. In 2016, she completed this degree awarded by MDSU, Ajmer, with a second division pass. When we spoke about this in early 2017, Chinu explained to me frankly that although she was enrolled in the degree program through Kekari College, where she was in residence, there was not one teacher posted in Kekari who was actually qualified to instruct students in the areas to be covered on the exam. Except for the "practicals" for which there was some supervised, hands-on laboratory work, students had to study on their own.

To make matters worse, the study guides—which are absolutely critical to education practice in provincial Rajasthan and much of India— were in English. With rueful humor Chinu told me about seeing prep books for the M.Sc. in the Kekari College library. These English books sat untouched and pristine on the library shelves, unlike Hindi study guides which would be dog-eared and continuously in demand. No Kekari student found the English books of use.[6] Moreover, the M.Sc. exam questions were in English and students were expected to write answers in English. Chinu said frankly that she would read the questions and if she understood a single word in an entire line, she would guess at answers that she could only hope would address the actual question.

Chinu spoke cynically of the whole process by which these exams were graded. As she related it, students in the sciences believe it is most important to fill all thirty pages, to make nice topical headings, and to make attractive, precise diagrams. The latter, of course, are more than cosmetic, and allow students without a command of English to display their scientific knowledge. According to Chinu, the anonymous graders in Ajmer never read the full prose answers thoroughly. Whether these speculations are true or not, Chinu did pass which under the circumstance seems most impressive.

In 2016 Chinu successfully obtained a RS-CIT or Certificate in Information Technology from Vardhman Mahaveer Open University, in Kota, with a good score of 65%. In addition, she has sat for multiple competitive exams that would qualify her for teaching at various levels, or for other government service jobs including the police. So far she has not done well enough on any for the results to lead to the desired outcome of a salaried secure job. She had one offer from an NGO school in a remote location with minimal pay and chose not to accept it.

For several months early in 2017 Chinu lived with a girlfriend in Jaipur cramming for yet another competition for teaching positions, one she had described to me as "bahut [very] tough." The toughness

resided not so much in the questions but in the discouragingly dis-
proportionate quantities of students taking the exam compared to the
number of actual jobs at stake. Later in 2017, several months before
writing her piece of this chapter, Chinu—more than six years after her
wedding—decided to reside with her husband Shaitan. They share a flat
in Bhilwara with Madhu, Madhu's husband Amit (who is Shaitan's elder
brother), and Madhu and Amit's little boy Nandu.

Born in 1994, Ghumar is the youngest of the three sisters. At the time
of my 2010–2011 fieldwork she was still in high school. I never asked
her to work for me, not only because of her age but because she rarely
spoke in Hindi, preferring her mother tongue of Rajasthani. Madhu and
Chinu both readily conversed fluently in schoolbook Hindi. Recently
when visiting Ghumar, I have found her spoken Hindi notably improved,
doubtless a result of her college major in Hindi.

Ghumar received a first division pass from the Government Girls
School in Ghatiyali. Unlike her sisters, she was able to take all four
years of high school (9–12), in Jahazpur. There, like Chinu, she chose
Agricultural Science for her specialization and again received a first division pass at the end of twelfth grade. After her marriage, Ghumar joined
Dev Kanya Mahavidyalaya in Devli for her B.A. Now she departed from
both her sisters' paths, taking Political Science, Hindi and Geography as
her three specializations.

Although her marriage to Omji has been successfully compatible,
and her in-laws are good, kind people, Ghumar's experiences as a young
bride took a toll on her health and on her studies. She lost her first child
shortly after giving birth at the hospital in Devli in 2013, and suffered
a painful infection after the delivery. One of her exams, on which she
received a low score, was taken when—according to her father and sisters—she was still ill and unable to sit up. Ghumar had special permission
to dictate her answers to Madhu.

A second pregnancy led joyfully to the birth of a healthy girl in spring
of 2017, but disrupted Ghumar's studies once again. She had begun but
not completed her B.Ed. from Tejasthali B.Ed. College in Nagaur, and
intended to complete her practice teaching, before her delivery. When
her doctor prescribed bed rest for several months this plan had to be
abandoned.

Among the three young women, then, Chinu was the only one to
have avoided clashes between education and reproduction. Yet Chinu's
path was not psychologically easy. Her family sympathized with and

supported her in her determination to succeed in the field of education, but they also worried about the protracted delay of married life.

ON BEING SCHOOLED

Around May of 2017, I sent an initial letter to each of my three co-authors, framing this chapter's aim and asking them to reply to a set of questions. I wrote:

> Each of you has a separate experience in schooling, studying, and seeking or gaining employment. Each of you can tell a special story about how education affects women's lives. You have female friends and close family who are non-literate (*anparh*); you have friends and family who are educated (*paṛhī-likhī*).

At the time, all three of them were preoccupied—with studying for exams, applying for jobs or learning new jobs, with their father's health, with the death of two uncles, with the birth of Ghumar's little girl, among many other events. One-half year later, I received their hand-written answers on lined notebook paper, transmitted to me by Bhoju as multiple image files. Madhu wrote eight pages; Chinu wrote thirteen pages in the smallest hand-writing; Ghumar filled nineteen pages but in larger script. As I read and translated their contributions I realized several things I had not anticipated.

Most impressive to me was that all three have an almost stunning sense of the transformative power of education; moreover, they see it as something nearly achieved in rural Rajasthan. Not one of them expressed an iota of disillusionment. In spite of years of disappointment in the severely competitive market for government jobs, all three continue to state that to become teachers is their ultimate aim in life. Rather than frustration, they emphasize achievement and perseverance. Their respect for teachers is also notable. Orally all three had critiqued some of the worst teachers in their schools, but only Ghumar in her written text is unforgiving of a teacher's flaws.

My questions were somewhat elaborate, and they made every effort to respond with care. Even when I had inadvertently produced overlapping themes requiring repetition, they were diligent to attend in detail to each query. The exception to this diligence is telling. I asked them to list the things in daily life that educated women had in common with uneducated women, as well as the differences between the two. Not one of them actually produced a list of similarities! This was the only one of my queries they ignored.

It is interesting to compare their separate responses on each topic, and so I present these translations according to topic; within each topic, with just one exception, responses are similarly ordered in the three sisters' birth order: Madhu, Chinu, Ghumar.

PERSONAL EXPERIENCES OF EDUCATION: BEST AND WORST TEACHERS; MAJOR SUBJECTS

Madhu

Teachers have held great importance in my life. All teachers educate children according to their own capacities. But each has a different method. Some teachers impressed me as poor, but children obtain knowledge even from a bad teacher's lessons. No teacher wants the children to do badly.

In my life I have had both experiences. When I was studying in middle school (grades 6–8) there was a female teacher, Tekha Telar, who taught us science. She treated me with so much affection. Her style of teaching was very easy and good, and I was easily able to understand.

I chose Hindi, Sanskrit and Political Science as my main subjects, because ever since childhood I have been interested in pedagogy. I wanted to be a teacher. And for this reason, I chose these subjects. My greatest interest is the study of Sanskrit, because from studying Sanskrit we can gain knowledge of our own ancient culture including the Vedas. This is why Sanskrit was my favorite. I completed a B.Ed. degree in Sanskrit. I really like to read Sanskrit, and I want to become a teacher and teach Sanskrit to children.

Chinu

It is like this, teachers can't be bad, but we sometimes think of those teachers who have sharp tempers, or who are strict disciplinarians, as bad. They force us to study, to cram, and even beat us. But they do this because it is their nature (character, *svabhāv*). We may fear such teachers, yet their behavior may also cause us to advance. Out of fear, we do everything connected with our studies right on time. When I was in school I thought such teachers were terrible. Now, looking back, I imagine that were it not for such teachers' actions, we could have become slackers (*lāparvāsī*).

A good teacher explains things to the children lovingly with discernment and patience—even difficult lessons. With good, compelling instruction, such teachers stimulate children's enthusiasm for their studies. A teacher always ought to seek the well-being of the children. They always should make efforts to stimulate students to advance. Thus they keep on encouraging students: whatever you want to do you will be able to do. That's all there is to it! Such a teacher will always keep pupils thinking in a positive fashion.

For me, in our village Ghatiyali, there was one female teacher who was the best of all. Her name began with *Sukh* [happiness]. But when she punished us or scolded us, then I would think that her name ought to begin with *Dukh* [sorrow]. When she was teaching us she explained everything very well. But sometimes if we didn't get it, in spite of her explanations, we were punished: "Hold your hand up, and stand, and pose like a rooster!"[7]

I chose biology for my major, because I like to learn about living things and their ways of existence. In the future, I would like to teach life sciences to children. From this study I have also learned a great deal about the human body, and about what the body needs to stay alive. I learned about problems connected with health, and ways that the body can find relief from these. So I am able to help others. I am also able to tell others a lot about plants—such as which plants are beneficial for us. And in general I understand how humans should behave towards other forms of life.

I have read a lot about plants' inner structure and I like studying this. From the beginning, I thought about this subject, and I am still studying it: I always want to learn more and more, about all kinds of life. For example, I have studied flying insects.

Ghumar

In my experience of teachers, the best teacher was Daksha Sharma. She always was able to increase children's enthusiasm, and always told them what they had to do to advance, and how to do it. She always told good things, and she never discriminated against any child. She always treated all the children equally, viewed them equally.

The bad teacher was Rajendra-ji, because he discriminated among the children. He never told the children instructive things. He cared only for himself and his own work. With blind faith in tradition, he always discriminated between boys and girls [favoring boys]. Because of this the children really didn't like him.

Good teachers are definitely important. Because just as the teacher is, so a student's education will be. Children are influenced by their teachers. If the teacher is good, a child's mind can be influenced for the good, and in this way transformed.

I chose Hindi for my major because, from the beginning, I liked learning about it. I liked to learn all about the authors and poets who wrote in Hindi. And I have quite a lot of interest in reading Hindi, because it is our mother tongue. And no matter what city we live in, we can easily speak Hindi with the people there. This is the reason I chose it—so I myself can teach Hindi to others.

EDUCATION AND THE GUJAR COMMUNITY

Madhu

Within Gujar society today, little by little people are beginning to pay attention to education. And we have begun to educate our daughters. In earlier times, people did not pay much attention to the education of girls. This is what people thought: "What use is a daughter's education? One day she will go to another's home." Because of thinking in this way, people didn't educate their daughters. But now this way of thinking has begun to change. Nowadays people wish this: "My daughters should go forward, and not become burdens to anyone, but become self-sufficient so that in their lives, there will never be any troubles or confusion. They should be able to stand on their own feet, and not require others to support them. They should be able to accomplish their own work themselves."

And you can see plainly that today without education, human life is incomplete. The times have already progressed enormously. So the uneducated person suffers many difficulties. Gujars are counted among the "backward communities" in the field of education. And this, alas, is true. Gujars have fought with the government to demand a reservation for government jobs, but I don't know when this matter will be settled.[8]

Chinu

Within Gujar society, women's education has had a major impact. It used to be that in Gujar society, one encountered very few women who were educated. However, nowadays just from looking around me, it seems that the majority are educated. If women are educated then they will cause the whole family to be educated. And nowadays even among the Gujars there are many such women. Women hold posts, for example in the Indian Police Service; and many women are teachers.

Because of educated women, the number of illiterate persons has decreased. Perhaps in the future there will not be a single illiterate person left among the Gujars. Among the Gujars some people are leaders and ministers, and they all continuously make efforts to awaken others to the need for education. And this has had quite an influence on Gujar society. Being thus influenced, people started to send their daughters to study. Because of women's education, the Gujar caste (*jāti*) has improved a great deal. And I hope that in the future there will be still greater improvement as people become increasingly aware.

Ghumar

Previously, in Gujar society women were not sent to school, for the following reasons. In earlier times, all women were illiterate, and all they could do was housework. Women stayed inside the four walls of their houses and did not even speak with others. In previous times it was thought that it would be futile to educate women as they would go to their in-laws' homes and have to do housework. For this reason it was necessary only to teach them housework.

But nowadays in Gujar society just as in other communities, change has come. Today, all girls are educated. And they are even sent "outside" [that is away from home to boarding schools etc.] in order for them to get ahead with their education. Thus we are able to brighten our own reputation and our community's reputation.

In Gujar society, education has this importance: Gujar women's situation today has improved because of education alone. Today there are Gujar women in every field. They are progressing and achieving a glowing reputation. In sum, education is of huge significance in Gujar society.

How Their Lives Differ from Their Mother's

Madhu

All three of us sisters' lives are totally different from our mother's. And our own children's futures will be different from ours. Because change alone is the truth of life. The coming generations' lives will be different from the life we are leading now. The style of life shifts according to changing times.

My mother is not literate. And for this reason, she had to be financially dependent on others. Moreover, she does not possess the knowledge that she ought to have. Even when we were small, she wasn't able to help us study. She had no knowledge of how to read or of what we were reading. But today, we pay attention to our children's studies, to how they are reading and to what they read. I am constantly trying to make sure that my son, as he grows, will never lag behind anyone, so that in his future he will have no difficulties.

Chinu

All three of us sisters' lives are quite different from our mother's. And, in our generation, in our society, in our village, a lot more change will come. For example, we three sisters are literate, and because of being literate, conveniences are available to us. But someone like our mother never experienced such conveniences. Within our mother's family there was nobody who was able to explain to her about education, to tell her its importance. She just didn't know any of this. Because our mother's family was not literate, they themselves did not know the value of education. If our mother did not attend school, moreover, there were no consequences. So her family members thought, "If she doesn't go, no matter! And what use is studying anyway?" But for us, if we didn't go to school, our mother herself ordered us to go. She came to understand the importance of education, and she always says of herself, especially, "it would have been a good thing if I were literate." She herself is not literate, yet she impelled us to go to school.

My mother never had the kinds of amenities that are available to us today. Our family members always provided all of our necessities. In these ways, our mother's life was quite different from ours. And future generations will have even more conveniences than we do. Moreover, they will have the opportunity for a good education. In our society a lot of change will take place in the villages. No one will remain illiterate, nor will bad customs endure. If everyone in rural society is educated, then there will be plenty of development, and perhaps even in the village all conveniences will be available. Thus no one will experience hardship. Moreover, village people will not need to leave home to study at school or college. In this way, a great deal of development will take place.

Ghumar

All three of us sisters' lives are different from our mother's. This is because she is not literate, and her mother and father also were not literate. For this reason they paid no attention to her education. And in the old days, there were not even any arrangements to obtain education, or they were scarce. For this reason our mother is different from us.

Because of being non-literate, she has "blind faith." She quickly believes in anything, accepts anything. But our father is literate. For this reason, he paid full attention to our studies, and to everything connected with education. For example, he made sure to provide us with school supplies that would be useful to us. For this reason, today our way of thinking and our thoughts are different from our mother's. Because of being non-literate, our mother cannot read a letter; she has to have it read to her. Our mother did not think about how to make the three of us progress in our future lives. But today we are able to think about our own children's interests, and encourage them, and stimulate them.

A Comparison Between Literate and Non-literate Women

Madhu

In my own family and among my friends' families too, there are non-literate women. But non-literate women in today's times are forced to confront many difficulties. For example, today instead of going to the bank, we are able to obtain cash directly from the ATM. This is quite a convenience. But non-literate women encounter difficulties in using the cash machine. Nor can they read the newspaper; nor can they do online work easily. For many kinds of work, they have to get help from others.

Chinu

In my own family and among my friends, there are both literate and non-literate women. What kind of difference is there between their lives? People say that if you educate one man, one person is educated. But if a woman is educated, then the whole family is educated. Women are the axle of the family.

An educated mother devotes attention to her own children's education along with ensuring that they have good influences and good health. But a non-literate mother is not able to help with her children's studies, nor is she able to say what would be a balanced diet for them.

In my family, there are educated girls. They themselves, thanks to being educated, can do every kind of work, such as making deposits and withdrawals, at the bank. But to do such things, a non-literate woman is always dependent on others. An educated woman reads the paper; and watches the TV news. She gets all the news about what is going on in the country and the world. But a non-literate woman knows nothing about these things, and they have no meaning to her. So her thoughts are limited to her home, to her fields, and to raising children. She has trouble even traveling from one city to another: "How shall I go?" But an educated woman can travel easily, and she is not dependent on anyone. In these ways, nowadays, non-literate women suffer many difficulties. A literate woman does not accept bad customs, traditions such as child marriage and the mistreatment of widows.

Ghumar

In my family are both educated and uneducated women. The uneducated women, whatever matter they need to understand, it takes them more time; and they are not able to read letters and messages, but have to take them to others. Non-literate women cannot attend to their children's reading and writing. And non-literate women because of "blind-faith" are too gullible, and quickly believe what anybody tells them.

But literate women are capable of running their households, competent in whatever work needs to be done. They pay attention to their children's studies, and after school, they can attend to their homework. Outside of the house whatever work is necessary they are able to do themselves. And they can tell the difference between what is right and what is false. A literate woman is not someone with "blind faith." She doesn't keep her eyes shut and believe in any old thing. Moreover, she is capable of directing her children towards an appropriate future.

In these times, non-literate young woman are always dependent on others. They have to get help with every kind of paperwork. But today's educated young women, in every field, are equal to men, and are working with men, shoulder to shoulder, contributing to the country's development, along with maintaining their home and family nicely.

Specific Fruits of Education

Ann

In my original queries I suggested seven possible fruits of education and asked my co-authors to add others that came to mind. Each of them chose to elaborate only on the seven I had suggested, often in very similar fashion. They ranked these benefits quite similarly as well, with a few variations I flag in brackets. For each item just one elaboration serves.

Madhu

Economic self-sufficiency [ranked first by Madhu only]. Today the literate woman is already quite self-sufficient. She can hold a salaried job herself and help her family economically. She can fulfill her own needs and not have to live dependent on others. Today women are needed in all fields, whether government or private. In all areas, women are equal to men. For example: I myself after completing my education, obtained a job in the post of sales promoter for the Himalaya Baby Care Company. And I receive quite a good salary. With this, I am helping my family.

Chinu

Ability to read the newspaper [ranked first by Chinu and Ghumar] Educated women easily can read the newspaper. And from reading it we learn what is going on around us. We also learn what is happening in the world, and gain all kinds of knowledge about many things. In the newspaper we find all different types of news, and we receive motivation from reading it, it stimulates us. Also, we obtain a lot of information about politics, such as which minister is in which field. And we learn about progress in our country's development.

Ghumar

Capacity to fill out forms [ranked second by Ghumar and Chinu] Today's women have taken into their control the capacity to fill out forms. It used to be that women were dependent on others to help them complete all forms; for every kind of paperwork they had to have it done by others. But today they can do every work themselves, including filling out forms by hand as well as online. From education, women's self-confidence increases. And in every field they have the ability to succeed. So women need not rely on others.

Chinu

Capacity to contribute to development This capacity also is obtained only from education. An educated person will know when an election is taking place in their village, and they will know that they ought to vote for the kind of candidate who is able to undertake development; the kind of candidate who can inform the public truthfully—for example about bad social customs; someone who will work to rid society of them. Moreover, if there are some children in the village whose families don't want to send them to school, then we can teach those children in the evening, and make sure that they get appropriate knowledge. Moreover, we can expansively tell them about education, and thus motivate them. And thus we instill in those children an awareness of education's value, and they too will join us in this effort. Moreover, non-literate women, can study along with their children.

Madhu

Ability to help non-literate women I am able to give non-literate women information about new things, or read aloud to them the news from the newspaper. I can help them fully complete any other kind of work that, because they are non-literate, they are unable to do.

Chinu

Capacity to earn equally to one's husband I have the capacity to earn equally to my husband. And I would like to make sure all women have this capacity. We are not only able to educate the children in our families, but we can also provide a good family environment. Moreover, we can help our husbands economically. Today, it is necessary for both husband and wife to be educated. If one person must stay outside the house to work, then one stays home and takes care of the house in a good way. If both get government jobs, then this is the best thing. Children will be well educated, and the house's financial situation will be quite comfortable. We can provide our children with a good education and good health. And people will be able to recognize us, and acknowledge our contributions.

Ghumar

Capacity to take care of their children's lives Previously, because of being uneducated, women were not able to pay attention to their own children's studies: they were unable to judge what was correct and what was a mistake. But today because of education, every woman, or at least those who are educated, is aware of these things. She is able to give full attention to her children's studies. Every day she supervises homework. She pays attention to their interests and to what they ought to do. She supports them, and strives to push them towards a bright life.

IMAGINE THE COMING TEN YEARS OF YOUR LIFE: WHAT DO YOU THINK YOU WILL BE DOING AND HOW WILL YOUR EDUCATION HAVE AFFECTED WHAT YOU DO?

Madhu

I like the job I am doing today. But this field is not connected with my education. I never thought that I would be doing this kind of work, but everyone has to flow with the times and their situations. Along with my job, I am also studying. In the ten years ahead, I want to become a government teacher and to educate children. This is my primary goal. I have a lot of interest in teaching. I also pay full attention to my son's education. In the coming ten years, a lot is going to change, and I don't want my son to suffer any difficulties.

In the coming ten years I want to gain this much competency: I shall be dependent on no one and I should be able to help my family's financial condition.

Chinu

In the coming years I will do the following things, related to my education. The first thing is this: I want to have a government job. Even now this is my aim. And if I get this job, then I will keep studying and go forward. In my life, I want to do the kind of work from which I not only improve myself but I also am able to help others. I think the very best thing would be if, after getting a job, I could open a school myself, English-medium, in which those village children who don't want to leave home could study. Moreover, there are quite a few literate unemployed persons, and my school could give them employment. Now there are no English-medium schools in most villages. As a result, many families have to send their children elsewhere to study. And because of this, families and their children experience a great deal of hardship—having to send small children away from home—all for the cause of education! I would make a major effort to open such a school.

And for myself, besides a job, there are other things I want to do. In order to do them, I would even be capable of leaving my own country. I want to gain recognition. Most people know my father. In his life he has had many struggles, and he receives recognition now. Like him, I want to distinguish myself.

Ghumar

In the coming ten years, I will be able to do a number of things. When some vacancy opens, I can fill out the form to apply for it, because I want to get a job. Moreover, in order to get a job the next time one falls vacant, I shall prepare myself. In order to prepare sufficiently for a competition, if I need to go out of my home, I will.

If You Had the Power to Change One Thing for the Next Generation, What Would Your *Hukam* [Command] Be?

Madhu

If I had power, in my community and for the coming generations, I would want to change a great deal. Today, people are earning well according to their capacities. And my own elders are living out their lives in comfort. But today, there is increasing distance between family members. Nuclear families are breaking away from the joint family, and other things that are not good are happening. Children growing up may lack the good influence from their grandparents. It is often out of necessity, we can say. But let's say that along with the good, bad things are also happening. For example, persons with aged parents ought to take care of those parents.[9] But some children leave their mother and father alone, because they are busy with their own work, and nobody has time. It ought not to be like this. I want children to keep their mother and father with them in their old age, and along with doing their own work, they should serve their elders. I know that human beings need to earn money. But along with earning money, they should not forget their responsibilities to their family.

Also, if I had power I would want my community and my future generations to be addiction-free, free from the curse of intoxicating substances. People should forget their suspicions and jealousies and live in love and brotherhood. I would like to make a society that is free from terrorism.

Chinu

I would like to see plenty of change for future generations in my society. I think that the coming generations will advance even more than we have, and their way of thinking will be very good and effective, so that for those generations to come, improvement will be there from the beginning. Enough, they will have good plans and understanding. However, they always ought to remain connected to their families. Along with their own advancement, they should attend to their own family's well-being, and continue to care about them.

While society has already improved, in coming times I would like to see more improvement. Bad social customs should be completely wiped out, and good development should take place. In future generations, no one will be illiterate and all will be independent. Whether male or female, all must be educated equally, and receive the same amenities, and have the same opportunities to advance. Having gained awareness they will help others to gain it. Social conditions should be improved, and we also need to pay attention to social development.

Ghumar

I want everyone in our society to be literate. Not a single woman should remain unschooled, but every woman should be educated. This will affect future generations, because if women are educated then children will be educated. And the future generations will take over the country's and our society's economic progress. All the future generations will be fully educated, and this alone will keep our society on the right track. We will make our contribution to our country's development efforts.

Thoughts About the Future

Madhu

In future generations, no one will remain non-literate. Even rural people now are educating all their children so that these children will not have to confront the problems that arise from being uneducated. What they have had to suffer, their children will not have to suffer. This is because, at present, education has already become an essential part of human life. Without education, people's lives are imperfect. And the future will be different from the present. In every home every person will be educated, and because of being educated, they will be able to lead better lives. With new technologies, all kinds of chores will be easily completed.

Chinu

Education has done much for us in the present life. And my expectation is that in the future it will do still more. I have received the fruits of education my whole life. And still it is said that one continues always to receive the advantages of education. I understand that in life, you need bread, clothes, and shelter; if a human needs anything else in addition to these, then it is education. Because no matter how much money, how much wealth we might possess, if we lack the wealth of education, then money and property hold no significance. An uneducated person will not be able to use wealth in the right ways.

If a person is educated, then even persons of superior status will ask them for help. The way I understand it is this: if girls and women are educated then perhaps there will be no work that women are not able to undertake. My expectation is that in future times because of education, no woman will remain illiterate. And unemployment will be ended, if women are educated. Suppose they do not get government positions, they are able to do other kinds of jobs. They can initiate any business. In the future, women will be involved in every branch of work (Fig. 5.4).

Fig. 5.4 Author Ghumar Gujar, left to right: radiant, the day before her wedding, 2011; as a small child, watching her mother decorate a ritually significant cow dung patty, 1997

Ghumar

Among the many fruits of education are these: we improve our lives, we contribute to the progress of our society, village and country, We can make our own futures bright. Through education, human beings recognize themselves and gain reputations among others. An educated person can remove afflictions. From education we learn to think about how to improve society in our village and our nation. Education makes human lives easier. And education is what gives us the ability to think about our futures.

NOTES

1. For a few notable and informative if not wholly satisfying exceptions, see Dutta (2016), Mehta (2000), Verma (2014).
2. Helen Ullrich (personal communication, 2018) reports that in her fieldwork area women who study may be exempt from housework. I have not

seen much of this in Rajasthan. Sometimes schools offer a study-retreat camp for young women before a major exam. The explicit reason for these camps is not tutoring but simply to free these students from the daily grind of domestic chores.

3. See Vijayakumar (2013) for the adjustments made by working wives in another region of India and a rather different social context.

4. See Gold and Gujar (2002): 165–181 for the lives of Bhoju's parents and the ways that Bhoju's own father made unusual choices, altering his family's history.

5. I checked with Bhoju and learned that even in 2017, although some local private schools do send buses to pick up students in Ghatiyali, there is no transportation facility for students attending the government high school in Sawar. These students, therefore, must travel with the crowds on the regular bus. For unaccompanied adolescent girls this can be unpleasant and risky enough to lead to a decision against further schooling.

6. See LaDousa (2014), Verma (2014) for the implicit hierarchy English competence creates at higher levels of education in various regions of India.

7. An illustrated Wikipedia page describes the "rooster punishment" as common in South Asia. https://en.wikipedia.org/wiki/Murga_punishment (accessed 6 January 2017).

8. Officially Gujars are classified as OBC (Other Backward Classes), a status garnering significantly less government reservations than ST (Scheduled Tribe) or SC (Scheduled Caste). In the past decade Gujars in Rajasthan have engaged in social movements demanding benefits similar to the ST Mina community, but thus far their demands have received only token acknowledgement; see Mayaram (2014).

9. Literally, to do their service: *sevā karnā*; there are moral implications to *sevā*, a term used for attending to deities as well as to elders. Another more mundane verb that translates as "to take care of" is *sambhālnā*.

REFERENCES

Dutta, Satarupa. 2016. The Changing Patterns and Lived Experiences of Women Pursuing Higher Education Post-marriage in India. *Journal of International Women's Studies* 17 (1): 169–185.

Gold, Ann Grodzins. 2001. Shared Blessings as Ethnographic Practice. *Method and Theory in the Study of Religion* 13 (1): 34–50.

Gold, Ann Grodzins. 2002. New Light in the House: Schooling Girls in Rural North India. In *Everyday Life in South Asia*, ed. Diane Mines and Sarah Lamb, 86–99. Bloomington: Indiana University Press.

Gold, Ann Grodzins. 2017. *Shiptown: Between Rural and Urban North India*. Philadelphia: University of Pennsylvania Press.

Gold, Ann Grodzins, and Bhoju Ram Gujar. 2002. *In the Time of Trees and Sorrows: Nature, Power, and Memory in Rajasthan*. Durham, NC: Duke University Press.

Gold, Ann Grodzins, Bhoju Ram Gujar, Madhu Gujar, and Chinu Gujar. 2014. Shared Knowledges: Family, Fusion, Friction, Fabric. *Ethnography* 15 (3): 331–354.

Gujar, Bhoju Ram, and Ann Grodzins Gold. 1992. From the Research Assistant's Point of View. *Anthropology and Humanism Quarterly* 17 (3): 72–84.

Jeffrey, Craig. 2010. *Timepass: Youth, Class, and the Politics of Waiting in India*. Stanford: Stanford University Press.

Jeffrey, Craig, Patricia Jeffery, and Roger Jeffery. 2008. *Degrees Without Freedom? Education, Masculinities, and Unemployment in North India*. Stanford: Stanford University Press.

LaDousa, Chaise. 2014. *Hindi is Our Ground, English is Our Sky: Education, Language, and Social Class in Contemporary India*. New York: Berghahn.

Mayaram, Shail. 2014. Pastoral Predicaments: The Gujars in History. *Contributions to Indian Sociology* 48 (2): 191–222.

Mehta, Prem. 2000. *College Girls and the 21st Century: Their Changing Social Values and Futuristic Perceptions*. Delhi: Indian Publishers Distributors.

Raheja, Gloria Goodwin, and Ann Grodzins Gold. 1994. *Listen to the Heron's Words: Reimagining Gender and Kinship in North India*. Berkeley: University of California Press.

Verma, Smita. 2014. Women in Higher Education in Globalised India: The Travails of Inclusiveness and Social Equality. *Social Change* 44 (3): 371–400.

Vijayakumar, Gowri. 2013. 'I'll Be Like Water': Gender, Class, and Flexible Aspirations at the Edge of India's Knowledge Economy. *Gender and Society* 27 (6): 777–798.

CHAPTER 6

Refashioning Futures: Dalit Women's Education and Empowerment in Maharashtra

Shailaja Paik

Since the end of the nineteenth century, Dalits ("Untouchables") struggled for the right to public spaces, including temples, streets, water tanks, and schools. Like other battles, Dalits' quest for education was filled with contradictions, triumphs, and reversals. What did education mean to Dalit men and especially women? Why was it so important to them? How did parents, relatives, and significant others support or hinder women's education and employment in twentieth century Maharashtra? How did women deal with double patriarchy: private and public, inside and outside their homes, and double discrimination—of caste and gender oppression? To engage these questions, my essay focuses on the life histories of three Dalit, Matang, middle-class women from Pune, Maharashtra—Dr. Sarita Waghmare, Gangabai Kuchekar, and Nima Jadhav.[1] I concentrate on their experiences and their own understandings of their lives.

S. Paik (✉)
University of Cincinnati, Cincinnati, OH, USA
e-mail: shailaja.paik@uc.edu

© The Author(s) 2019
H. E. Ullrich (ed.), *The Impact of Education in South Asia*, Anthropological Studies of Education,
https://doi.org/10.1007/978-3-319-96607-6_6

111

Matangs or Mangs in Maharashtra are erstwhile "Untouchable" outcastes who traditionally engaged in basket-weaving, rope-making, leather-work, execution of convicts, and so on. Matang is a sanskritized version of Mang, and the women I represent in this essay identified with their "Matang" caste background. Matangs are classified as Scheduled Castes (SC). Although, the category "Dalit" has acquired international currency and has emerged as an umbrella term for all SCs, Matangs, Charmakars, Dhors, and Valmikis rarely used the term and instead preferred their caste-specific names. I use the category "Dalit" for "SCs" and caste-specific names wherever appropriate.[2]

In this essay, I draw upon my book *Dalit Women's Education in Modern India: Double Discrimination* (2014) to provide details of ordinary Dalit women's lives, particularly focusing on education, employment, Brahmani (Brahmanical) hegemony, and *new* patriarchy in Dalit households in the post-colonial city, Pune. While Jadhav and Waghmare were second-generation learners, Kuchekar was a first-generation learner.

Dalits are not a homogeneous group of people. They have their own internal differences, hierarchy of sub-castes, and separate endogamous communities each with its own tradition and culture. The two predominant Dalit communities in Maharashtra state and the city of Pune are the Mahars and Matangs. In Pune out of the total population of the city of approximately 4 million in 1991, SCs constituted 631,063 (15.78%); out of which 287,795 (7.19%) were Mahars, and 193,629 (4.84%) were Matang (Census of India 1991: 66–67).[3] Socially and politically, Matangs are becoming more self-assertive on their own terms. For example, see Figs. 6.1, 6.2 and 6.3. In Fig. 6.1: a billboard from Yerawada slum advertises the celebration of birth anniversaries of Matang leaders, such as the wrestler-activist Lahujibuva Vastad Salve (1811–1881) and the communist activist-poet Annabhau Sathe (1920–1969). Figures 6.2 and 6.3 also celebrate the leaders and also include Raj Thackeray, the leader of Maharashtra Navnirman Sena, a wing of the militant Hindu-right-wing political party, Shiv Sena.

Matang women have excelled in their own education and now have good careers in Pune, the second largest city in Maharashtra, after Mumbai. Pune was the center of power during the Maratha Empire, and also the capital of the Brahmanical Peshwa rulers since the seventieth century. As a result, the city has served as a social, cultural, religious, and educational polis. Historically, Pune has also been segregated on lines of caste (Paik 2014: 196). Popularly known as the "Oxford of the

Fig. 6.1 Lahujibuva is in the left hand corner and Sathe on the far right, with historical figures—Non-Brahman and Dalit leaders—King Shivaji (the leader of the Bahujans), Shahu Maharaj (Prince of the Princely State of Kolhapur), and Dr. B.R. Ambedkar. The picture of the tiger is adorned by the slogan "Jai Lahuji (Victory to Lahuji)" and symbolizes the ferocity and bravery of Matangs

East," it is also an educational center. In the 1960s, industrial development started in Pune, and from the 1990s, it emerged as an Information Technology (IT) hub.

My book and several articles (Paik 2009, 2011, 2014, 2016, 2017) focus on the ways Dalit women in modern Maharashtra both shaped and were in turn transformed by the *incremental interlocking technologies* of public and private realms, in terms of education, caste, class, gender, and

Fig. 6.2 This billboard showcases a joint celebration of Annabhau Sathe and Lahujibuva Salve in the year 2015. As part of these festivities, successful business-men and meritorious students will be celebrated with a community meal. Beside the standing Lahujibuva Salve in the photo is Raj Thackeray, the son of the reknowned Shiv Sena leader Bal Thackeray. Shiv Sena, literally the "Army of (King) Shivaji," is a right-wing, regional, political party established in 1960s Mumbai. Shiv Sena demands preferential treatment of Maharashtrians, advocates pro-Marathi and a Hindu national agenda, and has strong supporters in different parts of India. Significantly the big and bright billboard of Matang festivities forms a background to the relatively smaller, but permanent board of Raj Thackeray's new political party—Maharashtra Navnirman Sena (Army for the new creation of Maharashtra)

sexuality. To uncover this story, I have deployed interdisciplinary investi-gations, analyzed a variety of "official," "non-official," "trivial" sources, and most significantly, centered oral life histories, which are a necessary condition to document the histories of ordinary Dalit women. Such sources are less important for the ruling classes who have always con-trolled reading and writing and archived abundant written records (Paik 2009: 177–185, 2014: 19–24, 2017: 177–179). This essay specifically focuses on the hitherto unexamined life experiences of Matang women.

Fig. 6.3 The billboard announces and pays homage to Annabhau Sathe on his 95th birth anniversary. Sathe is in the left and Lahujibuva is in the right hand corner. The group also calls itself "Tiger Group."

EDUCATION AND EMANCIPATION OF DALITS

Since the middle and particularly from the end of the nineteenth century, Dalits fought for their human and civic rights to gain access to public and religious spaces, including schools. They saw education as a particularly important means for their self-assertion as well as for their inclusion as citizens in the Indian body politic. Although the British colonial government permitted Dalits to study in state schools and issued an order on 23 February 1923 that "no disabilities were to be imposed"

(Paik 2014: 56) on them, many who attended the state schools experienced humiliating and discriminatory treatment from both teachers and higher caste pupils. The ostensible public right to education turned in practice into a right merely for a segregated education for Untouchable students. In this manner, the site of education became an arena of struggle between Touchables and Untouchables, thus perpetuating the Dalit body as a historical and contemporary object of pain and suffering in modern India. As a result, for Dalits the battle for education became a struggle for individual and collective freedom and political power. The situation was particularly problematic for Dalit women because caste discrimination was compounded by prejudices against female education.

Leaders such as Jotirao Phule (1827–1890), a pioneer of Non-Brahman, Dalit and women's education and Dr. B.R. Ambedkar (1891–1956), a social activist and ideologue critically analyzed how high-caste men tricked both Dalit men and women of all castes by excluding them from spheres essential to their human rights, including education. Most significantly, Phule and Ambedkar combined a critique of caste and gender hierarchies in ways that opened up new spaces for women. Analyzing these realities from the perspective of Dalits, I seek to understand the ideas, actions, and changing values, which have revolutionized Dalit women's lives. Despite Dalit leaders' promises and efforts to expand and democratize educational opportunity, their rationale held unsettling implications for Dalits and particularly Dalit women whose place in the body politic remained contested and uncertain.

Inspired by dreams of economic development through the application of technology and industrialization, and fired by the ideals of democracy, equality, abolition of caste, and by the vision of their country as a strong, integrated, and advancing nation, the planners for independent India set a high store on education. They saw education as a basic human right and as an instrument for economic, political and social change and development. Article 45 of the Indian constitution thus promised free and compulsory education to all children up to the age of fourteen years. Recently, India has endorsed the UN-inspired project of "Education for All (in Hindi Sarva Shiksha Abhiyan)."[4]

The desire for education has been growing amongst Dalits over the decades. In a study of Dalit college students carried out in the 1970s, M.B. Chitnis (1973, 1986: 47–49) found that while 85% of the parents and guardians of the students were illiterate, 75% showed a strong interest in the educational progress of their wards.[5] This finding struck a blow at those who blamed Dalits for their own illiteracy and ignorance. Although parents might be illiterate and unable to afford to buy books for their children, they still have a very positive attitude toward education (Chitnis 1973: 47–49).[6] Nevertheless, although educational uptake amongst Dalits has certainly improved greatly in recent years, there is still a long way to go (Chitnis 1981).

Scholars have argued that economic liberalization in many countries, including India in the 1980s and 1990s, have had an adverse impact on the quantity and quality of education (Shukla and Kaul 1998). In this respect, it seems that many states are increasingly abdicating their responsibility of providing equitable access to education. Craig Jeffrey (2008) and Veronique Benei (2008) have cautioned that amidst imageries in the contemporary global media of India's more accessible and much improved system of education, population growth, rapidly rising educational enrollment, and the failure of the Indian economy to create large numbers of secure jobs, has created a vast problem of educated unemployment among Dalit youth.

Some scholars have argued that certain Dalit communities are more motivated than others (Kurane 1999; Abbasayulu 1978; Sachidananda 1976; Singh 1969). It is also well known that only a relatively small upper stratum of Dalits make full use of the opportunities that are opened up through education (Dushkin 1972: 165–226, 1979: 661–667; Beteille 1992). Several studies have brought out the ways in which education, and the resulting economic betterment, creates internal divisions amongst Dalits. The Dalits who move upwards in this way are more likely to be oriented toward the higher caste groups. Some educated who have risen high in their social hierarchy have snapped their ties with their past (Abbasayulu 1978: 26) and there are instances of illiterate Dalits being treated with contempt by educated members of the community (Paik 2014). Sachidananda has found that, by and large, a great number of the Dalit elite in Bihar have taken little interest in bettering the lot of their less fortunate brethren.[7] Suneila Malik's (1979: 50–55) work in North India and my research in Western India showed that the educated members among the Dalits pointed out that they did not like to use their caste names, because if they did, the outlook of the people whom they were interacting with would change and they would be looked down upon as inferior.[8]

In the context of Maharashtra, two volumes of the Marathi magazine *Sugava* focused on Dalit elites or the so-called "Dalit Brahmans" who have snapped ties with their communities. This is an increasing concern for many Dalits (Wagh 1986, 1994). A related issue is that the increasing interest in education has also led to competition among Dalits for reserved positions. The sociologist G.G. Wankhede (2001: 1553–1558) has argued that the Mahars obtain most of the reservations. As a result, other Dalit groups, such as the Matangs and Charmakars dislike them. Thus, internal differences and competition among Dalits result in conflict.

Jadhav, a second-generation learner mentioned that her family was doing well.[9] One of her brothers is an Indian Penal Service (IPS) officer and the other is a military officer; her sister is in the first year of college. Jadhav also referred to the competition between the two communities for education and jobs: "as it is, far more Buddhist [Mahars] than Matangs are progressing to higher levels of education and also fetch [more] jobs" (Interview). Some Matang and Charmakars feel aggrieved when Mahars predominate in receiving the reservation quota at the expense of other Dalit groups. This thus inhibits Dalits unity.

Dalit Women Speak Truth to Power

As a part of my historical fieldwork, I interviewed some Matang women in different slums and middle-class neighborhoods of Pune during a few months from 1999–2006. I engaged with Jadhav who served as Police Sub-Inspector in Pune in 2001. This was the first time that I interacted with a Matang woman police officer and I was in complete awe of her. I re-connected with her in 2005 and followed up on the earlier interview. Jadhav had been promoted to the position of Assistant Commissioner of Police (Interview). We chatted away in different spaces—her private home (near Svargate) and the public regional police office (Kasba Peth, Pune)—at times in isolation and sometimes in the midst of people. Sarita Waghmare was another rare woman who played cricket during her school and college days in the 1980s. We grew up in the same Yerawada slum in Pune, but she lived in the middle-class apartment of Ramnagar when I interviewed her in 2004. My uncle introduced me to Gangabai Kuchekar with whom I interacted in her middle-class apartment on Sinhagad Road in the year 2002. I recount some experiences of these women below.

SCHOOL: A PRIVILEGE!

Many Dalit girls who were the first generation of learners were *highly privileged to go to school in whatever circumstances*. The fact that they could enter the portals of school at all became most important. Jadhav commented, "The standard and medium of the school did not matter at all. We could attend school; that was more than enough" (Interview, 2001). Grinding poverty, unemployment, and community distress all restricted the kinds of support and recognition that parents could allocate to their children's education.

Both, Kuchekar and Jadhav attended vernacular Marathi medium municipal schools. Kuchekar reported that the municipal schools she attended had very poor physical infrastructures. She added, "The classroom was dark and dusty. Many a time the ground was also unkempt, damp, strewn with firewood, bugs, and ants crawling around" (Interview, 2002). Other women agreed that most of the time their schools had dilapidated buildings, leaking roofs, and mud floors, a depressing atmosphere, few basic amenities (for example, no toilets for girls) and an inadequate number of teachers. By contrast, Waghmare, a second-generation learner was educated in an elite English medium convent school.

The depressing school atmosphere fed into the dry educational curriculum, which further dampened children's enthusiasm for knowledge. Some girls mentioned that they were bored and disliked the routine school life. Jadhav said, "I did not find any subject utterly boring or interesting. I just knew that there was no way out (Interview, 2001)." Sometimes even the serious students became bored and did poorly in their higher class examinations. They just wanted to scrape through their education. This spoke volumes about the quality of the educational system that broke the back of students. They were over-burdened and hated the sight of books.

INCULCATING HABITS AND DISCIPLINE

Historically, both the upper-castes and the colonial British government stereotyped Dalits as "docile" or "indifferent" to education. To challenge such a psychological colonizing, Dalits sought to inculcate discipline and "good" habits (Paik 2014, 2016). Toward this end, parents embodied the old Marathi proverb, *"chhadi lage chham chham, vidya yei gham gham"* (Paik 2009). They often used corporal punishment to compel their children to attend school and study hard. Parents often cited examples from their own lives to teach their children. Jadhav said that, "my father saw to it that I was never at home, that I never missed school" (Interview, 2001). Thus, Dalit parents saw it a moral failing on part of Dalits to express any dislike of school. Although the educational theorist, Ivan Illich has rightly criticized this disciplinary attitude toward education (1971),[10] and the women revealed a certain ambiguity on the issue—they abhorred the discipline, but understood their father's wider motives.

Because of such training, some girls studied independently. They devised strategies for themselves. Waghmare asserted, "I preferred to do it all on my own. I did not like to learn things by heart. I preferred to start from scratch, and that is the way I understood it well" (Interview, 2004). She further reported, "the male [cousins] did not study and left school in class ten and twelve" (Interview, 2004). Unlike her, however, her male cousins did not do well. Waghmare's educated parents, convent training, and excellence in extra-curricular activities bolstered her confidence. By contrast, many first-generation learners, like Kuchekar could not depend on parents, teachers, or relatives for any kind of help with studies. They somehow managed to move on from one class to another.

At this point, Waghmare's mother joined us and said that children should be nurtured in a "proper" home atmosphere. She continued,

> Our relatives who did not study did not get this [proper] atmosphere, and [hence they] are not doing well. However, the present generation kids study in good English medium schools. They are doing well. When I was studying there were [only] six Backward Class girls in a class of 50. They were studying, the community did send them to school, and now they are more progressive.[11]

Thus, Waghmare clearly connected education with progress, and individual, and community uplift.

Along with strict discipline, many lower-middle and middle-class Dalit parents also emphasized decent manners, propriety and "respectable" (Paik 2014, 2016) behavior to train themselves and their children for success in education and employment. They wanted their children to be well behaved. They also wanted the dominant castes to know that their children came from "cultured," "good," homes, and that they themselves were people of "good" character. In this way, they sought to counter the many negative stereotypes about Dalits. They saw a respectable demeanor especially necessary for girls to ward off dangerous attention from men. Many middle-class Dalits tried to portray a good image, rather their best one, to the upper castes in the hope that they might be accommodated within the hegemonic structure of power. This strategy, in turn was also important for building their self-confidence and self-respect. In the process, Dalits went beyond their individualistic concerns to embrace the needs of their larger community.

Many first generation pupils in municipal schools rarely read anything beyond their textbooks. Indeed, some Dalit parents actively discouraged wider reading habits, believing that schools offered the "perfect" knowledge and anything besides that was a waste of time and hence, irrelevant. Jadhav's father reprimanded her when she tried to read storybooks; she said, "We were to engage in studying school text books only. Everything else was a waste of precious time" (Interview, 2001). Thus, to many first-and-second-generation learners accessing education and exceling at school was the primary goal. For most, however, reading was confined to newspapers, some Marathi magazines, and light books. Reading serious novels and more intellectually demanding books was a rarity. Lengthy books aroused fear and awe.

However, many second-and-third-generation learners also engaged in exceling not only in the routine educational curriculum, but also in extra-curricular activities. Some Dalit women were involved in other activities, such as sports, singing, or playing the guitar (Pawar and Pawar 2004; Waghmare 2004). Waghmare was a rare woman who played cricket during her school and college days in the 1980s. During our childhood days, I watched her every Sunday, on her way to practice in her freshly ironed "manly uniform"—white shirt and trousers. She walked proudly with her cricket equipment on her shoulders. She always looked professional, alert, and seemed to be absolutely untouched by people and happenings around her. Waghmare also practiced regularly with her father. Thus, many middle-class Dalit parents attended to the overall development of their children. Such extracurricular activities rarely existed for first-generation learners. In this way, some second- and third-generation Dalit women learners acquired interest in activities outside the curriculum to a greater or lesser extent; some turned it into a habit. Some parents realized that involvement in such activities might give their children an extra edge in their school careers. They encouraged them to participate in crafts, dancing, music, drawing and sports, and to take pride in their achievements. Hence, Waghmare's father, a cricketer himself sowed the seeds of the sport of cricket in his daughter. She also responded favorably and developed a passion for the game. Her father was a role model and encouraged her interests.

HIERARCHY IN MEDIUM OF INSTRUCTION: ENGLISH AND MARATHI

The question of modern English or vernacular Marathi medium of instruction vexed many women. Jadhav said, "if I had attended an English medium school, I could have attempted the national level Union Public Service Commission exam. I would not have limited myself to the state level Maharashtra Public Service Commission" (Interview, 2005). Jadhav thus felt that her lack of English education had made it impossible for her to have any chance to gain entry to the highest cadre of the administrative service—the Indian Administrative Services. Many English medium educated second-and-third-generation learners thought highly of themselves. They seem to be at an advantage compared to those who do not understand the language. Many children are no doubt able to rattle off some English poems or songs at the insistence of their parents, but without prolonged English education, they lack that air of confidence that impresses everybody. In this way, the English language has become an obsession for people of all classes in India, as well as transnationally.[12]

Jadhav, who studied in a Marathi medium school, said that she purposefully admitted her children in an English medium convent school of the highest quality. She reasoned,

> In Marathi-medium schools, even the highly prestigious ones [located in the polis of Pune], caste discrimination is practised and I did not want my children to face *that* [caste discrimination, emphasis is mine]. Hence, I put them in English-medium schools and more significantly convents where *this* [caste discrimination, emphasis is mine] does not exist. We also want them to be prepared for a competitive future and English medium instruction is good for developing a well-rounded personality. (Interview, 2004)

Marathi medium in itself stigmatizes Dalit pupils. Most women who attended only Marathi-medium schools felt that an English-medium school would have positively affected their life and careers. As a result, they would have been more confident, outgoing, bold, and outspoken. Most significantly, they thought that English was analogous to prestige and a sense of superiority—something they had to constantly work upon taking into consideration their Dalit background. Significantly, Jadhav avoided the use of the Marathi word "jatibhed (caste discrimination)" and referred to it as "that" and "this" thereby mitigating and making caste-based prejudice banal.

This hierarchy in the education system is an insidious one, stretching even to the reputation of different English-medium schools. Girls from certain "better" convent schools are thus supposed to have "higher" standards. Most of the students studying in convent schools—the highest in the hierarchy—look down upon the rest of the students who attend a private/government school or any other school for that matter. Such educational hierarchies are found in many different countries of the world, and it invariably parallels the socio-economic hierarchy.[13] In India, the preponderance of upper caste/class pupils in convents/private schools, and lower caste/class pupils in government-run municipal/public schools exacerbates caste and class tensions.

BRAHMANI (BRAHMANICAL) HEGEMONY AND HARASSMENT OF DALITS

The Brahmani hegemony harassed Dalits and penetrated every miniscule aspect of their history, culture, language, and education.[14] The Brahman dress code, standards of hygiene (not to mention the stuffy and unclean Brahman households one comes across that reek of stale ghee), food habits, consumption of ghee, sanitized and nasal toned Marathi, and even the style of draping a sari is thought to be the best. Jadhav said, "We liked to dress up like them. *Ti brahmanan saarkhi sadi nesayachi*—we want to drape our saris like the Brahmans did" (Interview, 2005). Jadhav like other Dalits thus desired for the particular style of Brahman's dress, food, and so on. She, however, did not question why this Brahman style of draping a sari was supposed to be the best. I agree with Ambedkar who forcefully noted, "Brahmin enslaves the mind and Bania the body" (1991a, b, c). I am concerned with ways the dominant castes have mentally enslaved some Dalits.

A Dalit student, Chetan, who is studying genetics, stated emphatically: "Things can be learnt only from the Brahmans. They tell you how to live, how to fight and progress in life. I would marry only a Brahman girl alone, even if I have to undergo a second marriage" (Interview, September 11, 2004, Ramtekdi, Pune). Thus, many middle-class Dalits, like Chetan, were constantly troubled by their internal colonization of Brahmani hegemony over their Dalit personhood and yet wanted to be with Brahmins. They compared themselves with Brahmans and looked upon them as the "best." They tried to imitate the Brahmans who were and are at the helm of all social, cultural, and educational affairs.

Dalits negotiated these dominations in everyday practice in different ways, and theoretical conceptualizations and political consciousness emerged out of their historical and lived experiences. Upper caste hegemony is extended and their symbolic power is executed through "Pedagogic Actions" that incorporate the education system, along with other systemic agencies.[15] Eventually, the prevailing common sense marginalizes, illegitimates, suppresses, and annihilates the lower classes (the subalterns, Dalits). As Bourdieu emphasizes,

> The sanctions, material or symbolic, positive or negative, juridically guaranteed or not, through which Pedagogic Authority is expressed, strengthen and lastingly consecrate the effect of a Pedagogic Action. They are more likely to be recognized as legitimate, i.e. have greater symbolic force. (Bourdieu and Passeron 1977: 10–11)

In this manner, pedagogic practices reproduced Brahman hegemony in social and cultural domains. Brahmani practices seek to sharpen some Dalits' sense of cultural unworthiness and an extirpation of their acquirements, even if they themselves at times do not consider the dominant culture as the legitimate culture. This psychological violence undermines Dalit identity. This is reflected in the everyday lives of some Dalits; they then delegitimize their own culture. They disparage their own medicinal knowledge, art works, traditions, culture, and crafts and they imitate the so-called "purer" and "softer" forms of language, dress, food, occupation, culture, and pedagogy. For example, in terms of food, elites preferred *varan/dahi/tupa-bhat* (dal/curd/ghee-rice) or inculcated the Brahmani habit of consuming *tupa* (ghee) and abandoning *bombil-bhakri* (dry fish-bread). Though such a Bourdieuan postulate denies agency to the subaltern, this tendency of annihilating the caste identity is nonetheless a reality in some Dalit lives. Although many Dalits were co-opted, nonetheless, history has been witness to how many Dalit radicals either gradually developed cracks in or openly subverted upper-caste hegemonic ideology and practices. These complicated emotional upheavals animated the lived and everyday experiences of some Dalits. While some elite Dalits found the pungent smell of *bombil* extremely nauseating, others experienced a waft of *bombil* and *sukat* (small dry fish) as particularly appetizing. In other words, *bombil-bhakri* was a delicacy for lower-class Dalits that the elites disparaged. These contrasts put Jadhav in a predicament that forced her to skip a school picnic. She reported, "I was scared that, unlike my upper-caste classmates' mothers, my mother could not afford a packed lunch or delicacies for me. And if she did, I could not show to or share my *bombil-bhaakri* crumbs with anybody but my caste-girls" (Interview, 2001). Thus, Jadhav either hid her lunch or mingled with her own caste group with which she could identify and felt comfortable.

Some Dalits observed Brahman habits and characteristics and tried to emulate them in their own daily lives. They perceived Brahmans' food habits such as their vegetarianism (not to mention that historically the Brahmans were beef-eaters, as argued by Ambedkar) (1991a, b: 323–328, c: 334–349),[16] consumption of ghee and culinary skills—to be matchless. Similarly, they tried to avoid jazzy colors and clothes. They imitated "Brahmani" "shuddha (pure)" Marathi with the "correct" and "proper" accent and tone of speech that was also taught in the schools. I noted during my interviews with Dalits that sometimes shuddha Brahmani Marathi intruded into the Mahari-Mang voice and tone. I discerned this process in some women from all of the three generations.

Many middle class Dalits are ambivalent about these everyday practices and have a split consciousness in this respect. On the one hand, they know that their Dalit identity has economic and political benefits. On the other hand, they want to erase the cultural markers of such an identity. For example, some Dalits shed their last names, which signifies their Dalit origin, and take up the caste-neutral "*kar*" (literally, coming from a village) suffix which is associated with the upper castes. An example is the family of Nagares. Some Nagares are Christian converts from Ahmednagar District (commonly known as Nagar) who have changed their last name to "Nagarkar." Maharashtrian last names are generally constructed using place names. Some with "Kambles" and "Salves," which are Dalit-specific names changed to caste-neutral "Punekar," and Sankpals changed to Ambavadekar (Paik 2009).[17] Along with the problem of caste-specific naming, women also have to negotiate gender trouble.

CASTE AND GENDER DISCRIMINATION AND RISE
OF THE *NEW* WOMAN

Dalit women struggled against their double discrimination on lines of caste and gender, in order to carve out their own personhood and womanhood. Some parents practiced gender discrimination. As a result, some fathers admitted their sons to convent schools and sent their daughters to Marathi-medium schools. At the same time, however, some fathers and brothers did not interfere in "private" affairs of domesticating their daughters or sisters. Universally, men who have been in the public have left the private domain to their women. However, a few fathers understood that housework interfered with their daughters' studies, and insisted that they not be made to work at home. Jadhav's father always reminded his wife, "Nima has a lot to study, so do not ask her to do household chores" (Interview, 2001). Thus, Jadhav's father actually protected her from her mother who wanted her daughter to learn domestic skills to use later on in her life.

Many girls faced humiliation at school because of their caste background. One Meena Sathe was troubled because, despite earning higher grades, her teachers encouraged the "others" (upper-caste students) and not her. She stated, "In my case they never acknowledged that I was doing well. I did not like it, but still I studied to prove myself" (Interview, Sathe 2005). School was a thus a double burden for Dalit girls. They had consistently to excel at academic as well as at other activities and prove themselves to be "fit." Hirabai Kuchekar (2002) remembered a Brahman teacher during her Class 7: "He was really harsh. He asked me, 'What are you going to do with education?' He further continued, '*These* people will never improve. *You* will never understand this Maths; it is not meant for *you*. [Emphasis is mine].'" In this manner, teachers often discouraged Dalit students by encouraging them to drop out of school.

In municipal schools with majority lower-caste pupils, however, discrimination among pupils was rare. Kuchekar's daughter, a second-generation learner reported the following:

> I did not face *anything* in school, because it was a corporation school dominated by Dalit children. The teachers also, even if from the open category [upper-caste], did not practice caste discrimination. My friends also know my caste and are fine with me. They come home with me and I go their houses, and we are quite close. I have never hidden my caste. (Interview, 2002, emphasis added)

Thus, Kuchekar's daughter did not face caste discrimination as such. This could be because Dalits outnumbered non-Dalits and both students and teachers were aware of these facts. Also, it could be that students and teachers promoted a just environment that allowed individuals and communities to interact freely with each other. However, historically, when high-castes were in greater numbers, they would humiliate and discriminate against Dalits in both overt and covert ways. Kuchekar (2002) and others were familiar with such caste discrimination. The socialization of many upper-caste children by their parents and teachers led to discriminatory practices toward their classmates. Again, like Jadhav, Kuchekar avoided the word caste-discrimination substituting "anything" in its place. Women did not assertively use the words "caste prejudice," but mentioned it in subtle ways.

Women encountered more hurdles in the arena of employment. Jadhav reported,

> The bosses from other castes favour their candidates, and so I was not promoted for a long time. They spoiled my confidential report [service record] and that affected my service. Because we belong to lower caste, we have to work harder as they already call us names. Even our community does not understand our problems. I used to commute daily and the officer from our caste used to complain that I was not punctual. They also try to transfer me to police stations in slums or ones, which have lesser facilities. However, I have learnt to give back now. (Interview, 2005)

Thus, Jadhav illustrates how upper-caste men support their caste fellows and discriminate against Jadhav (or Dalits). She emphasizes that Dalits (or SCs and STs) constantly had to prove themselves and work harder than the dominant castes. As a result, once again they are psychologically burdened because they have to prove to be "fit" for particular jobs. Most significantly, Jadhav also highlights that even Dalits may not support each other, and discriminate on the lines of sub-caste, gender, and even class.

Some elite men discouraged women from taking up challenging jobs like administrative services, police, engineering, scientists, and so on. Patriarchal norms have held that women do not have the "caliber" and "commitment" required for these "masculine" jobs. However, these arguments failed to take into account the patriarchal expectations of family obligations, which come first *only* for women and not for men.

This was precisely the *new* phenomenon that most second- and third-generation Dalit women experienced in the recent fifty years or so. Women described their potentials and pitfalls, fears and frustrations, and ended with a sense of both despair and accomplishment, confidence and courage to stand and fight oppression. These Dalit women and others downtrodden had come a long way in fighting atrocities, at times giving up, negotiating, questioning, and politicizing issues. They were working hard every day and dreaming of bright futures for their future generations.

Women articulated how public education was responsible in shaping their **new** emotionally contoured political practices and overall lives. Kuchekar had obtained a good job at the Jilha Parishad (District Office) because of her education. She argued that,

> while education was a primary factor in my pursuit of employment, even entry into the public domain made me confident, bold and assertive. I was almost a **new** [emphasis mine] woman. (Interview, 2002)

Thus, the quality of education they had was not so important for many women. Rather and most significantly, the process constituted their **new** personhood.

Kuchekar further emphasized, "women have to manage everything and work hard to get out of the mundane daily rut." She and her daughter asserted,

> we do not have equal status with our men. Our employment is taken for granted; there is nothing special or unusual about it that would command any special status or respect within the family. (Interview with Kuchekar and her daughter, 2002)

Kuchekar had to take care of the household while employed outside, while the males of the family engaged only with their employment and in paid labor. Although women gained new experiences in the process of their education and employment, their oppression was also reinforced in a different way. This was especially significant for Dalit women.

Increasing levels of education for men and women at times had contradictory effects on marital family life. Due to these struggles and dynamic processes many unmarried second- and third-generation women hoped to find educated, understanding, and cooperative companions. They reported difficulty finding such partners. In some instances, as in non-Dalit families, contradictory gendered practices prevailed in the selection of brides and bridegrooms: for a prospective bridegroom, the essential criteria were level of education and earnings, whereas for brides it was some education and domestic skills. The second and third generation of unmarried women hoped to find educated, understanding, and co-operative companions. However, they noted the great difficulty of finding such men. Waghmare responded,

> I think education makes a big difference and significantly affects the home environment. Further, the mother's education is very important. She has a voice to an extent and can influence her husband and children. There has to be an understanding between them, however. A few educated and well-settled Dalit boys proposed to me. They were doctors and engineers who wanted their wives to be at home. I was surprised with these views and I instantly refused them. [But] this is a mentality of some men even today. What is the use of studying then? My medical degree will otherwise be wasted if I do not practice medicine. I am happy I refused that marriage proposal. I run my clinic today and I am doing very well professionally. Yes, some families from the upper-castes have a different atmosphere, *saunskar* [culture], and the parents are very co-operative. (Interview, 2004)

Waghmare rejected prospective husbands and thus challenged Dalit men who recorded their antipathy toward women as income earners and sought to restrict her public participation. Some elite men embraced the dominant conceptions of male and female respectability, in which the man was the breadwinner who decided the confines of the private and public domains. To them, the housewife was the linchpin of domesticity; women and children were "nonworking," "dependent," and "to be protected." They were still grappling with radical changes in the community. While Waghmare was talking about herself, her mother interrupted,

> However, with the Brahmans the situation is different. Women dominate men in their households. At the same time, by taking them into confidence and making them do what they themselves want, in a comfortable manner, using their sweet tongue, men also dominate their wives. Our [Dalit] men fight and their ego is [also] very big. They will not touch housework and expect things to be done fast. (Interview, 2004)

Thus, Waghmare compared Dalit and Brahman households and found the woman–man relationship in the latter to be egalitarian and companionate. She criticized Dalit men who prided themselves on their practice of patriarchal norms. They regarded the educated and unemployed wife as a better nurturer than a non-literate and employed one. Some of the "well-educated" ones also desired to keep their women at home and look after them and their children. Perhaps, some men believe that an educated and employed woman develops "*shinga*" (literally, horns) to fight as perfectly argued by Urmila Pawar (Interview, 7 September 2004). Suvarna Kuchekar agreed that "many a times men's education is only on paper. In practice it did not change their mental make up. Some men merely acquired higher degrees" (Interview, 2002). Waghmare's mother approved of Dalit women's subjugation. Nonetheless, most of the women also agreed that relationships were also changing.

Conclusion

In this essay, I analyzed contradictions in new Dalit women's lives under incremental interlocking technologies. I concentrated on Dalit women's formal education as it was interlocked in supplemental ways with social difference, caste discrimination, class conflict, patriarchal pressures, and Brahmani hegemony. Education is not an isolated process, and hence, it cannot be studied in a vacuum. Dalit women's lives record these complex interconnected circuits of the "domestic" with the "public" in the most intriguing manner. Secular education had an immense instrumental value for women. Dalit women, who carved out their new personhood and agency while fighting against caste and gender prejudice, disrupted dominant discourses. They gained immensely on social, material, emotional, and psychological grounds.

Although women gained new experiences in the process of their education and employment, their oppression was also reinforced in a new way. Women did not have a real share in the power in these structures; nonetheless, they agreed that things were changing. There was also the problem of the continued stigmatization of single women, often rejected for marriage due to their higher age. They faced caste discrimination in their workplaces, but they also reported that relations between the upper and lower castes were changing, and at times improving in a positive way.

Some middle-class Dalit men wanted to marry women who would conform to the new model of elite domesticity. New patriarchal norms would not allow the woman to work outside the home because she might become domineering, assertive, or very "free" in her behavior with other women and men. Such an idiom would also not tolerate the family surviving on a woman's income. In general, however, this attitude has shifted across time; many men prefer working women who could share financial responsibilities in addition to the traditional work of looking after the home and bringing up children. Some argued that work actually enhanced women's courage and confidence in the outside world as well as the family's prestige, and provided women with a purposeful activity.

Dalits are thus radical and conservative at the same time. Historically, Dalit women and men worked together in the public realm. However, especially in post-Ambedkar times, many Dalit men upheld norms of a new patriarchy and a new gendered morality. Dalits are struggling with many contradictory forces and are thus radical and conservative at the same time. As a result, especially in middle-class households, women's education and employment depended on men's approval. Yet, not all women conformed at all times. When women annexed new arenas of modern education and employment many women and men appropriated certain values associated with the upper castes and created new forms of hierarchies, including damaging effects on gender equality. However, in so doing, they were not merely imitating practices of upper-castes, in terms of food, clothing, honor, and respectability but twisting them for their own purposes. In the process, women resisted and consented at the same time; they constructed their own subjectivity and constituted themselves anew. Although there is an ambiguity, Dalits were well aware of the processes of social change, conflict, and continuity.

Through their everyday struggles for justice and power under the domination of the state and upper castes, women constituted themselves as significant agents. However, such a change was also restricted to individual women and has yet to affect the community as a whole. Ultimately, what mattered most was women's ability to educate themselves in hostile circumstances, struggle consistently against men's control of their social and sexual selves, refashion their personhood, and uplift themselves and their future generations.

NOTES

1. I have changed some names to protect anonymity. I interviewed Dr. Sarita Waghmare, M.B.B.S. on 12 November 2004; Nima Jadhav, B.A. on 16 September 2001 and again in June 2005; and Gangabai Kuchekar on 8 January 2002 in Pune.

2. For details on contradictions around naming see, Paik, "Mahar-Dalit-Buddhist: The History and Politics of Naming in Maharashtra," *Contributions to Indian Sociology* (2011), 45: 2, 217–241.

3. Census of India 1991, Series 14, Maharashtra, Part VIII (1): SC-1: Distribution of SC population by sex for each caste, pp. 66–67. The 1991 census is the latest one based on caste identity.

4. The Right of Children to Free and Compulsory Education Act or Right to Education Act (RTE) is an Act of the Parliament of India enacted on 4 August 2009, which describes the modalities of the importance of free and compulsory education for children between the age of 6 to 14 years.

5. M.B. Chitnis, "An Educational, Social and Economic Survey of Milind College Students", as in the Milind College Annual Vol. X, 1973 and in Barbara Joshi (ed.), *Untouchable! Voices of the Dalit Liberation Movement* (London, 1986), pp. 47–49; Suma Chitnis, *A Long Way to Go....: Report on a Survey of Scheduled Caste High School and College Students in Fifteen States of India*, A Project Sponsored by ICSSR (New Delhi: Allied, 1981).

6. Another study indicates that, though far, less educated and of poor economic means, and needing immediate financial help from the grown up members of the family, nearly nine-tenths of the students got encouragement from their father, mother, and brother. Thus, the members of the older generation, irrespective of their own educational level, understood the value of education; therefore, encourage the younger members of family to take up education. See Chitnis, "Educational, Social, and Economic Survey," pp. 45–46; S.K. Chatterjee, *Looking Ahead: Educational Development of Scheduled Castes* (New Delhi, 2000); and Jose Kananaikil, "Marginalisation of the Scheduled Castes," in Jose Kananaikil (ed.), *Scheduled Castes and the Struggle Against Inequality* (New Delhi, 1998).

7. Sachidanand, as quoted in Chatterjee, Looking Ahead, p. 277.

8. Ibid., pp. 279. Original in Suneila Malik, *Social Integration of the Scheduled Caste* (New Delhi, 1979), pp. 50–55. For Malik, as the level of education increases, the tendency to dissociate from their own caste groups increases because while, on the one hand, they improve their socio-economic conditions through their own achievements. On the other, the status, of the group to which they belong remains the same, which, in fact, lowers their own social standing and as a result, they tend to dissociate themselves from their own caste groups.

9. Jadhav, 16 September 2001.

10. Ivan Illich, *Deschooling Society* (1st ed., New York, 1971); Pierre Bourdieu and Paul Willis also critically analyze this disciplinary aspect of the education system.

11. Waghmare's mother, Buddhist, B.A., Officer, Vishrantwadi-Pune, 12 November 2004. She was busy with house work and I could not talk much to her.

12. For example, see an article 'How the Chinese learn English,' by Nazia Vasi who teaches English to Chinese in Shanghai. Vasi highlighted English as the new opium of the masses. See the *My Times/Times Review, Times of India* (Accessed on Mumbai, 25 March 2007).

13. Padma Velaskar, "Ideology, Education and the Political struggle for Liberation: Change and Challenge among the Dalits of Maharashtra," in S. Shukla and R. Kaul (eds), *Education, Development and Under-Development* (New Delhi, 1998), pp. 210–240. In another context, see Geoff and Whitty.

14. I am drawing upon Gramsci (1971) and Bourdieu and Passeron (1977) who have analyzed how dominant classes exercise power in European society through their hegemony.

15. I am deriving from Bourdieuan postulates in Bourdieu and Passeron, Reproduction in education, society and culture Translated from the French by Richard Nice (London and Beverly Hills, 1977).

16. Ambedkar has analyzed, 'Did the Hindus never eat beef?' According to him, 'that the Hindus at one time did kill cows and did eat beef is proved abundantly by the description of the Yajnas [in the various Vedas, Brahmanas, Sutras, and so on]. The scale on which the slaughter of cows and animals took place was enormous.' See Ambedkar, BAWS, Vol. 7, Chapter XI, pp. 323–328. Also see Vol. 7, Chapter XIII on 'What made the Brahmins become vegetarians?' pp. 334–349.

17. Ambedkar's father changed his family name "Sankpal" to "Ambavadekar."

REFERENCES

Abbasayulu, Y.B. 1978. Scheduled Caste Elite: A Study of SC Elite in Andhra Pradesh, Hyderabad. Ph.D. dissertation, department of sociology, Osmania University, Hyderabad, India.

Ambedkar, B.R. 1991a. What Congress and Gandhi Have Done to the Untouchables. In *Babasaheb Ambedkar Writings and Speeches*, vol. 9. Bombay: Government of Maharashtra.

Ambedkar, B.R. 1991b. Did the Hindus Never Eat Beef? In *Babasaheb Ambedkar Writings and Speeches*, vol. 7: 323–328. Bombay: Government of Maharashtra.

Ambedkar, B.R. 1991c. What Made the Brahmins Become Vegetarians? In *Babasaheb Ambedkar Writings and Speeches*, vol. 7: 334–349.

Benei, Veronique. 2008. *Schooling Passions: Nation, History and Language in Contemporary Western India*. Stanford, CA: Stanford University Press.

Beteille, Andre. 1992. *The Backward Castes in Contemporary India*. Oxford: Delhi.

Bourdieu, Pierre, and Jean-Claude Passeron. 1977. *Reproduction in Education, Society and Culture*. Translated from the French by Richard Nice. London: Sage.

Census of India. 1991. Series 14, Maharashtra, Part VIII (1): SC-1: Distribution of SC Population by Sex for Each Caste, 66–67.

Chatterjee, S.K. 2000. *Looking Ahead: Educational Development of Scheduled Castes*. New Delhi: Gyan Publishing House.

Chitnis, M.B. 1973. An Educational, Social and Economic Survey of Milind College Students. In the Milind College Annual, Vol. X. Reprinted in 1986 *Untouchable! Voices of the Dalit Liberation Movement*, ed. Barbara Joshi, 47–49. London: Zed Books.

Chitnis, Suma. 1981. *A Long Way to Go….: Report on a Survey of Scheduled Caste High School and College Students in Fifteen States of India*. A Project Sponsored by ICSSR. New Delhi: Allied Publishers.

Dushkin, Lelah. 1972. Scheduled Caste Politics. In *The Untouchables in Contemporary India*, ed. Michael Mahar, 165–226. Tucson, AZ: The University of Arizona Press.

Dushkin, Lelah. 1979. Backward Class Benefits and Social Class in India, 1920–1970. *Economic and Political Weekly*, 7 April, 14 (14): 661–667.

Gramsci, Antonio. 1971. *Selections from the Prison Notebooks of Antonio Gramsci*, ed. Q. Hoare and G. Nowell Smith (trans. G. Nowell Smith). London: Lawrence and Wishart.

Illich, Ivan. 1971. *Deschooling Society*. New York: Harper and Row.

Jeffrey, Craig. 2008. *Degrees without Freedom? Education, Masculinities and Unemployment in North India*. Stanford, CA: Stanford University Press.

Kananaikil, Jose. 1998. *Scheduled Castes and the Struggle Against Inequality*. New Delhi: Indian Social Institute.

Kuchekar. 2002. Interview conducted by author.

Kurane, Anjali. 1999. *Ethnic Identity and Social Mobility*. Jaipur: Rawat Publications.

Malik, Suneila. 1979. *Social Integration of the Scheduled Caste*. New Delhi: Abhinav Publications.

Paik, Shailaja. 2009. Chhadi lage chham chham, vidya yeyi gham gham (The Harder the Stick Beats, the Faster the Flow of Knowledge): Dalit Women's Struggle for Education. *Indian Journal of Gender Studies* 16 (2): 175–204.

Paik, Shailaja. 2011. Mahar-Dalit-Buddhist: The History and Politics of Naming in Maharashtra. *Contributions to Indian Sociology* 45 (2): 217–241.

Paik, Shailaja. 2014. *Dalit Women's Education in Modern India: Double Discrimination*. London and New York: Routledge.

Paik, Shailaja. 2016. Forging a New Dalit Womanhood in Colonial Western India: Discourse on Modernity, Rights, Education, and Emancipation. *Journal of Women's History* 28 (4): 14–40.

Paik, Shailaja. 2017. Mangala Bansode and the Social Life of Tamasha: Caste, Sexuality, and Discrimination in Modern Maharashtra. *Biography* 40 (1): 170–198.

Pawar and Pawar. 2004. Interview conducted by author in Mumbai.

Sachidananda. 1976. *The Harijan Elite*. London: Thompson Press.

Shukla, Sureshchandra, and Rekha Kaul (eds.). 1998. *Education Development and Under-Development*. New Delhi: Sage.

Singh, Anant Santokh. 1969. *The Changing Concept of Caste in India*. New Delhi: Vikas Publications.

Vasi, Nazia. 2007. How the Chinese Learn English. *Times of India*, 25 March 2017.

Velaskar, Padma. 1998. Ideology, Education and the Political Struggle for Liberation: Change and Challenge Among the Dalits of Maharashtra. In *Education, Development and Under-Development*, ed. S. Shukla and R. Kaul, 210–240. New Delhi: Sage.

Wagh, Vilas. 1986. *Sugava Special Deepavali Issue*. Pune: Sugava (November–December).

Wagh, Vilas. 1994. *Ambedkari Prerana Visheshank* (Ambedkar Inspired Special Issue). Pune: Sugava.

Waghmare. 2004. Interview conducted by author.

Wankhede, G.G. 2001. Educational Inequalities Among Scheduled Castes in Maharashtra. *Economic and Political Weekly*, 5–11 May, 36 (18): 1553–1558.

CHAPTER 7

"Government Brahmin" Caste, the Educated Unemployed, and the Reproduction of Inequities

A. R. Vasavi

It is now twelve years since I started to take competitive exams. I have cleared some written exams but did not make it through the interviews. In 2010, I cleared the exam and interview for the High School Headmaster's post. But, I am still waiting to get my allocated post. If I can get this job, then I will be secure and able to fend for myself and my family, including my mother and sister's family. I don't know if I can pursue my interests in art but right now a secure job and regular income are important.
Mallesha: M.A. (History); B.Ed.; artist and sign board painter; resident of Kollegal town; Karnataka, India.[1]

Mallesha exemplifies the complex trajectory of a person from a "scheduled caste[2]" seeking education, employment, and the security of a government job. His life represents the limitations of formal and institutionalized structures of educational opportunity for disadvantaged groups in India. Even as debates and public pressure for and against

A. R. Vasavi (✉)
Independent Scholar, Bengaluru, India

© The Author(s) 2019
H. E. Ullrich (ed.), *The Impact of Education in South Asia*, Anthropological Studies of Education,
https://doi.org/10.1007/978-3-319-96607-6_7

affirmative action in education and employment continue, the labeling of affirmative action candidates as "Government Brahmins"[3] highlights the attendant hostility and resentment that such programs invoke. Seen and labeled as undeserving recipients of government largesse, there is often ignorance of the multiple disadvantages such candidates experience.

Details of Mallesha's engagement and experience with varied institutions, established to create "equality of opportunity" and to facilitate the development and capability of citizens, indicate multiple complexities. The disadvantages of a sub- standard education, heavy family responsibilities, lack of social and cultural capital, and intensification of corruption in the very institutions which should enable equality of opportunity become hurdles in Mallesha's attempts at improving his life. What he stands to sacrifice are his own interests and skills, which governmental endeavors such as reservation/positive discrimination—forms of creating equality of opportunity—overlook in their emphasis on integrating persons into the mainstream, but substandard, models of development and equality. Perhaps what stands out the most in Mallesha's case—representing the situation and predicament of a large number[4] (up to six million) of youth who are seeking legitimacy, recognition, and integration into a dominant system—is his attempt to access and gain entry into the large government apparatus which is seen as a key source of not only economic and social mobility but also that of recognition and professional security. The spread of such a hegemonic model contains and reproduces several inequities and disadvantages.

The dominant economic model is built on the negation of plural and diverse practices and forms of livelihoods and life-worlds. In privileging a model in which both development and equality are premised on ideas of fostering the transition of a large mass of people from an agrarian or non-industrial/urban economy into a predominantly urban/industrial economy via opportunities for education, little attention is paid to the creation of alternatives in which multiple skills, abilities, and life-worlds can be created or sustained. At the same time, the emphasis on mainstreaming persons into the dominant education and employment model overlooks how long-entrenched structures of "graded inequality"[5] (Ambedkar 1945) work at micro and macro levels to reproduce forms of inequality. Such inequality includes the continued hold of caste-based disadvantages at a formative stage of people's lives as also the persistence of caste-based discrimination, corruption, and violation of rights even at the levels of formal institutions such as schools, universities, and recruitment agencies.

Both visible and invisible barriers exist that reproduce conditions of exclusion and deprivation. Even as the rhetoric of "inclusive growth" and "inclusive policies" gains currency, it is important to assess how the very agendas of inclusion strengthen pre-existing and entrenched forms of inequalities. For marginalized people, who are located primarily outside the privileges of a small but spectral and speculative economy that has grown since 1991, their disembedded and continuously eroded lives and livelihoods are the key markers of their personhood and being. Such trends indicate the need to recognize the voice and agency of disadvantaged groups and persons, especially in the context of understanding their experiences of public institutions and the impact of these institutions on them. Weis and Fine's notion of critical bifocality which seeks to "make visible the sinewy linkages or circuits through which structural conditions are enacted in policy and reform institutions as well as the ways in which such conditions come to be woven into community relationships and metabolized by individuals" (2012: 174) is useful and enables one to make inter-linkages between the macro policies that claim to promote equality of opportunity and the experiences of those that such policies seek to serve.

Contextualizing Mallesha's experiences at several levels and making the inter- linkages to macro structures, processes, and institutions is to enable disadvantaged persons to represent themselves through new forms of ethnography[6] that can encapsulate both objective structuring factors and subjective experiences. Drawing on details from his diary and supplementing these with discussions with him and with observations on trends related to his experience enables one to assess the realization of official pronouncements and the impact of these policies on the life-worlds of people.

Standard and official narratives disseminated by official bodies concerned with economic development and growth identify a range of factors and conditions that produce and reproduce inequalities. The World Bank as the dominant apparatus that claims to address forms of inequalities sees inequality as "objectionable on both intrinsic and instrumental grounds. It contributes to economic inefficiency, political conflict, and institutional frailty" (World Bank 2006: 9). Overlooking how inequality erodes the very sense of being for so many marginal and disadvantaged persons, the World Bank sees the creation of "equality of opportunities" as one of the key ways of addressing national-level inequalities. The opportunities are identified as access to education, health, resources, and infrastructure, all of which in the myriad policy documents and discourses are sought to be translated into objective and measurable criteria. Perhaps what has been missed in all these is the persistence and reproduction of "existential inequality" which Göran Therborn[7] (2013) identifies as inequalities which affect and mark individuals by denying them recognition and respect. The form and entrenchment of this type of inequality also erodes their agency and rights to self-respect and freedom. The resulting loss of dignity and limited options create not only uncertainties in their future but also disable them from challenging the very sources, structures, and agencies of debilitating inequalities.

Mallesha's life is marked by inequalities, the sources of which lie in the life conditions of family and community, schooling and education, and employment structures and processes. Locating the life narratives of such persons and their attempts to overcome the multiple disadvantages through the dominant system and its prescriptions will highlight the complex issues involved in addressing inequality through the mechanisms of education, employment, and integration into the dominant apparatus.

At age 32 years, Mallesha's life in Kollegal, a small town in Karnataka, India, has been marked by many of the inequities including the "poverty trap" that prevent him, his family, and also members of his neighborhood-cum-caste community from moving out of conditions of marginality and the multiple forms of inequality.

FAMILY AND COMMUNITY

I was born into a scheduled caste family and belong to the Madiga (leather workers) sub-caste.[8] My parents were uneducated. I am the eldest son and I have a younger brother and sister. When I was studying in Standard I, my father passed away. We had only one small shack as our own property. We had no other property or money. My mother and all of us (three) children moved into my paternal grandparents' house and we lived there for four years along with our paternal uncle. After that, because of the frequent quarrels in the family, we were separated from the larger family and started to live independently. My mother, who had no knowledge at all of the larger world, started making a living by working at construction sites, spinning silk reels at home, cooking food for sale, grinding rice, and millets for others, etc. Somehow she managed to bring us up. Observing all these problems, our maternal uncles sent our youngest uncle to look after us.

He worked as a head loader in the Kollegal bus stand and, together with my mother, looked after us (all text in italics are from Mallesha's diary).

Research has increasingly shown that class background, parental occupations, and living conditions influence both educational performance and aspirations (Booth and Crouter 2001; Lareau 2003). Yet research in India has failed to detail how intra-family locations and caste-community relations vis-à-vis the larger society and politico-economic factors act as deterrents to those aspiring and working toward educational achievements. Although there has recently been recognition of intra-family inequalities which go beyond the macro and structural sources of inequality, adequate attention has not been paid to the multiple burdens that individuals bear within these families and to the demands that families impose on children. For example, the World Development Report 2006, with its focus on "Equity and Development, highlights how '... income and expenditure are often controlled by the male members of the family and that this leads to underinvestment, especially in the health and education of girls' (World Bank 2006: 104)." The focus on intra-family issues, then, has been primarily on gender-related differences, with some attention being paid to how patriarchy and male dominance reproduce varied forms of inequality. What is missing in these narratives is the reproduction of family and community-based inequalities whereby the cultural and social reproduction of the very strategies of survival become barriers to opportunities to overcome inequality, poverty, and a range of disadvantages.

While Mallesha and his siblings were fortunate to have a larger extended family that sustained them in the early years he, like many of the oldest children in working class families, internalized the idea of acting as the de facto head of the family. The premature death of the earning parent becomes the single biggest burden on children, and is often the key factor in children dropping out of school and joining the pool of child workers. Children of single parents, in most cases those without fathers, often take on adult roles at a young age and act as parents to their younger siblings (NIAS 2002). Mallesha started working in standard/grade tenth itself (at around 16 years of age) to support his family. He worked as an apprentice to a painter and he contributed to the household even as he sought formal education and credentials. The life of several of his cohorts in the neighborhood also indicates how existential inequality eroded their abilities to break out of the cycle of poverty and disadvantage and to enable them to have better life chances.

NEIGHBORHOOD AND COMMUNITY

My neighborhood (a settlement of about 180–200 households, just off the Kollegal-Bangalore highway) has mostly Madiga (leather workers) households. When we were young, most of the men were occupied in leather-related work. My father purchased sheep and goats which were then sold for meat. Nowadays, many of the men work as head loaders, construction workers, drivers and painters, and some go to the cotton and sugarcane mills. Most of the women stay at home and do household work. Only in those families that have no earning male member, do the women go out to work in the mills or to the grain centers to clean grains.

There used to be a lot of alcoholism when I was growing up. There were frequent and violent fights in the families. Many children dropped out of school as their fathers were drunkards and either did not support the families or died when they were young. Nowadays, drinking has decreased. Some of those who suffered from this are now conscious and want to give their children a better life.

Most of the youth in the neighborhood are able to study only up to high school. Only some go on to Pre-University but many drop out from here also. There were about six to eight of us, all boys, who went to college. Nowadays, girls go for D.Ed. (Diploma in Education). There is pressure on girls to get jobs to help with dowry payments. Girls with jobs also find it easier to get husbands.

Such conditions and trends further explicate how existential inequality that emanates from family and community conditions and structures are transmitted to and made visible in the limited opportunities and life-chances that most of the members of disadvantaged communities have. The lack of support networks that could facilitate transmission of social advantage (Wall et al. 2010) combines with the lack of external social scaffolds to enforce the disadvantaged to submit to strategies of compromise or to internalize their disadvantages. Alcoholism and dropping out of school/college are key manifestations of the markers of the subjective experience and expressions of disadvantage.

EDUCATION AND "CAPABILITY DEVELOPMENT"

With the post-Jomtien Conference's[9] emphasis on education as the key driver of capability development, the dominant development discourse claims and promotes basic education as the foundation for future development. Echoing such perspectives and expressing popular sentiment, scheduled caste groups claim caste-based educational deprivation has denied them the right to formal learning (and literacy). They regard this as the single most important factor that is hindering their rise out of poverty, maintaining discrimination, and reducing them to low status. They seek education, as formal learning, to exit a life of hardship and see it as the single most important route to a better life. Families place great faith in education for addressing their multiple disadvantages and many even go hungry in order to provide education for their children. For Mallesha, school as an opportunity was a mixed experience.

SCHOOL

I studied in a school run by Catholic priests and we did not pay any fees. I went to this school regularly until Standard IV and they used to teach us very well. I was also a good student. The teachers were very strict and instilled fear and devotion in us. One day, in the fourth standard, a teacher caned me on my hand. Out of fear of this punishment, I did not go to school for a year. Because I did not attend school, they also beat me at home. My mother would give me a good beating and then cry. Once, they heated an iron rod and burnt me on my back. But still, I was very stubborn and did not go to school. Even when my classmates came to call me, I would not go. One day, some students from Standard VII came to my house and carried me to school. Still, I did not attend school. So, after all these attempts, they sent me to graze goats. After a year, my grandfather took me again to the school and readmitted me. All the teachers spoke to me gently. They advised me to come to school regularly. At this time, I was studying with students who were younger than me but still I did well in class. In the fifth standard, I was selected to go for a drawing competition. I did not know how to draw well. The other students, who had come from different schools, knew how to draw. They all had sketch pens, color pencils, paints and paint brush, etc. I had not seen any of these. Seeing all this, I had a desire that I too must learn how to draw and get all these things. From that day, I started to practice to draw. With this, I was able to distinguish myself from the others. I continued to learn and practice drawing even during my studies for various degrees. Some of the teachers supported me in this.

The trauma of entering formal educational institutions which are often hostile and are not particularly child-friendly is rarely documented. For many children from marginalized families, among whom formal and regimented learning is non-existent, such experiences become the bases for dropping out. Mallesha's case is exceptional in that his grandfather was insistent that he attend school and he was fortunate to have some sensitive teachers who recognized his interests and abilities and encouraged him. What Mallesha's case highlights is how supporting individuals such as parents, grandparents or teachers can make a difference to their lives and enable them to break out of the cycle of disadvantages. In insisting on his education and then recognizing his innate talent, a breakthrough from such existential inequalities was made possible.

ILLNESS

When I was in the sixth standard, I developed a severe allergy to dust. I would get fits of cough and cold and had to stay away from school. I had to be taken to the hospital frequently. My mother also took several vows to various gods and goddesses. She took me to several temples, mutts,[10] and religious fairs. I had several amulets around my neck, on my arm, and around my waist. Through all this, I would vent my anger on my mother and throw all the amulets away. Mother sold her brass vessels, her earrings, and also borrowed heavily to get me treated. It was only when I started going to pre-university college that the allergies subsided.

Ill-health resulting primarily from malnutrition marks the lives of many children from marginalized families. While health services and institutions are difficult to access, popular understanding of illness among the Madiga emphasizes treatment via appeasement of spirits, demons, and deities. Mallesha's early experiences traumatized him sufficiently to make him skeptical of such health seeking practices. Yet, his early childhood conditions made him vulnerable to frequent bouts of ill health and it was to be a setback later in his life. A feature of existential inequality, ill-health, and its recurrence acts as negative and inhibiting factors to Mallesha's full participation and engagement in education and employment seeking.

EDUCATIONAL INSTITUTIONS: SOCIAL SCARRING AND HUMILIATION

The expansion of the education system into a form of mass and public development agenda has meant that issues of education quality (in terms of learning levels and the functioning of the institutions) have become matters of serious concern. The very orientation and functioning of these institutions do not take into consideration the capability of different persons or encourage their intellectual development. Recent reviews and reports have consistently indicated the extant poor quality of education in government primary schools (ASER 2014) which are now largely attended by children of the low-ranked caste groups. Similarly, there are also studies that critique the lack of quality or the provisioning of relevant or employment-oriented education at the secondary and higher education levels. But there are very few studies that detail the negative atmosphere and the severe limitations of the new mass educational institutions. Policy discourse that focuses on promoting increased access to higher education completely overlooks these considerations and issues.

The development discourse also lays much faith in the ability of institutions to endow and entitle individuals and disadvantaged groups with a range of new capabilities. Institutions of education especially are seen and represented as acting as carriers of development and as addressing inequalities. Where there is recognition of the very problematic nature of institutions, it is qualified and identified as emanating primarily from either political or economic institutions. For example, although the World Bank report recognizes how "... complex historical processes, combined with inequalities in influence and power, may lead to bad political and economic institutions which severely impair the development of poor countries" (2006: 8), there is little recognition of the social scarring of marginalized individuals and groups in and by these institutions.

Although Mallesha and his friends, as members of the socially low-ranked and officially scheduled caste groups, are admitted to the university and its hostels on the bases of "affirmative action" or educational "reservations," their experience of the educational institution and its endowment does not further their capability development or their knowledge and skills to compete in the employment market. The lack of attention to providing quality education and the general limitations[11] of India's affirmative education policy (Weisskopf 2004) are also manifest in Mallesha's experience of university life. More specifically, the expansion and even the emphasis on equity through affirmative education policies have not addressed the "institutional handicaps and handicaps in life-history" (Bögenhold 2001: 833) which continue to mark the lives of even educated persons from disadvantaged backgrounds.[12]

Since I was interested in art and many of the teachers recognized this, I thought I should join CAVA (a fine arts training center) in Mysore. I had saved about Rs. 6000 and gained entry to CAVA after passing the tests. I had also spoken with my paternal uncles and they promised to help pay the fees for the two-year course. However, I was able to be there for only three months. The materials (paints, brushes, sketch books, etc.) were very expensive. As a Scheduled Caste student, I received a stipend of only Rs. 150 per month. This was not adequate. When I approached my uncles for financial help, they dithered. So, I dropped out of CAVA.

I later joined the Bachelor of Arts course in Kollegal itself. The classes were only in the morning and I worked in the evenings. Since I stayed at home, there were no extra expenses for hostel or food. But, even after completing my B.A. course here, I was not able to get a job. I then decided to enroll for a Master's course in History. I enrolled in Mysore University. The teachers were indifferent. They rarely took classes. We had a few textbooks and only some of us went to the library. There were no discussions or good interactions between the teachers and the students. We, as students from small towns and villages, were always hesitant. They (the teachers) talked down to us.

Every month, there were at least two strikes and classes were cancelled. On the non-strike days, classes were conducted only until the afternoon and after that most students whiled away time in the hostels. The facilities were also not good in the hostel. I used to try and be preoccupied with drawing or writing banners but I did not get such work continuously. The students had groups, and caste associations were strong. Friendships and alliances were made on the bases of their links with their villages and/or their caste groups. I did not join any of them.

Our hostel life in Mysore was very difficult. I stayed at the "Backward Classes Hostel" run by the Department of Social Welfare. Every student who had gained entry legally had to support at least two or three friends who had entered through the "back door." They ate at the mess (dining facilities) and also lived in the rooms. The running of the mess was auctioned to outsiders and they always sought to make money and gave us food that was inadequate and of poor quality. There were often fights over this. The authorities accused students of misusing the mess and bringing in friends. The students accused the authorities of being corrupt and of "swallowing" the money allocated by the government for them. The hostel also did not have any library facilities. Since classes were held only until the afternoon, we whiled away the time after that. We could not afford to buy our own books. No one cared for us and the students in turn became indifferent to rules and to their own lives. I think we wasted our time there. There was little learning and many students picked up bad habits (of drinking, gambling, and wasting time).

Exams were held only once a year. But, our performance in these was not always even. Only a few among us did well. Many would fail or get low marks. There were always fights over this, just as it was about the food and the hostel. General caste students often referred to us as "Government Brahmins" (Government Brahmanaru). We know that even some teachers did so. They considered us unworthy of the reservations and believed we were there only because the government was supporting us. There was always tension about this.

"Government Brahmins"

The overall tensions in the campus are compounded by the general limitations of inadequate and poor quality of educational programs. These include failure to engage the students adequately or to provide updated syllabi and content and the submission to populist demands in which the overall content and quality are further eroded.

The affirmative action or reservation policy and the program designed to address inherited disadvantages fails to develop the abilities and skills for these aspiring youth. Hostilities and rivalries between caste groups lead to the labeling of scheduled caste students, and those who receive reservations in institutions, as "government Brahmins"—as members privileged by the largesse of the government. Intense competition over limited educational seats, deep-rooted prejudice among upper-caste students and faculty, and the institutional failure to facilitate inter-caste integration have led to some of these hostilities. Popular constructions that low-ranked castes are undeserving and unable to utilize educational opportunities fail to assess the deep problems which result in largely inadequate and poor quality education, and which also limits or prevents disadvantaged groups or persons from breaking away from their conditions of disadvantage.

Such tensions in the politics of redistribution and recognition are noted by Nancy Fraser: "'Affirmative Redistribution'... aims to redress economic injustice, (but) it leaves intact the deep structures that generate class disadvantage. Thus, it must make surface relocations again and again. The result is to mark the most disadvantaged class as inherently deficient and insatiable, as always needing more and more. In time, such a class even more comes to appear privileged, the recipient of special treatment and undeserved largesse. Thus, an approach aimed at redressing injustices of distribution can end up creating injustices of recognition" (1997: 25). This is precisely what has become the norm in most educational campuses in India, with a rhetoric that "undeserving," "non-merit," and "poorly qualified" students from low-ranked caste groups have now gained entry and are largely responsible for the decline in the standard of education. These are compounded by hostilities between student groups which are drawn largely on caste lines. In what is a cruel misnomer, reserved category students begin to be referred to as "Government Brahmins," mocking them as unqualified for their reserved seat privilege. High dropout rates among the reserved category students and growing hostilities and tensions in various institutions over academic performance and the treatment of such students have become rampant across the nation.

DREAMS OF ENGLISH

Submitting to regional language politics, which by the 1980s had gained momentum in the state, many universities diluted their standards of teaching in English as the medium of instruction in higher education. The first casualty of this was the large mass of first-generation college students, primarily from rural and low-ranked caste groups, who were permitted to receive education in the state language, Kannada. While the numbers of graduates increased, their worth in the job market decreased dramatically. Ruing the lack of English language teaching and the fact that he, and his friends and classmates are unable even to converse in English, Mallesha expresses deep regret and discomfort.

In school, we were taught English from Standard V onwards. The teachers themselves did not know English. They memorized a few words and sentences and pretended to read. They let us write the words in Kannada over the English words so that we could read them. We mostly memorized the passages and could barely understand anything. We could not speak it, even though nowadays some of us can read… the newspapers. It was the same at college. They allowed us to read, write, and take the exams in Kannada. We found this easy and did not have to struggle. But, we know that knowing English helps get jobs. Many of those who have failed in the tenth standard did so because they failed in English. In college also we were not encouraged to know English. Now, we try. But, we can only dream about English.

UN-EMPLOYABILITY

Policy documents and reports which focus on criteria such as increasing the number or proportion of graduates etc., are singled out as key to the assessment of development, but lack of attention to the quality of education and to the sacrifice of quality over assertions of quantity mean that the disadvantaged become doubly disadvantaged. Lack of knowledge of English prevents them from being employed in the urban and new service sectors. In the contradictory and complex turn of an increasingly globalizing economy, Mallesha and his friends read about new job opportunities in the nation's metropolises; where a booming IT and IT services economy in the regional capital, Bangalore, has taken off and where jobs are a plenty for all those who can speak English. But, many of these unemployed youth, mostly those with poor quality education and lack of skills for the new economy are described as "unemployable;" often assigning individual blame for such limitations. Even mainstream discourse overlooks the institutional and structural limitations due to which these disadvantaged youth are rendered "unemployable." These youth desperately forge multiple strategies to gain entry into mainstream or government jobs. Distanced from any possibility of gaining entry into the new global economy, unwilling to do agricultural work and/ or engage in manual labor or in their caste-based work as it is considered demeaning and insulting for educated persons, many youth wander between educational institutions, courses, and short-term assignments that provide them little or no skills for employment. Caste-based skills such as smithy, carpentry, tanning and leather work, stone-work, weaving, etc., are neglected or forgotten as none of these skills are recognized even in the vocational training courses offered by the Institutes of Technical Instruction (ITI). The expansion of the higher education system, primarily through a network of colleges and regional/state universities, has been at the cost of providing quality and relevant education. Outdated in content, orientation, and training, most institutions cater to producing graduates who remain unemployed, underemployed, or unemployable in the new economy. The lack of competence in English is only one of the key handicaps faced by those who receive this type of mass higher education. For many, formal education does not provide them the capability to compete in the job market or be skilled enough to become independent entrepreneurs or workers.

THE SPECTER AND TREADMILL OF COMPETITIVE EXAMS

Over the years, Mallesha acquired several degrees. Apart from completing the two- year pre-degree course in Arts (History, Kannada, and Geography), he worked to get a Bachelor's degree (B.A. in

History), a Master's degree in History, and a B.Ed. (Bachelor's degree in Education). Like many of his compatriots in his neighborhood, he appeared for several competitive exams in order to get a government job. Each attempt, a prolonged process often taking several years (between applying for the post and receiving the final decision), marks every aspirant as having either 'passed' or 'failed'.

For most of us in the neighborhood, a job in the government is seen as the best opportunity. Government jobs (government kelasa) are considered to provide security (badrathe), are permanent (khayam) and also have prestige (gaurava). Even a low-level government employee has high status and is regarded with respect. Most of the boys start to take exams for government jobs as soon as they pass Standard X. Many take the exams for first division and second division clerks. Others also take the many exams for teachers' posts, for the forest department, and the revenue and police departments.

Over the past ten years, I have taken several exams. I have appeared for the High School Teachers' exams thrice, once each for the posts of preuniversity college lecturer, revenue inspector, hostel warden, and first division clerk. I have taken the Karnataka Education Service Exam once and the Karnataka Administrative Service exam twice.

Mallesha provides details of the dates and the process for the exam on which he pinned his hopes:

1. Submission of application: December 2007
2. Preliminary exam (objective type): February 2008
3. Results of Preliminary: June 2008
4. Main (descriptive) exam: December 2008
5. Results of main exam: July 2009; call for interview
6. Interview: September 2009
7. Final list of selected candidates: February 2010
8. Appointment letter: Sent in June 2012

The process, stretching over four years, involves the assessment of a large number of applicants. For the final 629 posts which were available, at least 60–80 thousand applicants took the exams. Of these, only about a thousand were able to clear the exams and qualified for the interview. Even as the whole process is delayed and no details or dates for the final selection are shared with the candidates, the issue of recruiting new teachers becomes contested.

Over the years, the increasing demand for such government jobs and the gradual shrinkage of these posts has meant that the very institutions that process such examinations and job allocations have also become very corrupt. Even as formal and mechanized processes (objective type questions assessed by computers) of examinations are introduced, the final selection (interviews) becomes the key stage in which influence and money power work to get candidates the job. Applicants seek support from caste-based politicians or organizations to either support their candidacy or negotiate the system in terms of bribing selection officers. In Karnataka, the state's Public Service Commission became the object of much public ridicule and speculation.[13] Set up to be an institution with the responsibility of recruiting and allocating government jobs, the state's Public Service Commission has become an antithesis of its very mandate. Far from being open and public or service oriented, it has become an institution run by successive governments as an agency for realizing party or caste-affiliated ambitions and expanding the pool of government employees who will owe allegiance and support to them. Malpractice and irregularities in recruitment led the former chairman, responsible for recruitment over a period of years, to be investigated and served a notice and imprisoned.[14] Between 2010 and 2011, the selection of external headmasters, the post for which Mallesha applied, became contested. Even as 629 posts were declared to be filled through competitive exams, older teachers who were also eligible for the posts of head masters as part of their career advancement, filed a petition in court challenging the Education Department's recruitment of outsiders. As the court case dragged on, some of the aspirants who had cleared the exams went on a hunger strike. A compromise was sought to be hammered out between the Teachers Association that opposed the new recruitment and the new recruits who were still awaiting appointment.[15] Such delays, confusion, and lack of transparency make the whole process of state-based recruitment for employment even more fraught with tension.

'Competitive exams' or exams for professional educational courses or for government jobs, have become a specter in the lives of marginal youth. They immerse themselves in applying, preparing, taking, and then waiting for the results of several competitive exams and focus their aspirations on being successful in any one of these exams. Even as they witness the booming urban economy, their own opportunities have not only shrunk but are marked by processes which deny them their individuality, creativity, and interest. In the increasingly competitive and corrupt context of gaining government jobs, the youth experience multiple forms of humiliation and degradation. Much of the discussion and preparation for the exams are to anticipate, guess, and discern what the contents of the exam will be and who will be on the interview board. Preparations for written exams focus on purchasing 'guidebooks', especially those which focus on preparing candidates for a range of exams. Gathering in friends' homes or in public places, groups of youth try out 'model exam papers' and discuss ways in which the exam can be 'cracked'. In all of this, in-depth knowledge of issues and subject matter are completely bypassed. For those taking multiple exams, the focus becomes on gaining competence in the different types of exams (objective type, or written essays) and in seeking extra help in order to succeed in the exams.

Mallesha himself becomes one such 'government job seeker'—an appellation that has gained currency and even legitimacy among the youth as they await jobs. A lower age bar for scheduled caste candidates means that he is eligible to take these exams until the age of thirty-five years. This extended age entitlement is also the basis on which Mallesha and his friends pin their hopes of gaining entry into the government sector. It also means they neglect to seek other avenues and fail to seek opportunities elsewhere. For the disadvantaged youth whose singular objective in adult life is to get into a 'government job', the delays, the lack of transparency, and the entry of questionable and inadequately trained persons into the system compel them to see the whole edifice and process of recruitment for government jobs as a corrupt enterprise. Scams that break out indicate not only nepotism but also the purchase of jobs through bribes paid to members of the selection committees. Among the disenfranchised youth, the exams become the new loadstone, a holy grail in which the bar for each year seems higher and more difficult to navigate and overcome. If passing the written test and interview and the declaration of his eligibility for the post of school headmaster acted as a boost to Mallesha's self-confidence, the long delay in getting the appointment letter leads to tensions. Upset over the uncertainties and his state of unemployment, Mallesha falls ill. His old childhood illness of wheezing and sinus returns. He spends nearly six weeks recuperating from this and has to borrow money for his medical treatment.

After several months of waiting for information from the State Public Service Commission (nearly 25 months since he applied for the post) and then despondent, Mallesha returns to work as an independent signboard painter and a freelance artist. He gets work only intermittently.

His family relationships deteriorate. His mother expects him to get a full-time job and to cater to her and the daughter's family and their needs. He would like to join a non-profit organization where his interest in art and education can be pursued but his wife refuses to work in a rural area. He now has a young son to look after as well and his limited income is inadequate to cater to the growing family. He longs to be able to do creative work, to integrate art in education, to read, and to write. But much of his daily life goes in preparing for exams, discussing strategies with friends, and earning some income through occasional painting jobs. Mallesha's condition is representative of the experience of many educated unemployed youth, which Craig Jeffrey identifies as 'futureless waiting' which is "a condition that marks the lives of millions of educated youth, who wait for jobs and appointments. Neither despondent nor wholly optimistic... their openness to possibility can be glossed as a form of waiting that is neither straightforwardly purposeful nor purposeless but shares elements of both forms" (2010: 91).

In seeking to make a transition from the world of non-literate, informal economy to that of being recognized as an 'educated' and employable person aspiring to be a 'government employee', Mallesha experiences multiple forms of humiliation and degradation. It is not so much his failure or inability to have the 'capacity to aspire' (World Bank 2006) as much as it is the distortions created by the dominant model as to what capabilities and skills will enable him to be employed and, therefore, become 'developed'. In the creation of an education-employment funnel that is narrow and limited, Mallesha remains marked as a 'failure', a man unable to gain the respect of his family and community. These represent what Craig Jeffrey notes to be experiences by the educated unemployed which are "... a triple temporal hardship. First, they are unable to conform to dominant visions of how people should comport themselves with respect to linear, clock time—they 'miss years' or have 'gaps' on their resumes.... Second, they are unable to obtain the social goods, such as a secure white-collar job, which connote development.... Third, they are incapable of moving into gendered, age-based categories, especially male adulthood, such that they come to be labeled or label themselves as 'dropouts', 'failures' or people on the shelf" (2010: 13).

Even as dominant discourse and theories recognize the multiple complexities and nuances of inequities, 'durable inequalities' (Tilly 1998), inequalities of opportunities, and the persistence of the 'poverty trap', there is a lack of recognition of the hegemony of the dominant model and its imprint on the life-worlds of those it seeks to integrate into its system. The failure to gain entry into this dominant model and its system becomes a marker of failure and the reproduction of the multiple forms of inequities especially for the disadvantaged. As a hegemonic model that privileges only one trajectory for life and recognition, it becomes the basis for the erosion of their plural life-worlds. In experiencing this loss of the plurality of life-worlds and in the subsequent marking of those who have 'failed' (through competitive exams, or through the inability to have those criteria), lie the reproduction of a generation of people who stand as eroded and as 'wasted' (Bauman 2004). The significance of the presence of the educated unemployed on families, communities, and on the larger society have not been adequately understood or represented. Only a few scholars have pointed to the implications of such prolonged unemployment for inter-generational and gendered relationships which, in many cases, lead to the possibility of enhancing membership in caste and religious associations and to tensions in marriages (Chowdhry 2010).

Mallesha—talented, sensitive, intelligent, and sincere—stands as a test case for the millions who are only known in official language as the 'educated unemployed'; a category of persons who must either be retrained or refitted to suit a new economy and its new orientations. What Mallesha experiences as loss—of not being able to pursue his own interest and skills in fine arts, of being subjected to a process that demeans his worth and abilities, of gaining certain 'capabilities' despite the very arduous process, and which in reality do not serve his own needs and desires—are issues that do not translate into objective, measurable criteria. Mainstream discourses in policy-planning, and the deployment of agendas and programs mostly recognize only those inequalities that can be addressed through a provisioning of education, health, access to resources, and more recently to a range of rights.[16] What of the hidden forms of exclusion which in the apparent rhetoric of rights dissemination, capability development, and collective welfare orientation miss the very foundation of the erosion of individuals? It would not be right or easy to say that Mallesha's life-world could have been drawn on the world of his ancestors and that a life of being 'the shepherds-cum-leather workers' would have been his legitimate or better world lending itself to a plurality of non-modern life-worlds. The limitations and depredations of such a world have only been too well elucidated and are not the grounds for recommending a return to caste-based occupations. But, what marks Mallesha's life is not only the inability to realize himself or the burden of existential inequality but also the stigma of being a failure despite having the certification that should have assured him success. He, like so many others in his cohort group, is the bearer of the loaded promise of development which in its unilinear and universalistic directives is increasingly a crucible in which the life, opportunities, and being of so many are being tested.

In being removed from a life-world of knowledge and skills that were drawn from his family and caste background, and further being denied the ability to realize his own interests, and in being measured against the dominant paradigm of being 'developed', Mallesha experiences multiple dislocations and humiliations. Such subjection and disorientation by the larger system also denude Mallesha and his compatriots of a sense of agency and creates another circle of 'inequalities of agency' (Rao and Walton 2004). Subscribing to the dominant narrative and directives of being 'educated', 'developed' and 'employed' and seeking legitimacy through these parameters, Mallesha and his friends do not seek to critique, challenge, or disregard the system of education, examination, and job allocation. Instead, the long periods of waiting, preparation, and strategies to gain government employment make them passive participants in the system and they also seek to play it in its own game.[17] This alone accounts for their silence despite the long years of stress, open violation of codes of conduct, and the questionable methods in which the much sought after jobs are allocated.

Mallesha's background of multiple class/caste and cultural disadvantage compounded with the social scarring by modern institutions and his own inability to fully comprehend it or challenge it represents a form of 'hermeneutical injustice' which Miranda Fricker describes as "... the injustice of having some significant area of one's social experience obscured from collective understanding owing to persistent and wide-ranging hermeneutical marginalization" (2011: 42). His life and its tribulations represent the tensions of being caught between the disadvantages of a family, a community, and a regime of rights and development programs which fail to address the very fundamental bases of inequality. Located within the very contradictions of a system that seeks to alter him and his life conditions and yet retains him within its complex of disadvantages, Mallesha internalizes the very norms of the larger apparatus and seeks to negotiate it through its own terms. The impact of this on Mallesha is personal and significant. He becomes subjected to processes of submission, co-option, and compromise. The limitations of the macro structures and their apparatus of institutions, processes, and rules mark the life-world of an individual who is also labeled as an 'educated unemployed'. Much of the outer promises of the agenda and programs of mass and inclusive education then become forms of new sources of inequalities. For every outer promise made by the larger system, there is increasingly an inner denial.

In 2014, close to ten years since I first met him and started discussing his education and employment issues, I visited Mallesha at his home in Kollegal. He had finally been appointed as a high school headmaster (four years, ten months after his application) in a remote village (to which he commuted daily). He expressed that he did not find satisfaction in his job. Being a headmaster entailed primarily bureaucratic work and he rarely got to teach. Neither did he have time to paint or engage in art activities. Yet, I observed a sort of newfound assurance about himself. And, as he noted, his family and his fellow caste persons now recognized (*guruthu*) him.

I am now an official and part of the government. People recognize me for that. One cannot have what one would have liked… a job doing what one likes. For people like us, being accepted (sweekara), and recognized (guruthu), by what society expects rather than being ourselves become our life's path. Mine has also been one.

Acknowledgements This paper was developed as part of the German Historical Institute London's Transnational Research Group on 'Poverty and Education in India' and was a Working Paper in their series.

NOTES

1. 'Mallesha' is a pseudonym but all other details are factual. In 2004, Mallesha joined a research-cum-advocacy project that I was co-coordinating. In 2005, I noted his interest in applying for government jobs and we discussed his skills and interests, family life and pressures and I requested him to keep a diary. The research project closed in 2007 but we retained contact and he visited me often in Bangalore. I was privy to his struggles to focus on his art and education work and yet gain entry into a government job. In 2009, when he quit his temporary painting job, I provided him with occasional financial support and part-time work in a research project. In 2010, we reviewed his diary and notes and I reframed several questions. We followed details of the case of the recruitment of headmasters, both through his personal experiences and through discussions and reports in the press. In writing this essay, I have translated selections from

his diary (written in Kannada) and shared the draft versions of the essay with him. He approved the essay in its entirety but requested the use of a pseudonym for his name. He continues to maintain a diary about his life as a government school headmaster.

2. The term 'scheduled caste' is drawn from the official schedule which identifies persons from former 'untouchable castes' and also from other low-ranked caste groups who are entitled to a range of government-based protective measures. The term has now gained social currency and many of these groups use it to identify themselves as 'Scheduled Caste' or use the abbreviation 'SC' rather than the term Dalit.

3. An autobiography, first published in Kannada and then translated into English, by Aravind Malagatti (1994) called *Government Brahmana* refers to such labeling. But, the label is widely and covertly used by upper-caste students and faculty to refer to reserved category students and employees (including faculty). Such labeling and name calling increased after the anti-reservations agitations, also called the Mandal agitation in 1990.

4. Estimates for the number of youth in India vary depending on the definition of youth. Currently, based on a definition of youth as ranging from 15 to 24 years, there are approximately 240 million youth (Government of India 2014) who constitute the world's largest bodies of youth. Of these, only about 20% make it to high school and only about 11% to the college or university level. Numbers for educated unemployed also vary but reliable assessments indicate it to be around 6.5 million (Dev and Venkatanarayana 2011).

5. B.R. Ambedkar referred to 'graded inequality' as a specific form of caste-based inequality in which hierarchical caste ranking and ordering meant that each caste was relatively unequal to those above it.

6. Although this may be seen as representing a form of "para-ethnography" (Marcus and Holmes 2005), I do not draw from this genre of social anthropology. Instead, I draw on the use of diaries and frequent discussions with the interlocutor along with observations of structuring issues and public debates as a form of engaged fieldwork in which anthropological questions of not only culture but also that of structures (and their political economies), and the agency, voice, and representation of the subject are sought to be addressed.

7. Göran Therborn (2013) identifies three types of inequalities: "vital inequalities" that pertain to inequalities of health and death; "existential inequalities" which mark individuals and marginal groups and refer to the multiple ways in which their personhood, autonomy and dignity are eroded or denied; and "resource and material inequalities" which refer to material deprivations.

8. Madigas (also spelt as Maadigas or Maadhigas) were originally associated with leather (or handling dead cows) and are akin to the north Indian

group of Chamars, the Madiga of Andhra Pradesh, and the Chakliyars of Tamil Nadu. In Karnataka, they account for the second highest proportion of Scheduled Castes and are considered to be 'untouchables' by many caste groups. As a group that has taken to various non-caste occupations, the Madigas of Karnataka are relatively well-organized in terms of political mobilization. Those who are organized now subscribe to the 'Dalit' identity and assertions that mark many of the Madiga youth associations.

9. The Jomtien Conference was first held in 1990, and India was a signatory to this conference and much of the recent directives for elementary education have been set by terms of the Jomtien Conference.

10. Mutts are Hindu religious orders established and run by various sects and orders. Many have spiritual leaders who are seen as both religious and temporal leaders.

11. See Weisskopf (2004) for a comprehensive overview of the limitations of the affirmative action program in the US and India. See also Deshpande (2011) for an argument that contextualizes the tension between the new trends in the growing privatization of education and the continued demand and need for affirmative action programs in education.

   Although Rohith Vemula's suicide at the University of Hyderabad in 2016, and the nation-wide agitations called 'Justice for Rohith' brought to public notice and debate the extant discrimination, neglect and humiliation that reserved category students experienced in institutions of higher education, no substantial changes have been made in the institutional cultures.

12. Bögenhold elaborates on Blossfeld and Shavit's work in thirteen different countries that rapid educational expansion did not reduce inequalities of educational opportunities. They concluded: "As a consequence of educational expansion, societies can produce a higher average level of educational attainment from one birth cohort to the next, without changing the educational opportunities of children from different social strata.... Thus, the modernization theorists' hypothesis of educational opportunities must be turned on its head: expansion actually facilitates to a large extent the persistence of inequalities in educational opportunity" [1993: 22] 2001: 838).

13. The State Public Services Commission is responsible for the recruitment of all government employees. While the process is supposedly open and exam-based, the biases and corruption enter at the time of interviews for which a substantial proportion of marks are allocated. In addition, in recent years, allegations of corruption in the very constitution of the board of members of the Public Services Commission have made the legitimacy of the Commission dubious.

14. H.N. Krishna, Chairman of the Karnataka State Public Services Commission, along with three others, was indicted by the Criminal Investigation Department for irregularities and illegalities in the recruitment of public servants in the years 1998, 1999, and 2004. After filing charges, he was arrested in October 2011 and imprisoned before being granted bail.

15. See newspaper reports in *The Hindu*, *Deccan Herald*, and the Kannada newspapers *Udaya Vani* and others between the period of 12–22 October 2011.

16. India has, over the past few years, been implementing a range of rights. While the Right to Information (RTI) and the Right to (Elementary) Education (RTE) bills have been passed more recently (August 2009), a range of bills pertaining to rights to food and housing are on the anvil. This is in addition to the establishment of a number of commissions to safeguard and promote human rights. As critics have pointed out, the promulgation of these rights, which have gained currency in discourses of governmentality, are ironically matched by a decline in the functioning of public institutions which are meant to safeguard or ensure these rights.

17. Common friends alleged that Mallesha had, along with some of his neighborhood friends, bribed one of the interviewers so as to guarantee him the job. When I discussed this with him, he denied this and so I am unable to ascertain whether this took place or not.

REFERENCES

Ambedkar, B.R. [1936] 1945. *Annihilation of Caste* (With a Reply to Mahatma Gandhi). Mumbai: Government of Maharashtra Press.

ASER. 2014. *Annual Status of Education Report 2013*. Mumbai: Pratham.

Bauman, Z. 2004. *Wasted Lives: Modernity and Its Outcasts*. Cambridge: Polity Press.

Bögenhold, D. 2001. Social Inequality and the Sociology of Life Style: Material and Cultural Aspects of Social Stratification. *American Journal of Economics and Sociology* 60 (4): 829–847.

Booth, A., and A. Crouter. 2001. *Does It Take a Village? Community Effects on Children, Adolescents and Families*. Sussex: Psychology Press.

Chowdhry, P. 2010. *Contentious Marriages, Eloping Couples: Gender, Caste, and Patriarchy in Northern India*. New York: Oxford University Press.

Deshpande, S. 2011. Social Justice and Higher Education in India Today: Markets, States, Ideologies and Inequalities in a Fluid Context. In *Equalising Access: Affirmative Action in Higher Education in India, United States and South Africa*, ed. M. Nussbaum and Z. Hasan, 212–238. New Delhi: Oxford University Press.

160   A. R. VASAVI

Dev, M., and M. Venkatanarayana. 2011. Youth Employment and Unemployment in India. Working Paper 2011-009, Indira Gandhi Institute of Development Research, Mumbai.

Fraser, N. 1997. From Redistribution to Recognition? Dilemmas of Justice in a Postsocialist Age. *Justice Interruptus: Critical Reflections on the 'Postsocialist' Condition*, 12–39. New York: Routledge.

Fricker, M. 2011. Powerlessness and Social Interpretation. In *The Philosophy of Social Sciences Reader*, ed. D. Steel and F. Gualla, 39–50. London: Routledge.

Government of India. 2014. Census of India: Provisional Population Data. www.censusindia.gov.in.

Holmes, D., and G. Marcus. 2005. Cultures of Expertise and the Management of Globalisation: Towards the Refunctioning of Globalisation. In *Global Assemblages: Technology, Politics, and Ethics as Anthropological Problems*, ed. Aihwa Ong and Stephen J. Collier. Malden, MA: Blackwell.

Jeffrey, C. 2010. *Timepass: Youth, Class, and the Politics of Waiting in India*. Stanford: Stanford University Press.

Lareau, A. 2003. *Unequal Childhoods: Class, Race, and Family Life*. Berkeley: University of California Press.

Malagatti, A. 1994. *Government Brahmana. Ondu Atmacharitre* [Government Brahman: An Autobiography] (in Kannada). Manasagangotri: Kuvempu Institute of Kannada Studies, University of Mysore.

National Institute of Advanced Studies. 2002. *Urban Poverty and Schooling: Local Education Report for Bangalore*. Bangalore: NIAS.

Rao, V., and M. Walton (eds.). 2004. *Culture and Public Action*. Stanford: Stanford University Press.

Tilly, C. 1998. Changing Forms of Inequality. *Sociological Theory* 21 (1): 31–36.

Therborn, G. 2013. *The Killing Fields of Inequality*. Cambridge: Polity Press.

Wall, Karin, Mafalda Leitão, and Vasco Ramos. 2010. Social Inequality and Diversity of Families. Working Report, Institute of Social Sciences, University of Lisbon, European Commission, European Research Area.

Weis, L., and M. Fine. 2012. Critical Bifocality and Circuits of Privilege: Expanding Critical Ethnographic Theory and Design. *Harvard Educational Review* 82 (2): 172–201.

Weisskopf, T. 2004. *Affirmative Action in the United States and India: A Comparative Perspective*. New York: Routledge.

World Bank. 2006. *World Development Report, 2006*. Washington DC: World Bank.

CHAPTER 8

Schooling, Identity, and Belonging in a Tamil Lutheran Congregation

Geoffrey L. Burkhart

Preface: A Personal Note

It is the fortunate undergraduate student who encounters a professor who markedly influences the direction his or her professional life takes. Pauline Kolenda was the first to open doors for me both to Indian studies and to anthropology with her enthusiastic, masterful teaching and her steady encouragement guiding me to social anthropology. Over the 50 years that I was privileged to have her tutelage and friendship, I came to appreciate especially several aspects of her work. Among these are her insistence on thorough documentation, her impatience with the misuse of analytical categories as answers rather than as tools for ethnographic enquiry, and her persistent concern with the dilemmas of the disadvantaged, notably women and Dalits. The last is especially notable in her writings on the lives of Chuhras, a Dalit caste in Uttar Pradesh, whom she first came to know in her mid-1950s' research (1958, 1987, 1989, 1990). These guiding concerns suggest something more in regard to her presence in the field: a critical human touch in establishing open, fully

G. L. Burkhart (✉)
American University, Washington, DC, USA

© The Author(s) 2019
H. E. Ullrich (ed.), *The Impact of Education in South Asia*, Anthropological Studies of Education,
https://doi.org/10.1007/978-3-319-96607-6_8

engaged connection with the people she was interviewing and with how they, in their several places, make their way from day to day. In this essay, I present several case studies which I trust begin to acknowledge some aspects of Pauline Kolenda's influence on my own field practice and suggest my debt to her teaching.

INTRODUCTION

Scholars of various disciplines have paid considerable attention to the reconceptualizing of locality and of groups grappling with the influences of global systems on local identities and ways of life. For example, Rob Wilson and Wimal Dissanayake problematize the relations of the global and the local by attempting to move beyond conventional framings, such as those that map center and periphery, that pose global hegemony against local resistance or that reinscribe the global as modern and the local as traditional. They comment, "...we are witnessing not so much the death and burial of "local cultural originality," as Fanon once feared within residually colonial structures of national modernity, as their rehabilitation, affirmation and renewal in disjunctive phases and local reassertions..." (1996: 3). Among others, James Clifford reminds us that the concept "native" has paralleled a conception of cultures as unitary which has tended to suppress concerns with external relations. He advocates reconceptualizing what he calls "dwelling" in particular times and places as cosmopolitan experience, focusing on "concrete mediations" of cosmopolitan and rooted experiences (1992: 101, 115).

As is well known, the surge of Protestant mission activity from the mid-nineteenth century importantly included providing schooling, otherwise denied, to disadvantaged groups. The establishment of primary and secondary schools (and also teachers training and vocational schools) gave added opportunity to persons of the lowest castes (though not limited to these groups). These institutions operated not only as environments that facilitated, if not encouraged, conversion but also provided models of family life, gender-definition, and other aspects of daily life which contributed to increased respectability of families (as Eliza Kent has detailed particularly well for southern communities: 2004 and as Karen Vallgarda has detailed in her account of Danish Mission Society (DMS) schools in the nineteenth century [2015: Chapter 1]).[1]

In this paper, I do not trace direct connections between the content of mission schooling and the ways of life of those whose education, in whole or in part, occurred in mission schools. Rather, my concern is with notions about the betterment of individuals, their families, and their social circles that were formed partly in this context and that are central to the aspirations and identities of members of a Lutheran congregation in northern Tamil Nadu. My focus is on how members of that Protestant religious minority express their identities, by which I mean both self-conceptions and self-representations in speech and action within the wider socio-religious setting of small-town life.[2] Keeping in mind broad methodological perspectives like those of Wilson, Dissanayake and Clifford, I am interested in the diverse identities represented among the members of a small congregation of Lutherans, an ostensibly homogeneous group. I begin with a comment on the conceptualization of Christian Indians as a distinct community by anthropologists and other social scientists.

One perspective, especially prevalent in older literature, was influenced by church- and mission-related purposes and narrative genres and emphasized differences between Christians on the one hand and Hindus and Muslims on the other.[3] This stance both suggested a fundamental "outsiderness" of Christianity (implicitly or explicitly linked to colonialist projects) and thus Christian marginality (Robinson and Kujur 2010). Consistent with concerns about an authentic Christianity was considerable attention to motivations for conversion, especially with so-called mass conversions (Cederlof 2003; Frykenberg 2008: Chapter 8; Manickam 1977; Pickett 1933; Robinson 1998; Webster 1992, 2012: 156–162). Regarding the DMS, the founding institution of the Arcot Lutheran Church I write about here, Henriette Bugge states that, in the late nineteenth century, their missionaries "...were constantly on their guard against anything that smacked of mass movements..." (1994: 68).

An instructive example of "concrete mediations," to use Clifford's phrase, of the relation between cosmopolitan and rooted experiences is the case of Anglo-Indians, that Christian community characterized by Lionel Caplan as "a medley of different ethnic and racial strains, Indian and European," in the sense of their being "somehow between and apart from" their original sources (1995: 745; see also Caplan 2001; Blunt 2005). Caplan remarks,

> Despite sharing a common religion, Anglo-Indians [in Madras] are quick to distinguish themselves from Indian Christians and vice versa. The latter are usually differentiated on the grounds that they are converts from Hinduism, belong to or come mainly from low castes, and are primarily Tamil-speakers;

Anglo-Indians, by contrast, have only ever been Christians, are a "Forward" caste, and speak English as their first language. During much of the colonial period, Anglo-Indians worshiped alongside Europeans; Indian Christians had their own vernacular churches (Caplan 1995: 759, n. 8).

Paralleling Anglo-Indian self-representations, social scientists have usually treated Anglo-Indians separately from other Christian Indians. Caplan's work, in treating Anglo-Indians as creolized, is instructive in being drawn to heterogeneity within the Anglo-Indian community and to the varied and even contradictory representations of identity.

An Arcot Lutheran Church Congregation

I turn now to a congregation of the Arcot Lutheran Church (ALC) in the town of Polur in Tiruvannamalai District of Tamil Nadu.[4] I carried out fieldwork there (then in North Arcot District) for eight months in 1983. My account here is of Lutheran life as I found it then.

In 1983, Polur was made up of about 15,000 Hindus, 5000 Muslims, 1500 Roman Catholics, several families of Jains and several committed atheists, in addition to just over 200 Lutherans. (The proportion of these categories is unlikely to have changed significantly since 1983.) The ALC as a whole had some 20–25,000 members in the northern districts of Tamil Nadu.[5] It became, in 1950, the successor church to that established by the DMS. The DMS first undertook evangelism in 1864 at Melpattambakkam, South Arcot District (Bugge 1994: 64–71). The church in Polur and a school for girls had been established earlier by the American Arcot Mission of the Dutch Reformed Church in America, but in 1921, under comity, the agreement which avoided competition between Protestant missions, it turned over work in the Polur area to the DMS (Arcot Lutheran Church 1964: 79; Wandall 1978: 88, 144). (There were in the pastorate seven village congregations and five primary schools previously established by the American Arcot Mission.)[6]

Although Danish missionaries were never resident in Polur, there was regular contact with them and their spouses. In Polur, most Lutherans' recent exposure to foreigners was limited to contact with the DMS missionary who managed the large mission station of Libanon at Tiruvannamalai, 30 miles to the south, with rarely visiting Danish missionaries, and with Danish engineers and architects working in mission- and church-related development projects.[7]

Many Lutherans are themselves individual converts or come from families which had converted in the past generation or two. I never asked anyone directly to which caste he, she, or a forebear had belonged to. A few Lutherans volunteered a former caste identification, in private conversations, and all of these named a middle or upper middle-level caste, e.g., Naidu, Nayakkar, and Vellalar. Some people spoke of their families having originally been Roman Catholics or members of other Protestant denominations.[8]

Since in South India most conversions deriving from mission work from the mid-nineteenth century to the present have been of disadvantaged people, as noted above, many middle and high caste persons assume that Christian Indians have so-called "untouchable," i.e., Dalit (Adi-Dravida, Scheduled Caste) origins. As is amply evident, that view is often accompanied by a prejudicial opinion of Christians. While it is clear that many Polur Lutherans came from Dalit castes, it is critical to note that many people were quite reticent to speak of their caste background and that some showed irritation when others brought up this subject, directly or indirectly. For example, when I was speaking with a few people about my visit to Lutherans in a nearby village, I mentioned that some there had used the word "kottu" to refer to local patrilines of a set of allied families. My listeners immediately bristled at hearing the term, which identified the speakers as former Dalits.[9] When I asked about their "native place" some people replied "Polur", though I knew it to be a nearby village. Also several people's accounts of village origins led me to present-day Dalit communities nearby.

Given this, a brief comment on the late-colonial and post-Independence cultural politics of caste is critical here. The central tendency on the part of most Polur Lutherans to avoid the identification of prior caste membership contrasted markedly with the political significance of a growing Dalit consciousness, including among many Christians elsewhere in Tamil Nadu (and South India more generally). For example, the movement to align Christian activism within the broader rubric of the Dalit movement and in turn to situate that struggle within larger social justice efforts was especially evident in the Church of South India (Ayrookuzhiel 1989; Carman and Rao 2014; Harper 2000; Mosse 1994b; Prabhakar 1990; Webster 1992). I return to this issue later in the paper.

Immediately after the DMS began its work in Polur, they established a boys' school. The boys' and girls' schools were subsequently combined into one school still called the Danish Mission School. The DM School, the church, the pastor's residence, and the residence of a few teachers were located within a small compound in the center of town. (Residences of Lutherans were not grouped in a street or neighborhood.) Numerous primary schools were found in the town: several Government schools (none English-medium), two private English-medium nursery and primary schools which Lutheran individuals founded, private Muslim schools for girls and boys, a long-established Roman Catholic higher elementary school, and a small private school run by a Pentecostal church, the Indian Christian Assembly.[10] In addition, there were a Sanskrit school training boys to be priests and a Government Girls' and a Boys' Higher Secondary School, with classes through twelfth grade. Students who attended English-medium private schools were able to begin English-medium study in the sixth grade at the government high schools.

Educational achievement is important to ALC members. Adults who have completed studies make up two loosely evident patterns. One consists of people who were born in nearby villages and a smaller number born in Polur. The former attended DM elementary schools or taught in them and later moved to Polur. Polur DM and other higher elementary and secondary schools (and those in nearby towns) have drawn students from these villages. In some cases, students commuted daily from the closer villages, and in other cases families moved to Polur. This movement is consistent with clear generational differences that are found in the educational attainment of sets of parents and children. This is also paralleled by shifts in occupations of both men and women of different generations. These people are also those who are likely themselves to be converts or whose parents converted.

The second pattern consists of people whose employment (or their spouse's employment), many as teachers and school heads and some as government workers, brought them to Polur from more distant places. These families tend to have been Christian for several generations and are likely to have attended Christian-founded schools elsewhere in Tamil Nadu or nearby in Andhra Pradesh. They typically were members of other Protestant denominations or may have been Roman Catholics.

Both these patterns include adults who have completed their high school education (which was 10th grade in earlier days), men outnumbering women, or with teachers training. Twice as many men as women completed bachelor's degrees (Appendices 1 and 2). The general picture that emerges here aligns with a summary statement that Caplan makes concerning mobility among Madras Christians: "Upper middle class Christian informants most typically articulate a three generation mobility model—from poor peasant in one generation to mission school teacher in the next to urban executive, university teacher, etc. in this". He adds, "Such a model faithfully represents the overall process, even if the time span is somewhat telescoped" (1977: 208). The histories of those native to the Polur area reflect initial steps in this model (Burkhart 1985). Particularly evident is the number of men as well as women who are teachers or heads of schools (many of whose parents or grandparents would have been agricultural laborers). For both men and women, the importance of these professions as "clean" work is clear, and for women in particular, teaching is seen as a respectable occupation even though of a quasi-public nature.

THE REPRESENTATION OF IDENTITY

I now present four cases drawn from a series of conversations of varying degrees of formality with five Lutheran men and women. My main concern is with the content of what individuals related to me, but I add some details on the tone of these ethnographic moments. I show, especially in the two longer cases, aspects of the speakers' views on contemporary events important to them and provide details of personal and family histories. I emphasize these people's thoughts and actions in demonstrating their places as educated, Protestant Christians within the Polur social setting.

MR. RAJ AND MRS. ROSE[11]

On a few occasions, when approaching the home of Mr. Raj (age 50) and Mrs. Rose (age 45), whom I felt I was coming to know well and in whose company I felt especially welcome, a family member called out to others something like, "Durai has come to visit!" I was uncomfortable hearing the term, "durai", given its meaning of "master" (akin to sahib in north Indian languages), a notion I associated with colonial times. It suggested to me more than politeness, seeming to set me apart, suggesting a gap in status between us. Yet, at the same time, the usage perplexed me because of what I understood to be a growing familiarity with this couple and their family. It was simplistic of me to understand it simply as a relic of the colonial in the post-colonial (my periodization, not theirs) or as primarily reflecting a divide in the informant/ethnographer relation. It took me some time to see that the usage suggested ambiguities, granting me an opening encompassing customary respect and assumptions about shared experience of worlds wider than Polur.

Equally puzzling to me was Mr. Raj's comment that I wore the South Indian dhoti better than he. He claimed his slipped. He said he needed a belt. He preferred pants. Might this kind, generous, and dignified man be gently mocking me or even implying that I was being patronizing by wearing a dhoti on occasion? As I came to know him better, other interpretations suggested themselves. Perhaps, he was invoking the legacy of his early childhood in South Africa where his family had migrated. Perhaps, it reflected his years of service in the Indian Air Force (after his family's return from Durban to their natal village near Polur) particularly during World War II when he had come into contact in Bangalore with British and American military men whom he had liked.

One day I had been telling Mr. Raj and Mrs. Rose about my first visits in Tiruvannamalai to the ALC Carmel Church, to several DM schools and to the Danish Mission station at Libanon to meet the Danish missionary. At one point, Mrs. Rose voiced, with a laugh, a proverb about a man of Chettiar caste: "Aatayam illaatu SeTTi aattril irangamaTTaar," more or less literally, "A Chettiar won't go down into the river for no reason". Mr. Raj, asking me if I knew what a Chettiar was, interjected vehemently: "Banias! Capitalists!"

Mrs. Rose explained the proverb's meaning: Somehow a Chettiar had drowned in the river. When his body was seen floating in the water, people said, "Leave him alone; he is up to something." I was perplexed about Mrs. Rose's implication. I diverted my attention from whether she was speaking about me by dwelling on the apparent caste-based stereotype of a wily, even grasping, businessman which the proverb's meaning suggests. The perhaps disparaging comment seemed out of character for my hosts. My concern with hierarchical distinctions, here caste-related, blinded me to the possibility that Mrs. Rose was gently provoking me. Clearly, she had not read critiques of anthropologists charged with complicity in colonialist enterprise or charges of anthropologists' profiting from marketing the cultural truths of others. After some time, I saw she used the proverb to chide, in a kind way, the luxury of my impractical work, while at the same time relating me and some aspects of my foreignness to local statuses. Mr. Raj's complementary, forceful comment, "Banias! Capitalists!" also suggests such a bridging.

Re-examining the layered nature of Mrs. Rose's use of the proverb allowed me to reinterpret the designation "durai," as a question: "Did I want to be treated as a 'durai'?" My failure to see this immediately distracted me from considering Mr. Raj and Mrs. Rose's cosmopolitan stance and their understanding of our relation.

When I asked about their families' pasts, Mr. Raj spoke about his father's migration to Durban early in the twentieth century and about the circumstances of the family's return in 1935 to his father's village of origin near Polur. He characterized his family's life in Durban, where, for example, he claimed, "British wouldn't allow Indian clothing," and where, he said, apples were so plentiful that boys used them as footballs. He spoke of his sister's returning to the village with "socks, boots, hats" only to be faced with poverty, due to the treachery of a relative who had purloined funds they had sent to purchase land.

In several conversations, Mr. Raj spoke of these early difficulties. He commented on the struggle to receive a good education, noting his attendance at the village Danish Mission elementary school. He described the subsequent conversion of the family, influenced by the teachers.[12] He noted his family's moving to Polur for access to the Government High School there. He cited his service in the Indian Air Force with posts in Bangalore and New Delhi. He commented on his marriage and current family concerns. Mr. Raj's tellings regularly framed past events as comments on larger themes of current relevance. The latter included his appreciation of the discipline of what he called "defense life" as opposed to the relative disorder of "civil life". To rearrange his topics into a chronologically arranged family history, as I first did, diminished the intent of his commentary. His central lesson was about the complexities of Lutherans' life paths.

Mrs. Rose appeared somewhat reluctant to talk to me about her family, in part, I think, so as not to appear presumptuous in the presence of her husband. Her family, which resided some 40 miles from Polur, was of some prominence in the larger Church. She surprised me one day when I stopped at the DM School, where she was headmistress, by inviting me into the school office and beginning to relate some details about her father's life. Her interest, like her husband's, did not fit my chronology-based category "family history." Instead her remarks stressed the importance of Christian community and articulated concerns about Christian education and the moral life.

I tried at first to conjoin Mr. Raj's and Mrs. Rose's accounts; yet their differences (and their complementary natures) prevail. He positions himself significantly as South African-born, in contrasting pants and dhotis and in references to "socks, boots, hats," in mentioning the abundance of food in South Africa and, one day in talking of World War II, commenting on the remarkable supplies of "tinned" food available to the American military establishment at Bangalore (canned salmon was his favorite). Mrs. Rose dwells more directly on issues of spiritual concern (though her husband was no less ardent a Christian) and on their expression through an ordered and principled social life. This complements the values that Mr. Raj espoused in his often repeated reference to "defense life."

Like Mr. Raj and Mrs. Rose, many Lutherans in Polur were not very interested in telling me what I thought of as their family histories. Such talk usually made sense to them only when phrased as questions about their parents and grandparents, and answers to them quickly turned to moral points about the character of deceased family members or about pressing personal matters, such as arranging marriages of children. They raised issues about problems of the present-day church, such as finances, the inroads of Roman Catholic proselytizing and worries about village Lutherans' reversion to Hindu practice.[13]

Mr. Raj's account, like those of numerous other Lutherans who are native to nearby villages, exemplifies Caplan's comment, mentioned above, regarding Madras Protestants' holding a three-generation mobility model. Mr. Raj's narrative also importantly embeds a shift from a caste identity to some version of "castelessness" which term Caplan, in an important discussion of Christian identity, uses "only to suggest that Christian values do not include notions of hierarchy, and so, of caste" (Caplan 1980: 216). The movement to a religious minority identity, with associated benefits of increasing educational levels and an accompanying change of occupation, leads to the expression of status in terms of class. Caplan and other anthropologists working in Tamil Nadu have pointed out at some length that the terminology for various clusters of status–group markers is extremely complex (Caplan 1987; Chapter 1; Dickey 2016: Chapter 2; Fuller and Narasimhan 2014: 17–21; Hancock 1999: 45–47). I use "class" here as a summary term to indicate the denial of or reassignment of meaning to customs conventionally signaling the maintenance of caste boundaries. Let me give three brief examples. As noted above, the majority of Polur Lutherans avoid the use of caste-linked names, titles, and other notions that indicate pre-conversion caste status.

This avoidance is not limited to those of former Dalit status (cf. Caplan 1980: 223). Secondly, all congregants in taking communion drink from the same cup, and at church festivities food appears to be shared generally. This indicates that widespread commensality is not negatively sanctioned. Thirdly, though there is a strong preference for marriages to be made within the larger Protestant community, they occur occasionally with Catholics and sometimes with Hindus (predominantly with Hindu brides who are then said to convert to Christianity).

MRS. DAISY WILSON

I never noticed Mrs. Wilson, a widow of 75, at the Lutheran Church of which she considered herself a congregant. She lived close to Polur's Sacred Heart of Jesus Catholic Church (though not in the predominantly Catholic neighborhood). She was born in a village near Tiruvannamalai, where she began elementary school. She then shifted to a school in Ranipet, when her father's work took the family there. She attended an American Arcot Mission high school in Chittoor, Andhra Pradesh, and received teachers training at an American Mission school in Madurai, about 200 miles to the south. She served as headmistress of St. Joseph's Middle School in Polur from 1948 till 1967. Her educational career is like that of many teachers in moving through a series of Christian schools, receiving teachers training at a Christian institution and teaching at several locations.

Her husband, who was deceased, was a Hindu born in Kolar Gold Fields who had converted to Roman Catholicism. Mrs. Wilson presented herself as staunchly Christian. She had wanted her daughter to become a nun and her son (who was married to a woman in Kerala) a "father". She said she went often to the Catholic Church at 5:30 in the morning, where it was convenient for her to pray alone, but she did not attend mass. She frequently punctuated her remarks with a "Hallelujah," revealing her familiarity with Pentecostal forms. She was one of the few persons for whom denominational distinctions, even those between Protestant and Roman Catholic, seemed to have little importance.

MRS. MERCY DEVAMANI

Mrs. Devamani, a widow of 78 in 1983, provided me with a recently written English account of her family history. It locates her forebears five generations earlier in Tirunelveli District in the far south of Tamil

Nadu. That area was characterized by extensive Protestant missionary activity early in the nineteenth century, which led to well established, and often well known, churches, schools, colleges, and medical institutions. Her family was originally of Nadar caste, and implicit in her account is her family's improved status as middle-caste owners of property. In her family's circle, marriages between Christian men and Hindu women (who then became Christians) were not uncommon. She stressed her family's early connections to the (Anglican) Church Missionary Society. She completed her education (10th grade) at a CSI high school at Srivaikundam. She considered herself a Church of South India member who, in the absence of a CSI congregation in Polur, attended the ALC.

Her history of her family emphasized a strong evangelical commitment, and in talking with me, she stressed her devotional activity. She noted her involvement with a Monday night devotional group which was praying for ALC church members, making their way, she said, through the whole of the church membership and even, she emphasized, including one man who had left the church. She characterized their activities as those that had earlier been carried out by Indian Bible women, who had been employed by missions as evangelists to work among women. She was also connected with a larger network of prayer groups, mentioning the Friends Missionary Prayer Band, which originated in Tirunelveli District and which she stated was active not only in Tamil Nadu but also northern India. What Mrs. Devamani so interestingly juxtaposes here is a set of "mainstream" Protestant practices and attitudes with the devotionalism of fundamentalism. Her written family history attests to miracles; for example, it records that her grandmother died and came back to life. In her conversations with me, she extended her widespread spatial references—to her Tirunelveli origins, to prior residence in Kerala State, and to prayer band connections in Madras—by mentioning that her brother resides in London, her nephew in Korea, her niece in the U.S.A. and other relatives in Saudi Arabia.

MR. RAJASINGH

a. Family Heritage and Christian Identity

I had lengthy conversations with Mr. Rajasingh (age 69) that enlightened me concerning the fusing of Christian and non-Christian elements which become the ground for his assertion of a Christian identity in the religious landscape of Polur. When I asked him about how his family came to be Christian, he pointed to a large photograph of his father hanging in the office of the English-medium nursery and primary school he had founded in 1974. He then mentioned the theological seminary of the American Madurai Mission in Madurai, where his family had lived for several generations. In a brief note which he wrote for me subsequently, he detailed that his father had earned a bachelor of theology degree there and had been its vice principal. He noted that his paternal great-great-grandfather had been a soldier, "a Rajput (Singh) sepoy" [soldier], presumably of North Indian origin who worked in the office of the European district collector at Madurai. That soldier's son became a Roman Catholic, presumably after association with the influential Jesuit mission established early in the seventeenth century (Thekkedath 1982: Chapter 10). He married a high caste Nayakkar woman. Mr. Rajasingh's note recorded that his mother's side were also Nayakkars, employed by the (Congregational, after 1870) American Madurai Mission. It appears that through this association, his mother's family became Protestant.

Mr. Rajasingh employed several registers to place his family socially for me. The long record of Christian affiliation emphasizes close association with foreigners in historically important Christian missions. The designation "Nayakkar" presents a claim to relatively high status. This parallels the high rank that "Rajput" implies, suggesting secular power of Kshatriya-like martial life, connoted by the title "Singh." Mr. Rajasingh has continued the tradition of incorporating the title "Singh" in the names of his sons. He remarked that his paternal grandfather's cousin had a degree in Western medicine, and he mentioned in his written note that his grandfather worked at the orphanage maintained by the Madurai Mission during the 1904 famine. These representations are consistent with his emphasis on educational and professional accomplishments.

b. A School Annual Celebration

My introduction to Mr. Rajasingh's family had begun with my visit to the Government Girls' Higher Secondary School. I visited a ninth-standard English class taught by Mrs. Selvarani, who, I learned later, was the daughter-in-law of Mr. Rajasingh. Mrs. Selvarani was explaining with spirit a Tagore poem, the theme of which was humility. She emphasized the unimportance of material things and stressed the importance of "soul". When she came to the word "bend," she asked some girls how "you pray". It was clear that she was posing the question to Hindu and Muslim students. She then asked the class whether they could "sing" the poem. When the class hesitated, she fit the poem to a tune which I recognized as not Tamil and that she identified as "our marriage song." I wondered whether she were Christian.

Several days later, a local printer showed me the newly produced invitation for the celebration of the "9th School Day," at Mr. Rajasingh's school.[14] On the page the school crest and a statement of invitation were followed by the names of guests who were to take part in the program. These included the ALC pastor, a Christian engineer, a Hindu board member, and a Muslim medical officer. Heading the list was my name, followed by "Ph.D., Prof., American Institute of Indian Studies", with the notation, "presides". I recognized the honor of being included, as my degree joined a melodious listing of others' degrees: B.Com., B.D., B.S., B.L., M.A., M.B., and M.Sc. These markings were put in the service of the celebration of students' accomplishments. (Yet, the name of the principal and notation of his degrees, Bachelor of Arts and Licentiate in Theology from Madras University, were modestly missing.)

In my first visit to the school soon after moving to Polur, Mr. Rajasingh had given me an overview of its operation and proudly showed me albums of photographs of previous School Days. The pictures recorded notable townspeople and guests from elsewhere who had been present each year. Being so new to Polur, I did not recognize most of the faces in the photographs, and so I was unable to read these visual compositions as representing one view of Polur's social order. The pictures of the student performances in the "cultural program", however, were more revealing to me. There, for example, was a student dressed as "Daniel in the lions' den". Numerous images with explicit Christian references were particularly evident. The albums also recorded tableaux of several Hindu deities as well as "fancy dress" skits. The photographs of students dressed as Hindu mythological figures were fixed beside others representing Tamil cultural heroes, the latter particularly evident in most recent pictures. It occurred to me that the shift in the constellations of themes represented by the photographs might signify understandings of nationalism, of Tamil nationalism in particular, and that their array constituted an argument for the place of Christians in the socio-religious spectrum of Polur.

On the evening of the celebration, I arrived at the school with two visiting anthropologists, one a British doctoral student, the other an Indian doctoral student at the University of Madras. When the Muslim medical officer noticed a sub-inspector of police, a Christian man whose daughter attended the school, sitting in the audience, Mr. Rajasingh immediately invited him to join other guests seated on the stage. Likewise, my British friend was asked to sit on the stage and to offer remarks.

The ALC pastor opened the celebration with a prayer, speaking in both Tamil and English. Mrs. Selvarani then introduced speakers and segments of the program in English. Next the school's annual report was read in English. It noted, "The elite of the town and educationalists are in the Board". It singled out the celebration of two national events, Independence Day and Republic Day. The Polur pastor and the ALC bishop, were mentioned in the context of building dedications. Five Hindu men were mentioned by name and thanked for gifts to the school. The report concluded: "We thank the almighty Father for turning His Grace upon us and enabling us to bring each child to God to be blessed by Him", thus asserting the Christian foundation of the school.

Following the distribution of prizes for excellent work, "cultural items", each a brief performance, were presented in a seemingly arbitrary sequence. The performances mixed a broad range of themes, paralleling the array of photographs in the albums: Christian and Hindu religions, Tamil nationalism, English nursery rhymes and English literary classics among them.[15] The cultural program, of course, is intended as a display of students' skills as nurtured by the school staff. "Cultural" is used here in a narrow sense, signifying the content of each performance, e.g., the moral of Daniel's faith upheld even in the face of lions' jaws and the children's skill at dance harnessed to spiritual devotion. From another perspective, the array of "items" was anchored in different, yet fused cultural traditions. I would argue that "Baa, Baa, Black Sheep" and "Solomon Grundy", also presented that evening, must be understood as recognizably Indian, or in a special sense "Anglo-Tamil" performances. The performances as a whole constitute several arguments about the integral place of Christian education. The first expounds the value of Christian sentiments, values and beliefs. The second demonstrates the worthiness and appropriateness of the school as a vehicle for the advocacy of Christianity. The third reframes Christian principle as a social, i.e., not only a religious, formulation. The fourth portrays the integral place that such a formulation should take in the conceptualization of Polur as a politico-cultural place, where a Christian perspective has parity with other religions.

I want to make clear that I am not arguing that either the school or any other Christian institution that I am familiar with in Polur works subversively or by covert insinuation. The willingness of Hindus and Muslims to send their children to this school, to the other private, Protestant, English-medium nursery and primary school, and to the DM School seems quite straightforward, as does the employment of Hindu teachers there. Complementing this is the employment of a Christian Tamil teacher in Polur's Muslim primary school as does Mrs. Selvarani's setting a poem by Tagore to a Christian melody for a class predominantly of Hindu and Muslim girls at the government high school. The School Annual Day is a conventional demonstration of the employment of Christian heritage and Christian standing in Polur, yoked to educational opportunities.

c. Social and Scientific Religious Custom

One evening I dropped by Mr. Rajasingh's office, finding him alone and reading a book by Oral Roberts, which he explained as being about making your own miracles. Our conversation turned to death and cemeteries, occasioned by the recent demise of an old friend, a much respected elder in the church. A few weeks later, we spoke again alone and at some length about rituals at death, burial and the celebration of the anniversary of a death. He frequently juxtaposed mention of a Lutheran or other Protestant practice with a comment on Hindu practice. For example, he claimed that Hindus hold a ceremony on the second day after death, but Christians carry it out on the third, because the resurrection of Christ was on the third day. Some Christian practices may seem to be quite similar to Hindu ones, he said, giving the examples of preparing the grave site, building up its level with dirt, and using dissolved cow dung and whitewash in preparing the site. Yet, for Christians, he said, there are "social" and "scientific" reasons for these practices. He gave the example of an act performed in the Madurai area (but not at Polur): the mourners' hands are washed by the pouring of milk over them at the grave site. This, he argued, is scientific in that milk is the purest thing possible and social in that "Enmity should be washed out". Thereby any family discord may be eliminated and all should "be peaceful afterwards." He stressed the significance of the prayer meeting commemorating the first anniversary of a death. Hindus, he claimed, don't remember the dates of deaths and hold noisy celebrations on New Moon days. Christian observances are calm, he observed.

He returned to the issue of the scientific basis of religious acts. He seemed concerned that much of what he was telling me about Christians might appear to me to be based in, or derived from, Hindu practice. His argument shifted slightly to one about the underlying scientific reasons for many practices, now including Hindu ones. He offered as an example the fact that many Hindu shrines are located at the summit of hills. Why? Because people get good exercise climbing them. They often have to go through eucalyptus groves or stands of other trees which are healthy places. The water at the top of hills is "medicated" and "pure", he said. His line of reasoning was that although Christians continued or adapted Hindu-like practices, they did so for the practical reason of enhancing health and family welfare and accord, thus detaching themselves from Hindu religious meanings. Yet, in this perspective, the distance between Christian and Hindu, more stark at the beginning of our talk, became lessened.

d. Discussion

The public performances of annual School Day celebrations with its varied representations on stage become concretized, formal moments dedicated to an idealized depiction of educational success. This activity parallels the freshness of Mr. Rajasingh's reflections in private on the relation of Christian and Hindu religious practices. These representations make up a significant part of an argument for understanding the integration of this Protestant Christian presence in Polur.

Summary and Conclusion

In this paper I have put forward two main arguments. The first concerns the absence of communal politics based on caste origins. As mentioned above, there has been a preponderant and long-standing attention in both the mission-based and academic literature to the fact that a majority of conversions in South India were of people belonging to Adi-Dravida or Scheduled Castes. In recent decades Christians in India have become increasingly involved in the cultural politics of caste by asserting solidarity, at the very least, if not identification with and active participation in, Dalit-centered struggles for social justice (Carman and Rao 2014; Mosse 2012: Chapters 5–6). At stake in these struggles is the removal of discrimination, regarding disrespect, humiliation and denial of eligibility for numerous practical benefits originating in the state. Given this larger context, the virtual absence of such a politics in Polur in 1983 appears anomalous. However, in examining the social context in which Polur Lutherans find themselves several explanatory factors may be found.

First, numerous Lutherans originate in castes of non-Dalit status, and, as I have noted, many readily claimed an original middle- or high-caste status. Thus, it is unlikely that such families would strongly identify with, though they might well have been sympathetic to, a Christian Dalit political movement. Complementing this situation is the reluctance of many others to acknowledge low caste origins. This may have a variety of bases, including a strong feeling that this issue simply should be irrelevant in the present day. Furthermore, Lutherans' distancing themselves from discourse about caste origins may contest beliefs held by some non-Christians attributing both backwardness and inferiority to Dalits and its inescapability despite conversion to another religion.

Second, relevant here is Bugge's argument that the Tiruvannamalai-Polur-Vellore corridor was characterized by greater urbanization and commercial development than was occurring in the twentieth century in other parts of North and South Arcot, the area of DMS work (1994: 167–172). Since caste distinctions in town and city settings have operated to some extent differently than in villages for some time (Caplan 1980; Singer 1972), especially as linked to occupational opportunities, self perceptions of many Polur Lutherans appear to have shifted to notions of socio-economic class. This fits with the increase in respectability of educated persons, especially women, which was gradually effected and tied in part to a shift in employment from agricultural laborer to "clean" occupations which has been facilitated by educational opportunities.

Third, to reiterate, a practical aspect of the assertion of Dalit status is access to state aid, among other forms as subsidies for schooling and reserved admission to colleges. The absence of participation in Dalit political movements by church members may suggest that their aspirations for betterment, channeled through emphasis on education, new avenues of employment and respectability, were judged realistic and that the benefits accruing from Scheduled Caste status were not worth the subordination that status carries.

A second argument I have made concerns the ways in which Lutherans place themselves in the socially diverse Polur setting. I have provided examples of ways in which some Lutherans voice and otherwise perform self-representations that situate themselves as cosmopolitan citizens. I have described above a public performance of Lutheran identity in the School Annual Day. In my depiction of private conversations with a prominent Lutheran elder, Mr. Rajasingh, I have tried to convey his very active thinking about how some Christian and Hindu practices are similar, while their meanings and significance differ, and how he determined the grounds for representing these differences. His counterpoising of elements drawn from different traditions is lively, resourceful and innovative, if not entirely consistent or resolved in its details. In examining the meaning of certain religious practices, implicating intentions behind them, he adopts a not uncommon distinction between "religious" and "social" (or in this instance, 'social/scientific') suggesting that specific thoughts and actions must fall within one category or the other. This signals an ongoing concern, and it has the sense of being continuously renewed. Furthermore, his comments emphasize his sense of his heritages being complex, yet complementary, a fusion of Christian and Hindu (or Western and Tamil) elements. What was conceived of as external, linked to foreign missionary activity, is brought, indeed is lived, as internal or domesticated. Mr. Rajasingh's splicing of educational discipline and the assertion of Christian social location refashions and continues a process of indigenizing elements of once-foreign Christian influences.

In the case of Mr. Raj and Mrs. Rose, Mr. Raj binds together "worldly" themes framing experiences as diverse as enjoying the luxuries of "socks, boots, hats" in urban South Africa—and the rise in class status that phrase implies—set next to an implicit reversion to an impoverished, degraded life upon his family's return to their natal village. Likewise his idiom, "defense life", suggests the value of orderliness to be sought in "civil" contexts, such as family life.

The content of Lutherans' representations, as Mrs. Wilson's, Mrs. Devamani's and others' accounts exemplify, displays dimensions of experience that they draw upon in situating themselves for various social purposes and constitute arguments about Lutherans' integral place in various social arenas of Polur. As is clear, especially pertinent is the provision of access to education to disadvantaged groups facilitated by mission schools, in this case by the DMS and maintained by the ALC. The lessons, implicit as well as explicit, in certain representations of respectable deportment, even if registered mainly regarding women in the domestic sphere, had important implications for the status of their families and kin circles. The models offered by the teachers, as well as the content of the curricula, encouraged a sizable proportion of students to look for greater opportunities, both in seeking higher education and in employment, than would otherwise have been available to them.

Acknowledgements I am deeply grateful to Polur ALC members for accepting me into their church community and families and for giving me to understand something of their lives. The Rev., now Bishop (retired), R.D. Vijayakumar, pastor in Polur in 1983, showed me good humor, much consideration and interest. I can express only inadequately my debt to Mr. D. Gnanamani, Mrs. Kanakarathinam and their family and to Mr. A.S. Mani, Mrs. Edith Lily and their family, who have shown me, in 1983 and since, innumerable kindnesses, steady encouragement and personal support. Mr. K. Rajendran worked most ably as my assistant in 1983. I thank Mr. P. Rattinakumar who conducted village censuses. The interest which the families of Dr. P. Paulraj, Mr. M.A. Jeyasingh and Mr. D. Durairaj showed in my work was unwavering. Mr. B. Narasimmalu and Mr. P. Sadhusiluvaidas most helpfully introduced me to a wide range of Polur residents at the beginning of my work.
In Vellore, Dr. Pauline King, at the Christian Medical College Hospital and the Family Village Farm, took an immediate interest in my work and welcomed me into her family. Miss Else Krog, DMS missionary at Libanon, Tiruvannamalai, was generous in speaking with me about the work there.
Prof. N. Subba Reddy, Head of the Department of Anthropology at the University of Madras in 1983, granted me a research affiliation and an institutional home for which I remain most grateful. The continuing support, beginning in 1983 of Dr. M.A. Kalam and his family and of Dr. V. Sudarsen, both of the Department of Anthropology at the University of Madras, has sustained me academically and personally. Mr. Vincent Peters generously conducted a census among the members of the ALC Madras congregation; his father, the Rev. Apolos Peter and his family welcomed me in Madras and later in Polur and Tirukoilur. Discussions in Copenhagen in 1985 and 1986 with retired DMS missionaries Mrs. Kirsten (Jensen) Lange, Ms. Lydia Larsen, Ms. Ingeborg Depping and Ms. Helga Olesen greatly expanded my understanding of the DMS and ALC settings of Polur Lutheran life. I am grateful to Mr. Leif Munksgaard, then Secretary of the DMS for his help and to Mr. Carl Rise Hansen who aided me in gaining access to the Danish Royal Archives.
I thank the American Institute of Indian Studies for the award of a Senior Fellowship and American University for a grant of sabbatical leave which funded my Polur field trip in 1983. An American University Summer Research Grant supported my 1986 Copenhagen research.

A comment of Dr. Malcolm Rodger's led me to examine the school celebration I discuss here. I am much indebted to Dr. Sara Dickey for encouragement and help in thinking about this paper. I thank Dr. Helen Ullrich for her excellence as editor of this volume and for her incisive comments on my paper.

NOTES

1. A brief historical account of the education of women in Tamil Nadu has been provided by Grafe (1990: 188–211). Frykenberg's historical overview of elite education in India as a whole is valuable (2008: 301–344) as are Caplan's comments on South Indian Christian girls' education (1980: 219–221).

2. Embedded in many discussions of Protestant communities is a conventional city/village dichotomy. This usage is, no doubt, a short-hand expression for differences of scale, economic complexity (especially the range of employment types), diversity of population and the like and may imply a difference in sophistication. The small town setting that I write about may usefully be viewed as a 'middle ground' of diversity between village and city and as depicting early stages in a social process of familial advancement.

3. This emphasis on difference may have derived partly from pseudo-biological or pseudo-racial colonial "investigative modalities" to use Bernard Cohn's phrase (1996: Chapter 1). Compendia of castes and tribes (e.g. Thurston and Rangachari 1909) employ categorization which downplays the richness and complexity of historical process. Mid-twentieth century studies in South India by missionary-ethnographers (e.g. Diehl 1965) and social scientists (e.g. Luke and Carman 1968; Wiebe 2010) are well worth a serious review in regard to the ways in which they treat Christian/Hindu/Muslim interchange (see also Brown and Frykenberg 2002; Frykenberg 2003). For recent studies in Tamil Nadu, see Lionel Caplan on Anglo-Indians (e.g. 1996) and 'elite' Christians (1980, 1987: esp. Chapters 5–6), David Mosse (1994a, 1996, 2012), and Nathaniel Roberts (2016). I examine elsewhere the attitudes of Danish women missionaries in the mid-twentieth century centering on their relations with Tamil women (Burkhart 1989). These women exhibit dramatically different ideas from those held by Danish Mission Society missionaries in the nineteenth century as Vallgarda documents (2015).

4. In previous publications I have used the pseudonym "Arulur" for Polur.

5. Like several other Lutheran churches in South India, the ALC chose not to join the union of several Protestant denominations which became the Church of South India (CSI) in 1947 (Paul 1972). Nevertheless, the ALC maintains close ties with the CSI and with other independent Lutheran churches.

6. The Tranquebar Almanac for 1983 indicates that Lutherans were found in sixteen villages in the Polur Pastorate. In 1983 I knew of small

congregations in only six villages. A census of these villages, conducted for me by a Polur Lutheran, Mr. P. Rathinakumar, showed 158 active Lutherans. Thus by my count the Pastorate contained about 365 self-identified Lutherans. Wandall records a population of 618 in 1960 (1978: 144). The Tranquebar Almanac lists 2047 for the pastorate, a puzzling figure.

7. Polur residents understood the aims of these foreigners, but my aims as an anthropologist were less clear. I had cards describing myself as a 'social anthropologist,' which many took to mean social worker. This prompted questions: 'Where were my projects?' and 'What funds might I make available from America?' One man suggested that I start my own church.

8. The son of the first Lutheran pastor in Polur, Rev. D. Perumal, told me he knew of only one Muslim convert there in the 1920s. No Christian in Polur ever mentioned Muslim ancestors to me.

9. One Lutheran, annoyed at the usage, said that "kottu" names implied degrading occupations. Michael Moffatt cites the use of "kottu" among Adi-Dravidas in a Chengalpattu village (1979: 173). Caplan comments on some Madras Christians' claiming original non-Dalit status by citing genealogical links to original converts who became prominent Protestant figures and were known to be of middle- or high-caste status (1980: 223–226).

10. Established in 1955, the Indian Christian Assembly opened an orphanage with a school in Polur in 1964 which also provides training for boys in a printing shop and in tailoring for girls. Its founding pastor died in 1979, and in 1983 it maintained a low profile in the town.

11. I use pseudonyms for Lutherans and other Polur residents, but not for other persons I mention. I use the titles Mr., Mrs., and Miss as these were regularly used by Lutherans.

12. About 20 families in the village had converted from the mid-1920s to mid-1930s. Also during this period a pastor succeeded in obtaining titles to small parcels of government 'wasteland' for some Dalit families (Viswanath 2014: Chapter 4).

13. During a visit to one village with two Polur residents, several men there argued that opportunities provided earlier by the DMS had diminished as support from it gradually lessened after Independence. These comments were coupled with a discussion (more freely expressed than I had heard in Polur) of the benefits of Scheduled Caste status and noted persons who had adopted Hindu names in addition to Christian ones in order to access such benefits (Mosse 1999; Webster 1992: 164–168). One of the Polur residents, who worked in social welfare programs, linked to this discussion the criticism that the ALC as a whole was split hierarchically between pastors, teachers and others benefitting from positions in church institutions and "laymen" who had become comparatively disadvantaged.

Another Polur resident summarized this issue saying, "A pastor has only [i.e. centrally] the Bible; don't give him money and power."

14. Annual school celebrations are common events, showcasing students' achievements. Clearly, they also serve to publicize the school and emphasize connections with important personages, thus helping in recruitment of students.

15. An annual day celebration at St. Peter's Nursery and Primary School, a second English-medium Protestant school in Polur included in its cultural program of more than 35 performances a Tagore poem, south Indian classical dance, Christian songs, the fable of the crow and grapes, a drama of Alexander and Porus, a cha-cha dance, and cinema songs and dances.

APPENDIX 1

See Table 8.1.

APPENDIX 2

See Table 8.2.

Table 8.1 Educational Achievement of Adult Lutherans in Polur

Highest level completed	Men		Women		Total	
	No.	%	No.	%	No.	%
1. Attended elementary/higher elementary school	4	7.3	14	25.0	18	16.2
2. High school not completed	2	3.6	2	3.6	4	3.6
3. High school completed (10th grade)	21	38.2	16	28.6	37	33.4
4. High school and further (non-degree) training (except teachers training)	3	5.5	1	1.8	4	3.6
5. Intermediate degree* (2 years)	12	21.8	11	19.6	23	20.7
6. Bachelor's degree**	11	20.0	5	8.9	16	14.4
7. Post-bachelor's degree or diploma	2	3.6	2	3.6	4	3.6
8. No schooling or none reported	0	0	5	8.9	5	4.5
Total	55	100	56	100	111	100

Note This table is reproduced, with minor modifications, from Burkhart (1985) with the kind permission of the editors of South Asian Social Scientist
*Includes PUC (pre-university course) and teachers training
**Includes LMP (licensed medical practitioner)

Table 8.2   Occupations of Polur Lutherans

Type of occupation	Men		Women		Totals
	No.	%	No.	%	
1. Self-employed	2	4.1	–	–	2
2. Private firm employee	3	6.1	–	–	3
3. Public firm employee	–	–	–	–	–
4. Medical professional	2	4.1	3	5.7	5
5. School teacher*	16	32.7	21	39.6	37
6. Government employee	12	24.5	5	9.4	17
7. Clergy	2	4.1	–	–	2
8. Domestic—in own home**	–	–	18	34.0	18
9. Unemployed***	6	12.2	–	–	6
10. Other	6	12.2	6	11.3	12
	(Retired teacher: 4 Church sexton: 1 Retired Military: 1)		(Retired teacher: 3 Retired evangelist: 1)		
Total	49	100	53	100	102

Note This table is reproduced, with minor modifications, from Burkhart (1985) with the kind permission of the editors of South Asian Social Scientist
*Includes government and private schools
**Includes unmarried young women who have completed their education
***Includes unmarried young men who have completed their education

REFERENCES

Arcot Lutheran Church. 1964. *The Arcot Lutheran Church Centenary Souvenir: Nutrandu Vizha Malar.* Madras: Diocesan Press.

Ayrookuzhiel, A.M. Abraham. 1989. Dalits' Challenges to Religious Systems—A People Ignored by Church History. *Religion and Society* 36 (4): 38–48.

Blunt, Alison. 2005. *Domicile and Diaspora: Anglo-Indian Women and the Spatial Politics of Home.* Oxford: Blackwell.

Brown, Judith M., and Robert Eric Frykenberg (eds.). 2002. *Christians, Cultural Interactions, and India's Religious Traditions.* Grand Rapids: William B. Eerdmans.

Bugge, Henriette. 1994. *Mission and Tamil Society: Social and Religious Change in South India (1840–1900).* Richmond, Surrey: Curzon Press.

Burkhart, Geoffrey. 1985. Mission School Education and Occupation among Lutherans in a South Indian Town. *South Asian Social Scientist* 1 (2): 97–118.

Burkhart, Geoffrey. 1989. Danish Women Missionaries: Personal Accounts of Their Work with South Indian Women. In *Women's Work for Women: Missionaries and Social Change in Asia*, ed. Leslie A. Flemming, 59–85. Boulder: Westview Press.

Caplan, Lionel. 1977. Social Mobility in Metropolitan Centres: Christians in Madras City. *Contributions to Indian Sociology* (n.s.) 11 (1): 193–217.

Caplan, Lionel. 1980. Caste and Castelessness among South Indian Christians. *Contributions to Indian Sociology* (n.s.) 14 (2): 213–238. Reprinted in Lionel Caplan. 1989. Religion and Power: Essays on the Christian Community in Madras, 117–147. Madras: Christian Literature Society.

Caplan, Lionel. 1987. *Class and Culture in Urban India: Fundamentalism in a Christian Community*. Oxford: Clarendon Press.

Caplan, Lionel. 1995. Creole World, Purist Rhetoric: Anglo-Indian Cultural Debates in Colonial and Contemporary Madras. *The Journal of the Royal Anthropological Institute* (n.s.) 1 (4): 743–762.

Caplan, Lionel. 2001. *Children of Colonialism: Anglo-Indians in a Postcolonial World*. Oxford: Berg.

Carman, John B., and Chilkuri Vasantha Rao. 2014. *Christians in South Indian Villages, 1959–2009: Decline and Revival in Telangana*. Grand Rapids: William B. Eerdmans.

Cederlof, Gunnel. 2003. Social Mobilization among People Competing at the Bottom Level of Society: The Presence of Missions in Rural South India, ca.1900–1950. In *Christians and Missionaries in India: Cross-Cultural Communication Since 1500*, ed. Robert Eric Frykenberg, 336–365. Grand Rapids: William B. Eerdmans.

Clifford, James. 1992. Traveling Cultures. In *Cultural Studies*, ed. Lawrence Grossberg, Cary Nelson, and Paula Treichler, 96–116. New York: Routledge.

Cohn, Bernard S. 1996. *Colonialism and Its Form of Knowledge*. Princeton: Princeton University Press.

Dickey, Sara. 2016. *Living Class in Urban India*. New Brunswick, NJ: Rutgers University Press.

Diehl, Carl Gustav. 1965. *Church and Shrine: Intermingling Patterns of Culture in the Life of Some Christian Groups in South India*. Uppsala: Almqvist and Wiksell.

Fuller, C.J., and Haripriya Narasimhan. 2014. *Tamil Brahmans: The Making of a Middle-Class Caste*. Chicago: The University of Chicago Press.

Frykenberg, Robert Eric. 2003. Introduction: Dealing with Contested Definitions and Controversial Perspectives. In *Christians and Missionaries in India: Cross–Cultural Communication Since 1500*, ed. Robert Eric Frykenberg, 1–32. Grand Rapids: William B. Eerdmans.

Frykenberg, Robert Eric. 2008. *Christianity in India: From Beginnings to the Present*. Oxford: Oxford University Press.

Grafe, Hugald. 1990. *History of Christianity in India: Tamilnadu in the Nineteenth and Twentieth Centuries*, vol. IV, Part 2. Bangalore: Church History Association of India.

Hancock, Mary Elizabeth. 1999. *Womanhood in the Making: Domestic Ritual and Public Culture in Urban South India* . Boulder, CO: Westview Press.

Harper, Susan Billington. 2000. *In the Shadow of the Mahatma: Bishop V.S. Azariah and the Travails of Christianity in British India.* Grand Rapids: William B. Eerdmans.

Kent, Eliza. 2004. *Converting Women: Gender and Protestant Christianity in Colonial South India.* Oxford: Oxford University Press.

Kolenda, Pauline. 1958. Changing Caste Ideology in a North Indian Village. *Journal of Social Issues* 14 (4): 53–65. Reprinted in Kolenda 1981, 104–125.

Kolenda, Pauline. 1981. *Caste, Cult and Hierarchy: Essays on the Culture of India.* Delhi: Manohar.

Kolenda, Pauline. 1987. Living the Levirate: The Mating of an Untouchable Chuhra Widow. In *Dimensions of Social Life: Essays in Honor of David G. Mandelbaum,* ed. Paul Hockings, 45–88. Berlin: Mouton de Gruyter. Reprinted in Kolenda 2003, 3–23.

Kolenda, Pauline. 1989. Micro-Ideology and Micro-Utopia in Khalapur: Changes in the Discourse on Caste over Thirty Years. *The Economic and Political Weekly,* 12 August. Reprinted in Kolenda 2003: 79–99.

Kolenda, Pauline. 1990. "Untouchable" Chuhras Through Their Humor: "Equalizing" Marital Kin Through Teasing, Pretence and Farce. In *Divine Passions,* ed. Owen M. Lynch, 116–153. Berkeley: University of California Press. Reprinted in Kolenda 2003: 33–78.

Kolenda, Pauline. 2003. *Caste, Marriage and Inequality: Studies from North and South India.* Jaipur: Rawat Publications.

Luke, P.Y., and John B. Carman. 1968. *Village Christians and Hindu Culture: Study of a Rural Church in Andhra Pradesh, South India.* London: Lutterworth Press.

Manickam, Sundararaj. 1977. *The Social Setting of Christian Conversion in South India: The Impact of the Wesleyan Methodist Missionaries on the Trichy–Tanjore Diocese with Special Reference to the Harijan Communities of the Mass Movement Area 1820–1947.* Wiesbaden: Franz Steiner Verlag.

Moffatt, Michael. 1979. *An Untouchable Community in South India: Structure and Consensus.* Princeton: Princeton University Press.

Mosse, David. 1994a. Catholic Saints and the Hindu Village Pantheon in Rural Tamil Nadu, India. *Man* 29 (2): 301–332.

Mosse, David. 1994b. Idioms of Subordination and Styles of Protest among Christian and Hindu Harijan Castes in Tamil Nadu. *Contributions to Indian Sociology* (n.s.) 28 (1): 67–106.

Mosse, David. 1996. South Indian Christians, Purity/Impurity, and the Caste System: Death Ritual in a Tamil Roman Catholic Community. *The Journal of the Royal Anthropological Institute* 2 (3): 461–483.

Mosse, David. 1999. Responding to Subordination: The Politics of Identity Change among South Indian Untouchable Castes. In *Identity and Affect: Experiences of Identity in a Globalising World*, ed. John R. Campbell and Alan Rew, 64–104. London: Pluto Press.

Mosse, David. 2012. *The Saint in the Banyan Tree: Christianity and Caste Society in India*. Berkeley: University of California Press.

Paul, Rajaiah. 1972. *Ecumenism in Action: A Historical Survey of the Church of South India*. Madras: Christian Literature Society.

Pickett, J. Waskom. 1933. *Christian Mass Movements in India: A Study with Recommendations*. New York: The Abingdon Press.

Prabhakar, M.E. 1990. Developing a Common Ideology for Dalits of Christian and Other Faiths. *Religion and Society* 37 (3): 24–39.

Roberts, Nathaniel. 2016. *To Be Cared For: The Power of Conversion and Foreignness of Belonging in an Indian Slum*. Oakland: University of California Press.

Robinson, Rowena. 1998. *Conversion, Continuity and Change: Lived Christianity in Southern Goa*. Walnut Creek: Alta Mira Press.

Robinson, Rowena, and Joseph Marianus Kujur (eds.). 2010. *Margins of Faith: Dalit and Tribal Christianity in India*. New Delhi: Sage.

Singer, Milton. 1972. *When a Great Tradition Modernizes: An Anthropological Approach to Indian Civilization*. New York: Praeger Publishers.

Thekkedath, Joseph. 1982. *History of Christianity in India: From the Middle of the Sixteenth Century to the End of the Seventeenth Century*, vol. II. Bangalore: Theological Publications in India for Church History Association of India.

Thurston, Edgar, and K. Rangachari. 1909. *Castes and Tribes of Southern India*. Madras: Government of India Press.

Tranquebar Almanac. 1983. Madras: Tranquebar Printing and Publishing House.

Vallgarda, Karen. 2015. *Imperial Childhoods and Christian Missions: Education and Emotions in South India and Denmark*. Houndmills: Palgrave Macmillan.

Viswanath, Rupa. 2014. *The Pariah Problem: Caste, Religion, and the Social in Modern India*. New York: Columbia University Press.

Wandall, Povl. 1978. *The Origin and Growth of the Arcot Lutheran Church*. Madras: Christian Literature Society.

Webster, John C.B. 1992. *The Dalit Christians: A History*. Delhi: ISPCK.

Webster, John C.B. 2012. *Historiography of Christianity in India*. Oxford: Oxford University Press.

Wiebe, Paul D. 2010. *Heirs and Joint Heirs: Mission to Church Among the Mennonite Brethren of Andhra Pradesh*. Winnipeg: Kindred.

Wilson, Rob, and Wimal Dissanayake (eds.). 1996. *Global/Local: Cultural Production and the Transnational Imaginary*. Durham: Duke University Press.

CHAPTER 9

Life Options Through Education: A Karnataka Village Study

Helen E. Ullrich

INTRODUCTION

Upon my 1964 arrival in the south India village, Totagadde,[1] the residents regarded themselves as educationally backward (Ullrich 2017: 1, 140). When I returned more than a decade later, the increased availability and utilization of educational institutions amazed me.[2] Women and men of all castes (but primarily Havik Brahmins) attended high school and one Havik Brahmin man was in medical school. Through narratives, the aim of this chapter is to portray the impact of education on a Karnataka village. The sections are arranged by decades from the 1960s to 2000. After a general summary of the state of education, each section will feature an individual narrative extending across generations. The 2000 section will include the impact of education on other caste groups with special attention to the Divaru[3] and the Scheduled Tribes (ST).[4]

H. E. Ullrich
Tulane University Medical School, New Orleans, LA, USA

© The Author(s) 2019
H. E. Ullrich (ed.), *The Impact of Education in South Asia*, Anthropological Studies of Education,
https://doi.org/10.1007/978-3-319-96607-6_9

This chapter focuses on the author's data from participation observation, interviews, and questionnaires over a 53-year period from 1964 to 2017. While the focus of this chapter is on the Havik Brahmins, members of all castes have been included in my research. I would be remiss to ignore the educational experience of other Totagadde castes. With each decade since 1964 the involvement of all has grown incrementally. In addition to personal gratification, education resulted in increased age at marriage, opportunities for employment, and travel to other countries. Kinship and ritual observations have become flexible to facilitate female education and to retain close familial relationships, while allowing intercaste interactions. Except for the Dalits, in 2011 younger Brahmins and many non-Brahmins had college educations. Younger Dalits attend school. The female microlending groups, organized by caste, encourage education. The group I regularly attended is the ST micro lending group. Many have borrowed for their children's school fees and for their own educational progression.

Through narratives over five decades, I propose to explore how education was initially a way for Brahmins to maintain dominance and later became an equalizer. By encouraging members of other castes to participate in education, the Brahmins provided a larger student body and showed their respect for the accomplishments of other castes as enhancing the Totagadde reputation. This, in turn, increased the respect for Brahmins who shared their power. This compromised dominance has been endorsed by some and proven threatening to others. By separating the paper into different time periods, I propose to show the positive impact of education for all groups in Totagadde with regard to job opportunities, as well as the consequences for the village that is in transition from caste exclusivity to an educationally based achievement culture. The last portion of each section will focus on a multigenerational case study of the impact of education on a different Havik Brahmin family.

ILLITERACY, NURSERY SCHOOL, AND PRIMARY SCHOOL IN THE 1960S

With the exception of Brahmin men, illiteracy was common in Totagdde. I know of one literate Divaru man and one literate ST man. At this time one older Brahmin opposed education for his sons, as he correctly believed if educated they would choose the option for a professional life over the life of a landholder (Ullrich 1975: 23–24). Older literate Brahmin women had husbands who taught them to read or had learned from their children who attended school. Women in their twenties generally had a primary school education which ended when their fathers arranged a prepubertal marriage. The daughters of the third generation completed their education before marrying. Until recently women's education ended with their marriage. Some of the daughters and granddaughters, who married at a later age, continued their education after marriage.

In the 1960s two institutions in the Totagadde area supported education: a nursery school, which the Haviks established, and a high school building established from the contributions of people from all castes in the surrounding communities. At the same time the establishment of a college in a nearby town allowed women to commute to college from towns and villages with bus service. Alas, Totagadde had bullock cart transportation and poor roads, so the option to commute to college remained in the future when bus transportation became a reality (Figs. 9.1, 9.2, 9.3, 9.4, and 9.5).

Although the Totagadde primary school included students of all castes, primarily Brahmin children populated the school. Brahmin men

Fig. 9.1 Government primary school in Totagadde

Fig. 9.2   Government nursery school in Totagadde

Fig. 9.3   Government high school for villages surrounding Totagadde

Fig. 9.4 High school student, 1970s

had started a nursery school in the temple. At that time since only Havik Brahmins entered the temple, the nursery school was open only to Brahmin children.[5] An unmarried Havik Brahmin woman was the nursery school teacher until her marriage when another unmarried Havik Brahmin woman took her place (Ullrich 2017: 142). These teachers gathered the Brahmin students in the morning and returned them home at the end of the day. By the 1970s when the nursery school had been relocated to the primary school complex, the government assumed responsibility for the nursery school and the employment of the teachers. At that time children of all castes attended the nursery and primary

Fig. 9.5 Woman in
the first graduating class
(1968) of L.B. College,
Sagar

schools. I overheard several Brahmin mothers chastising children of
the STs and scheduled castes (SCs) for wearing stained clothing. Those
mothers doing the chastising failed to remember that these ST and SC
children wore their Brahmin employer's children's stained hand-me-
downs (Ullrich 2017: 142). Although the mothers' goal was to emphasize caste superiority in terms of cleanliness and unstained clothing, the
result was to demean the SC and ST children. My concern was that these
children would feel so criticized, that they would stop attending school.
However, not only did they continue to attend school, but they began
to wear unstained clothing. For Brahmins to acknowledge non-Brahmin
and Dalit change in attire took years. In 2017, I heard Brahmins recognize changes that non-Brahmins and the SC and ST members had made
years ago.

When the government assumed the appointment of the nursery school teachers, a non-Brahmin secured the position. At that time

members of all castes found their own way to and from school or their parents brought them. A Brahmin woman cooked a meal for all the children and brought it to the nursery school. With a Brahmin cook, the food was considered ritually pure enough for every child (Ullrich 2017: 142). However, those who lived close to the school often went home for lunch. Children from the different castes tended to sit in separate rows, but they played together.

What began as a Brahmin maneuver to maintain dominance by encouraging education among all the castes resulted in a diminution of Brahmin power but initially the retention of Brahmin prestige. The nursery school is a prime example in which children from different caste groups began to associate with each other and develop respect for their different strengths. By the 1980s non-Brahmin academic excellence received village recognition. So from the initial multi-caste nursery school in the 1970s and Brahmin criticism of non-Brahmin cleanliness in assertions of caste dominance to respect for individual accomplishments, the Brahmin hegemony gradually changed.

In 1964, two men from poor Brahmin families were in college away from Totagadde while a third worked on his bachelor's and master's degrees via correspondence courses. Family events kept two men from wealthy families from completing their higher education. These five males valued their education and became proponents of higher education for future generations. During the 1960s, a primary school education was readily accessible for Brahmin women; college education was possible for men from families with financial means and for women from nearby villages that had public transport.

Illiterate women received recognition for their special skills, such as diagnosing illness or midwifery. After my hostess' four-year-old and the three-year-old had measles, she looked at me and thought I also had measles. Saying, "but adults don't get measles" she sent me to another hamlet for a consultation with an excellent diagnostician who scolded me for going outside with the measles. This illiterate woman had a son who would become a cardiologist in the 1980s.[6]

In 1995, her grandchildren, ignorant of her healing skills, mocked her Kannada pronunciation. Kannada in the 1960s and 1970s had no –f. By 1995, all the schoolchildren had –f in their phonology and distinguished –f from –p, as in fashion and passion. Even in the 1960s, language was an indication of education. When a woman gave a speech in imperfect Literary Kannada, her husband verbally and possibly physically punished her for embarrassing him and the family. Better to remain silent than to demonstrate one's linguistic incompetence.

At that time, an educated person had the ability to present spontaneously an elegant speech in Literary Kannada. Oral skills were evidence of an educated Karnataka individual. I was the outlier, as Totagadde residents discovered when they called upon me to present a speech. Even though I knew English, Literary Kannada, and Havyaka Kannada, I lacked the ability to speak spontaneously before a group of people in any language. The attitude toward public speaking changed between 1964 and 2017, with the change from an oral-based to a literacy-based culture. With higher education available, a high rank or a high first class in examinations took precedence over oratorical skills. The members of the ST micro lending group reported in 2011 that they "speak like Helen." I hope that means that expressing their views took precedence over eloquence. At the very least, even the illiterate had a vocal presence in the meeting. Telling themselves that they "speak like Helen," may have also allowed them to speak before groups (Ullrich 2017: 136).

Devi and Her Descendants[7]

Devi, an illiterate Havik Brahmin woman, was married at age 9 to her patrilateral cross-cousin[8] (father's sister's son). Until menarche, she visited back and forth between her maternal home (*tauer mane*) and her husband's home. She reported no psychological challenges at such an early marriage. Unlike other women of her age whose husbands or children taught them to read, she remained illiterate. She was wise in diagnosing childhood illnesses and in managing a household—under her husband's supervision. While raising her twelve children, she noted that her younger had more educational opportunities and married later than her older daughters, who married before puberty.

One of her sons in the 1960s had several firsts—the first to have a college degree, the first to have an intercaste marriage (to a Brahmin of another caste[9]) with family approval, the first to have a love marriage to a woman he met at work, and the first to provide his younger sisters with an opportunity for further education in Bengaluru. Upon marriage, Devi's banker son's wife stopped work to raise her family. Having a place in Bengaluru proved serendipitous for his younger sisters, as he provided for their education through the Pre-University Certificate (PUC)—catapulting them into the category of the most highly educated Totagadde women at that time. His marriage and independence obviously presented no problem, but brought honor to the family. This educated son with a profession helped his family by providing opportunities and financial assistance otherwise unavailable. Devi talked of this son with both love and pride.

Devi thought each change that provided more options for women improved the society. These included higher education, older age at marriage, and widows' inclusion within the culture. She admired the courage of the first widow in the region to refuse to shave her hair. Devi did not shave her hair when she became a widow, but she never again entered the temple.[10] Unlike women who had difficulty with their sense of identity at the time of prepubertal marriage, in spite of the deaths of two children (from plague and a smallpox vaccination), and widowhood, Devi retained her sense of self and her opinions about her culture. This is markedly different from many cases of challenges to the ego ideal upon widowhood (Ullrich 2011).

Her youngest son and his wife both had Pre-University Degrees (PUCs). Although Devi thought he married late for a man (33), the age difference between this son and his wife (5 years) was "just right." She was thrilled with this marriage, as she had worried that her youngest son might decide to remain single.

If Devi had lived long enough, she would have approved of her grandchildren's educational level. The younger ones married after finishing their PUC, B.A., or M.B.A. Some worked before and after marriage. Some continued their education after marriage until they started a family. Not all originally agreed with advanced education for women. The youngest son and his wife disagreed about educating their daughter when she was a toddler. This son thought his daughter would have no need for a college education. His wife thought her daughter needed a college education, but a master's degree would provide difficulties in arranging her marriage.

When the time came, Devi's youngest son sent her youngest grandson to a prestigious college and his daughter to the local college. Thinking his daughter was of ordinary intelligence—perhaps because she studied little in college—he was amazed at her high first class examination results when she graduated with her B.Com. Her older brother believed that she would have had similar occupational opportunities to his had she been sent to a good college (Ullrich 2017: 150) (Figs. 9.6 and 9.7).

Fig. 9.6 Devi's youngest granddaughter with Bachelor's in Commerce successfully finding employment

Like her father's sister's daughter (patrilateral cross-cousin), she held a job before her marriage—initially against parental approval. In this case her father approved the job in Bengaluru, while her mother felt she was losing her best friend. The job situation for unmarried women had changed so much by 2000 that her relatives joked that she set a record for quitting a job, as she stayed away but a month. Yet she found another job close to home where she worked until her marriage. After her marriage, she found working from home boring—so boring that she e-mailed me to discuss her work situation. Since then, with her B.Com. qualification, she has obtained employment at the Bengaluru Infosys in the finance department and is also studying accounting. For a reserved, unassertive woman, she is proving her brother's point about her intelligence. Although I regard her as successful in her employment endeavors, her brother's opinion is valid. If her education had been of the same quality as his, she would have had more opportunities. Sibling solidarity

Fig. 9.7 Devi's granddaughter and her husband, both with M.B.A.s and their daughter

in this case included recognition of a sister's intelligence, although the parents remained unaware of it. This has led to greater opportunities for women of the next generation.[11]

Her older cross-cousin had a scholarship to attend an M.B.A. program. With the highest rank in her division of the university, she was the only person in her graduating class to secure a job from a college interview. While working with the public in Chennai, she decided being stylish and well groomed was a part of her job description. After working for several years, she married and came to the United States where she and her husband are raising their daughter. After her daughter is settled in school, she plans to seek employment.[12] Her self-assurance and confidence have served her well and may be part of her family socialization as well as her academic accomplishments. While her parents were visiting in the United States, I asked her mother whether she had approved of her daughter's working in another state before marriage. Without dropping a beat, the mother commented, "She had the qualifications. Why shouldn't she work?"

The case study of Devi, her younger children, and her grandchildren illustrates how one uneducated woman had wisdom and her own opinion about cultural beliefs. She facilitated opportunities for her children and grandchildren and welcomed changes that provided them with greater autonomy. This case study also illustrates the role of education in the rise of a family from poverty. No matter what the caste of the individuals, poverty may be only marginally or unrelated to intellectual talent.

High School in the 1970s

Illiteracy was less common in the 1970s, with non-Brahmins attending school. One Brahmin mother-in-law told me in 1965 that her daughter-in-law had no reason to speak because her husband would always speak for her. This woman's death may represent a changing of the guard from women with no interest in education to those who valued education. A high school within walking distance of Totagadde had been built in time for those who were in nursery school a decade earlier. While parents urged education for their children, one boy delighted in playing hooky without his parents' knowledge. One Divaru and one Brahmin reminisced in 2017 about their lack of interest in school during the early 1970s. They tossed their books and homework in a corner upon coming home. The slackers obtained their PUC and do not regret neglecting their studies.

Relatives and family delighted in the success of the college student who became a well-respected teacher and a future headmaster in the local high school. In the future his daughter would become a mathematics professor, choosing profession over marriage—or so all the relatives believed. When the "right suitor" appealed to her, she then combined family and a career.

The Havik whose father refused to send him to college obtained his college degree in Hindi by correspondence courses. He taught Hindi to Havik Brahmins and brought new farming techniques and agricultural knowledge from South and Southeast Asia to all the non-Brahmin castes. By remaining in the Totagadde area these two college-educated men, the teacher-headmaster and the agriculturalist, used their education to benefit all the castes of Totagadde. By giving to all castes, they prolonged the Havik Brahmin dominance via respect rather than by wielding strict power. When there was a water shortage for irrigation, some Divarus allotted irrigation water for themselves and the Brahmins. When a Divaru took an excess of his water allotment for his own irrigation, other Divarus chastised him. He had ignored the consensus Divarus had determined was appropriate sharing between the two castes. This is an expression of Divaru appreciation for the Brahmins' sharing agricultural innovations and an indication of Brahmin dominance through respect. In time a class system would have priority over caste affiliations, as education independent of caste proved to be a route to socioeconomic success.

While men had "street smarts," Havik women and members of lower castes (except for Divarus) were socialized to passivity. In the 1960s even when husbands and wives had the same amount of education, a primary school education, husbands boasted that their wives need never leave home, buy their own clothes nor state an opinion. Indeed, one man forgot to ask his wife for the children's measurements when he ordered new clothes. Clothes made from the prior year's measurements were all too small. But who was to blame? The wife, of course.

The only 1960s literate Divaru man had one child, a daughter, whom he sent to school. She was literate and in school in the 1970s. She would earn her SSLC before her marriage. Her best friend, who lived next door, tried to show me she was also literate. However, there was one problem. Since I'm literate in Kannada, I noticed she was holding the book upside down. Her parents had no such regard for education, nor later did she and her husband. In the 1990s, they precipitated a permanent rupture with their oldest son, when they refused to pay the fees for his bachelor degree examinations. He moved to the opposite side of town—cementing a rupture with his parents. Other Divaru adults regarded his parents as unfair to their son, who had so much promise. At the time, these Divaru families were sending their children to college. Initially, some college-educated Divarus were unable to find jobs while others moved to Bengaluru for employment. The emphasis on education was obvious in the Divaru hamlet.

By 2011, the grandchildren of the first literate Divaru man had all finished college. Before her marriage the granddaughter worked, while the two grandsons set up their own business in town. Owning a car demonstrated their success. Other Divaru families with cars in their carports proclaimed prosperity, possibly associated with increased education.

In general, sons had priority over daughters' educations. One Divaru mother was even unaware that her daughter had completed her college education. This may be a further illustration of the Divaru women's loss of financial control and power within the family. With prosperity this caste has become more patriarchal and patrifocal (Mukhopadhyay and Seymour 1994: 1–33), a marked change from the traditional socialization of Divaru women to assertiveness and managing family finances. A mother's pride in her son's educational accomplishments including employment in Bengaluru contrasts with her educated daughter at home learning to cook and to do housework while waiting to marry.

Like boys, Divaru girls traditionally had a ceremony observing their first haircut. Havik women, in contrast, had ceremonies indicating their subservience. One was the Haviks' strict observation of menstrual taboos that contrasted with Divaru women's observing them in name only. (The Divaru practice reflected a superficial Sanskritization (Srinivas 1989: 56–72) rather than any belief in women's inferiority.[13]) Among the Haviks, at marriage, a husband could choose his wife's name. Many other customary Havik ways of showing deference to one's husband have shifted from an emphasis of a wife's inferiority to etiquette of her choosing.

In the 1970s, as with the primary school, the student body of the middle school and high school in a nearby village consisted primarily of Brahmins. No longer would Brahmin girls stay at home during their menstrual impurity. Upon return from school, Brahmin children changed their clothes to remove the everyday pollution. By 2017, however, those returning from school would change from their uniforms into play clothes. Ritual pollution had ceased to be of concern.

At this time some girls attending high school reported that they wanted a profession, rather than marriage. Listening to this, I asked one Havik Brahmin mother whether her daughter had a choice. This mother responded that only economic self-sufficiency would provide her with that option. However, this mother, who believed her daughter would change her mind, was indeed prescient, as her daughter did change her mind and married before taking her college examinations. Her mother wanted her daughter to postpone the marriage until after her examinations, but daughter and husband decided against a postponement. Although she wanted her own profession, she never finished college. After discussing her desire for employment with her husband, she decided seeking a job would bring marital discord. Since they had no need for a second salary, she chose the role of homemaker as her profession. Her two daughters-in-law in 2018 were both employed in their professions of choice.

In later years, I noticed some choosing a career before marriage; one deciding against marriage; and one wishing to remain single, but with a salary insufficient to support herself. Her brothers gave her no option— become financially self-sufficient or marry. She had an arranged marriage (Ullrich 2017: 147).

Case History: Suvarna

Suvarna was embarrassed at her lack of education. Both she and her husband had a primary school education in the 1940s and 1950s. Her 1960s certificate verifying expertise in Hindi provided her with some satisfaction. Her two daughters were more highly educated than she. The oldest married after completing her SSLC in the 1970s. Her younger daughter earned a masters degree in the 1980s. Neither daughter had specific household tasks, as was typical of unmarried Havik girls in their maternal homes.[14] The time was allotted to studying. Even then the younger daughter failed some classes, but her mother was proud of her for persisting in her studies.

A frequent topic of conversation between Suvarna, who married at age 13, and her mother, who married at age 11, was the difficulties an early marriage posed for women's education. They made no mention that their husbands also had primary school educations. Both thought a woman needed a high school degree. By the time Suvarna's older daughter married, they thought a college degree was necessary, as well as Hindi and English. Although the older daughter lacked the educational qualifications for a professional job, she, with her husband's blessing, started her own business. Initially, her father disapproved because he thought that his daughter's profession would detract from her husband's status as an executive.

Both daughters used their education. The younger one taught Hindi and English, while the older one closed her business when her husband retired in order to accompany him to other countries and other parts of India. Their children attended private English-medium schools and then earned advanced degrees in India. The older grandson received his doctorate in an English-speaking country where he readily found employment. Suvarna eagerly anticipates her daughters' weekly telephone calls with news of their grandchildren's education and professional endeavors. She welcomed her older grandson's choice of a bride engaged in similar work, though she was of a different caste and from a different region of India. He met her while working in an English-speaking country.

Suvarna indicated that his choice of a wife who was already adapted to life in another country was a wise decision.

EDUCATION IN THE 1980S: SECONDARY SCHOOL EXPECTED, COLLEGE A POSSIBILITY

In the 1980s Brahmin girls usually had a high school education (Secondary School Leaving Certificate, SSLC). Those who failed their examinations quickly married. Rarely did they reveal their lack of education. Some with a seventh grade education exhibited intellectual curiosity when they made visits to a neighbor's to read a daily newspaper. Often, pressed for time, they read the paper and returned home without conversing with the neighbors.

The impact of education was obvious from the independence to travel to town, often accompanying an older woman who lacked the experience and knowledge of how to negotiate the town. The newly recognized value of women's voices and opinions led to women's making their own decisions. The belief that an educated woman might be self-sufficient led the way for companionate marriages. Companionate marriages, the ability of a woman to seek employment, and the possibility of divorce all served as buffers against abuse.

Groups of students in co-educational colleges developed friendships, noticed compatibility, and suggested love marriages. Then, as in the future, if disapproving parents discovered a daughter's romance, they removed her from college. Occasionally daughters' choices in marital partners met with parental approval. Some parents even expressed the view that their daughters had found more appropriate men than they would have been able to find. With college becoming an accepted part of education, it ceased to be special. One Havik Brahmin grandmother, whose fondest wish had been for an education, expressed dismay when two of her college student granddaughters showed no inclination to study.

One woman contrasted her marriage with the current marriages among educated youth. She reported that at age 8 she had no idea of how to talk with a husband. The following shows her perspective:

> ...Now as soon as women marry, they talk with their husbands. Before women did not talk with their husbands as soon as they were married. Just as now, there were some good relationships and some bad relationships.

Then daughters-in-law looked after their mothers-in-law. Now each daughter-in-law attends to her own needs. Then the mother-in-law was like a god. If one did not do as the mother-in-law said, the mother-in-law ... would tell her son. He would ask, "Why did you not obey your mother-in-law?" Now the son does not pay any attention to his mother. Even an assertive daughter-in-law listened to her mother-in-law. Then daughters-in-law were afraid of their mothers-in-law....

...Now women are in their twenties when they marry. They are older than twenty when they start having children. They are grown. ...Then men had no use for women except for bearing children....Now there is affection for wife and children. Then there was none.

We were not educated then. I learned to read from watching my children learn. My elder sister went through the fourth grade. Then Mother and Father died and I had no opportunity for education.... field notes Oct. 18, 1995.

Families have different reputations. One family had the reputation of not sending their daughters to school. However, my field notes suggest that this appellation was unjust. At the time that the oldest daughter failed her SSLC, her mother developed severe asthma. The mother's asthma was so severe that she needed her oldest daughter for the housework. This daughter vociferously complained, yet one wonders whether the asthma was an expression of the mother's disappointment in this daughter's failure as her other daughters and son all have college educations. None did any housework while they were studying.

Jaya in the 1980s

Jaya was about to start college when I arrived in Totagadde with a computer. Her father visited me specifically to examine the computer. But the person who urged Jaya to study Computer Science was her mother who believed there was a future for those who majored in Computer Science. However, Jaya refused and instead chose to earn her Bachelors in Commerce (B.Com.). "When I was little, I was happy. After I grew up, I had many worries and concern about a hard life. When I started college, my mother died. At that time I became quiet and was very depressed" (Field notes).

At Jaya's mother's unanticipated death, both Jaya's and her father's grief was palpable. Although Jaya believed that women needed a degree, she failed two parts of her B.Com. examination and consequently was unable to register for a master's degree. She did retake and pass the examination and wanted to pursue her master's degree. At such a time, her classmates and Totagadde residents were extremely supportive. The close friends she had made while in college became the individuals upon whom she relied. This was characteristic of those who attended college.

After Jaya completed her education, she looked for a job. Meanwhile she visited classmates daily and spent even more time with them on weekends. This extensive visiting ended with her marriage. Otherwise in-laws would think that all one did was to visit friends. "If they continue (to visit) as before marriage, they will get a bad reputation." In addition to visiting, Jaya wrote to her friends. When asked what she had done that made her the proudest, she commented, "...doing the daily work. In some houses daughters don't do anything. They think they will start once they are married. I do all kinds of work. This makes me happy." Her response to what brought her the most honor was "I can do all the work alone." Her greatest regret was not earning her M.Com.

Jaya spent two years at home after completing her B.Com. That was the time she learned to cook and to clean house. She had spent two years unsuccessfully looking for a job and then decided she was ready for marriage. Consulted about her marriage, Jaya married an engineer. However, they lived in a non-Kannada speaking area. Her husband's job involved a lot of travel. Lonely and depressed, she requested a divorce. Rather than a divorce, Jaya received psychiatric treatment for her depression and marital therapy for her dissatisfaction with her marriage. Unlike older Totagadde Brahmin men, who called her a demoness, her husband and father remained supportive. Her husband changed jobs and moved to a Kannada-speaking area. This adjustment to her needs was the remedy she required to develop a happy marriage. They had one daughter, who became a child film star and later excelled in college.

This case illustrates increased female assertiveness and accommodation of husband and father to female assertiveness. The goal for a master's degree is an example of incremental education for women. Although the elders may disagree with a daughter's assertiveness, parental, and spousal consideration of their daughter's desires and needs have become more common.

EDUCATION IN THE 1990S: MARRIAGE AFTER COLLEGE

The only person in 1995 to refuse my request to tape her interview did so on the basis that her speech identified her as uneducated. Although she belonged to a younger generation, she had little education. The thought that people outside her community might hear her speech on tape embarrassed her, but she had no hesitancy talking with me.[15] Her daughters would have college educations and work before their marriages. She and her husband used their daughters' educations to demand educated, lucratively employed husbands. Other villagers considered her search for well-educated grooms from prosperous families as unrealistic. However, her determination illustrated that education is more important than poverty in arranging daughters' marriages. Other village women, ignoring these parents' efforts in searching for an acceptable spouse, tell me it was a matter of their daughters' fate written on their foreheads[16] to have considerate husbands from prominent families who respect and look after their wives' parents.

An SSLC provided girls with the opportunity for employment. Some chose housewifery as their profession, but others, equipped with shorthand, typing, and stenography (and later computer) skills, obtained secretarial or court jobs. If she worked elsewhere, in other cities, often a relative stayed with an employed, unmarried woman. Mothers and other female relatives often encouraged such women, and even appeared envious of their independence. In contrast, others whom the patriarchy dominated failed to comprehend women's desire for independence, a career, and also marriage.

Older women believed girls should receive an education. Some resented the termination of their education and so have encouraged their daughters and granddaughters. The granddaughter generation, unlike their daughters' generation, is more likely to complete their college education. Many girls at age 18 had earned their PUC and commuted to college in the town six miles away. Others resided in a hostel in the nearby town or in hostels at colleges in distant towns.

The pressure for good grades started with elementary school when parents and relatives asked whether a child, regardless of sex, was first in her class. If not, they inquired as to the reason. So the expectation was for academic excellence. The ultimate achieved status is first rank in one's class. Parents, especially fathers but also mothers, were supportive of educational endeavors. Some college students told me that their grandparents had no idea of what education involved, while other grandparents sacrificed to help their grandchildren obtain their professional goals, which may reveal the grandparents had longed for educational opportunities.

Sreya's Education

Sreya experienced difficulty in her PUC examinations. Although she received a first class, despite studying hard—arising at 6 and studying until 11 at night, she failed to receive a high first class. She reported that she becomes depressed when she gets low marks. She also becomes anxious when studying and taking examinations. For the first time in her life she developed allergies, colds, and frequent fevers, which were worse during examination time. If she forgot to put oil on her hair, she developed a headache, burning eyes, and was unable to read.

At age eighteen Sreya completed her PUC. She resided in a hostel for her first year of college. Like many of her Totagadde friends, she had chosen to study science, a subject she found challenging. However, she believed science would allow her greater job opportunities.

Her father had already paid the hostel fees for Sreya's second year, when a roommate hung herself. Sreya's account of the suicide is different from the one her elders provided. The elders commented that the examination results had yet to arrive. Moreover, she was the beloved only child of a wealthy family. As a result, her parents didn't care about their daughter's grades. Obviously the daughter cared. "What a shame that the girl was so worried that she did not wait to receive her grades," the elders reported.

In contrast, Sreya believes that the girl committed suicide because of poor grades. Moreover, her original SSLC marks, proof of her high first class, had been lost. She had brought those grades home, put them in a safe place, and then had been unable to find them. A Xerox copy was unacceptable. The fee for another original was Rs. 125, but negotiating bureaucracy is a daunting task. The girl would need such an important document to show any employer. Sreya volunteered that her roommate's was the first suicide to occur in the hostel. Sreya forgot to attend her roommate's memorial service.[17]

After the suicide, Sreya was afraid to stay in the hostel, as were her other roommates. She decided to commute from her maternal grandparents' home. Moreover, she regarded her mother's brother as a good tutor who could help her with her studies. She returned to the hostel for her final year of college.

She believed that single women should work. Sreya planned to work until her marriage, ideally at the age of 25. She had no worries about marriage possibilities. Indeed, suitors began making inquiries and requesting her horoscope from her paternal grandfather from the time she began college. Her grandmother was of the opinion that arranging marriages at older ages, such as after college, presented no difficulties. Her belief that Sreya would marry shortly after college graduation was correct. Sreya became engaged before and married a year after her graduation.

Sreya reported that early marriage, at age 13–14, was violence toward a woman (*himse*). Women needed an SSLC, a college degree, Hindi, and English. In her opinion, English was more important than Hindi. This proved the situation for Sreya, as she spent the first five years after her marriage in an English-speaking country. Her desire to raise her family in India near her parents and in-laws was the deciding factor in returning to India.

EDUCATION IN 2000: FROM CASTE TO CLASS STRUCTURE

The first Divaru to attend private school was a girl. In contrast, the first Brahmins to attend private school were boys and then girls. By 2011, there were two Brahmins, both girls, in the government school while all the others were in private schools. One Dalit girl was attending a special English medium government boarding school for the intellectually gifted, and one Divaru girl attended the English medium private school in the nearby town. All the other non-Brahmins, ST and SC attended the government school.

By 2000, members of all castes normally attended college or technical schools. One educated man of the potter caste had charge of the computers at the nearby college. His marriage to a woman of the potter caste who had her bachelor's degree impressed all of Totagadde. Perhaps not all, as she insisted in living in town and had nothing to do with the production of pottery. Her in-laws might have wished for a more compliant daughter-in-law. Educated members of other castes also refused to do agricultural work, even though they were unemployed and their parents and siblings would have appreciated their help farming the family land. Parents had educated their children, especially sons, with the idea that they would qualify for jobs and help the family out financially. Generally, exasperated parents remained proud of their children's educational achievements.

In the past Divaru women held a high position within their family, as they controlled the money and wore the key to the money chest around their necks. When education and land reform brought prosperity, men took control of the finances. A well-respected, charismatic Totagadde Divaru, who is a Member of the Karnataka Legislative Assembly, has added to the village reputation. The first reference in my field notes lists his educational level as an SSLC. His reported educational level has increased with his tenure in office.

In one Divaru family, both son and daughter had completed college, but in 2010 the mother only told me about her son, his degree, and his employment in Bengaluru. A neighbor who had been her daughter's college classmate reminded the illiterate mother to tell me about her daughter's college education. Her daughter, now at home waiting for her marriage, is learning household management skills. Younger Divarus, including college students, no longer wear their traditional jewelry or saris, which served to differentiate them from other castes. Divaru girls in college eagerly told me which Brahmin girls were classmates.

When I asked Totagadde Brahmin college girls about their Totagadde classmates from other castes, I was told there was no way to identify caste among college classmates, in spite of their attending each other's weddings and other events. One Divaru mother wearing the traditional Divaru sari and jewelry came to acknowledge her daughter's Brahmin classmate's son's first hair cutting. Seated on the outside stoop, she told me as I entered to inform the family of her attendance and to tell them that her daughter was out of town. The mother remained outside without any refreshments—uninvited into the home for the celebration—a poignant example of the transition between generations.[18]

Approximately, half of the ST micro lending group were literate; half were illiterate. One woman, who was earning her college degree via correspondence courses, obtained a job as a librarian. Since she would be at work when the group met, she left the group. She has held this temporary job for six years, and has every expectation that it will become permanent after she earns her Bachelor's degree. Before obtaining the job as a librarian, she took classes in tailoring, sewing, and Computer Science. She is qualified in xeroxing and knitting. In 2017, she was in her last year of a correspondence course for her B.A. She plans to continue her education with a Bachelor of Library Science (B.Lib.). She has enjoyed her work as a librarian, as well as the more than Rs. 5000 salary per month.

Her illiterate mother earns Rs. 100/day working for a Brahmin. Unlike her daughter, she had no interest in school. Her brother, upon completing the eighth grade, declared he wanted a job instead of an education. He obtained a job cutting lumber for Rs. 500/day. If he had chosen to work for a Brahmin, he would have earned Rs. 150/day.

When she left the group, she taught her mother to write her name and then her mother joined the micro lending group. They carefully distinguish those who are truly literate from those whose skills are limited to signing her name. The illiterate members of the micro lending group learn from those who have completed their SSLC or PUC. However, I have noted no arrogance on the part of the literate members. The micro lending group has given both illiterate and literate members self-confidence in navigating the world of banking. In 2017, the banking protocol changed so that men from the Dharmasthala organization now take the money to the bank. Women no longer travel to the bank, but they manage the financial aspects of dues, loans, and loan repayment. These are important functions of this group in developing accounting skills. Another important function is as a support group. The membership has remained stable.

When one member's daughter received a full scholarship to an English-medium school[19] that included boarding fees, food, uniforms, and all supplies, members of the group feared that her mother would miss her daughter so much that she would bring her home. The group was successful in providing the mother with the support necessary to insure the daughter's education. The daughter in 2017 was studying for her second PUC.[20]

Brahmins hold different views toward the academic and job positions reserved for Dalits. The more prosperous Brahmins support affirmative action in education and jobs, as an important way to help Dalits. In contrast, Brahmins on the edge of poverty and those denied admission in favor of Dalits resent the reserved seats. One Brahmin expressed the view that Dalits were uninterested in education, but my visits to their homes suggested a far different situation. One Dalit is a poet who has self-published but is discouraged because his audience is so limited. He gave me one of his books. Another one is a respected principal in a school located in a nearby town. A third Dalit, a woman, has her SSLC and is a nursery school teacher in the Divaru hamlet. The first Brahmin woman who chose to remain single was a nursery school teacher of Dalits. She has sponsored the most promising students by paying their education fees.

The earlier part of this section has focused on non-Brahmins and SCs. While non-Brahmins have obtained more lucrative jobs in nearby towns, Brahmins have secured employment throughout India and in other countries. Every Brahmin family has at least one person employed outside of Totagadde. Some have had their education and employment in other countries. Some have retired or plan to retire to Totagadde.

Momta's Education

When Momta's suitor saw her photograph, he showed it to friends and relatives including me, with the comment "This is the woman I hope to marry."

In her discussion with me, Momta had fulfilled her personal criteria in preparation for her marriage. After graduating from college, she had worked for two years. She told me "It is important for a woman to work one or two years before her marriage. Now it is important for all to have an education. Indeed, an education is the most important prerequisite for marriage." field notes Feb. 28, 2011.

Although Momta's suitor was enthusiastic about the possibility of marrying her, only after meeting and talking with him did she freely give her consent. The Havik Brahmin pattern by 2000 was to provide the potential couple with an opportunity to talk in private. The opinion of the couple is crucial and more important than that of parents and relatives. If her parents had approved and she was uninterested, she would have had the final say. This is in contrast to her mother-in-law, Padma, who has an SSLC. When Padma's parents asked for her consent, she felt she could not refuse her parents, even if she had wanted to reject the suitor they proposed.

Padma has experience with children choosing their own partners, as her daughter met someone in college whom she wished to marry. She discussed this with Padma and her father. They indicated that they could arrange a marriage with a man from a more prominent family. The current protocol for arranged marriages is initially to have relatives and parents discretely inquire about a family and the potential bride or groom, then to give the boy's family the girl's horoscope and photograph, and finally for the couple to meet each other in the presence of selected family members. At the meeting, the couple has a chance to talk privately in a separate room. Even if all the relatives consider the match an ideal one, both boy and girl need to agree to the match. Such meetings are kept secret and occur outside of Totagadde, so that if either the girl or the boy refuses the match, neither will lose face. If one or the other expresses no interest in a marriage, the search starts over. However, with a love marriage there is no need for the exchange of horoscopes. Padma's daughter was insistent, so her parents reluctantly arranged the marriage. Fortunately, everybody involved has been pleased with the marriage.

Both Momta and Padma are free to travel unaccompanied out of Totagadde. This is a sharp contrast with fifty years ago, when husbands did all the shopping. Momta and Padma both take the bus to town to buy coffee powder, tea, vegetables, and their own clothes. They stated their husbands don't know what they want or what clothing will suit them, so the men of the family provide them with the money to spend. Momta's son may go with her. When he does, she ignores his tantrums when she refuses to buy every toy he wants. At a fair she limited his purchases to a toy truck and some other small items, which he chose.

The period from 2000 to 2017 has shown increased independence for women with the cultural expectation of a college education for both men and women. Even the uneducated have expectations of respect for their vocal presence, their opinions, and their perspective. Many women work after graduation and even after marriage. Some believe women should obey their husbands and seek work only with their husbands' permission. For others the consideration of a wife's employment is part of the arranged marriage negotiations. Some may work after marriage when presented with an interesting job offer. Individuals may continue their education after marriage. All accept the idea that education provides women with increased independence.

Conclusion

Since the 1960s, education has brought prosperity to the South India village, Totagadde. All castes have benefitted financially with options for their own businesses or professional development. College and the workplace have increased personal interactions among people of different castes. There have been changes in the marriage system and some acceptance of intercaste marriage. For women, education has provided them with acceptable assertiveness. While the Divaru women traditionally were assertive, Havik Brahmin women socialized to passivity and silence have gained a vocal presence. The access to education has provided even the uneducated with the belief that their perspective is important. This major shift in Totagadde culture accounts for even the uneducated developing the skills for their enterprises.

Throughout the past fifty years education has had an impact on speech patterns. The Havik dialect of Kannada was such a prominent social language that Haviks restricted their dialect to other Haviks. In 1974, when I listened to the Divarus mimic the Havik dialect, I noted their version of the Havik dialect was unlike the actual dialect. Certain phonemes such as –f and –z were absent in Havyaka Kannada fifty years ago. Now all the school children are able to make the distinction. Non-Brahmins typically use –ś rather than –s. Not only have the Havik dialect and the Divaru dialect changed with regard to pronunciation, but the vocabulary has also changed. I am the object of teasing because I use the term telephone rather than phone. With intermarriage and schooling, the use of the literary form has become more common because it has no caste markers in pronunciation, lexicon, and syntax. Language use itself has propelled a hierarchical caste structure to a hierarchical class structure marking the educated from the uneducated. The literary language is the form of Kannada that students learn in school and everybody uses outside of their homes.

Education and professional options have had an impact on the strict caste hierarchy of the 1960s and have contributed to the shift from a caste to a class system. What began as a Brahmin movement to maintain dominance by encouraging education and modernization for all castes initially increased respect for the Brahmins followed by education as an equalizer honoring the accomplishments of all individuals regardless of caste. As Totagadde residents moved to urban areas and worked with members of various castes throughout India and in foreign countries, the caste system, while an integral part of an individual's social network, no longer determines how one interacts with others. One's classmates, friends, and compatible relatives may form the inner circle of intimacy through shared experiences. The intimacy of the husband-wife relationship has replaced the earlier mother-in-law power relationship over the daughter-in-law. Distance is a factor: continents may separate parents, children, and other relatives. Communication, frequently daily or weekly, is primarily through the Internet or the telephone.

From the perspective of cultural hegemony, the gradual change in the social order has taken more than fifty years and continues. In the area of education, the nursery school serves as a prime example in which the initial school occurred in the temple at a time when only Brahmins had access to the temple. Told that non-Brahmin children with predicted accidents of young children would pollute the temple, the ritual ranking of the Brahmins above others was clear. When the school moved to provide access to members of all castes, the children freely associated and played together. However, a Havik woman's preparation of food for the nursery school gave evidence of Brahmin ritual. As students of all castes mingled and attended college, they began to attend each other's weddings, children's first hair cutting, and other ceremonies. The profound ignorance of customs among Brahmin women of other castes decreased and was replaced with interest and curiosity. Some Brahmin elders decided welcoming their children's non-Brahmin classmates was more important than keeping strict ritual caste separation. In 1960 Totagadde society, the circle of ritual hierarchy included all spheres of life. By 2017, the areas of ritual hierarchy had diminished to individual hamlets of the village Totagadde. Education is but one factor, but an important one, in altering cultural practices, values, and perception.

Acknowledgements I express my gratitude to Suzanne Hanchett and the anonymous reviewers for their comments on my introduction and chapters, to Geoffrey L. Burkhart for his comments on my chapter, and to the people of Totagadde. The National Humanities Center provided an ideal place to analyze and write my research in the spring of 1988. The following granting institutions made possible my India research trips: American Philosophical Society: 1985, American Institute of Indian Studies Junior and Senior Fellowships: 1964–1966; 1975–1976; 1986–1987; 1994–1995.

NOTES

1. Totagadde is a pseudonym for a Karnataka village approximately 200 miles northwest of Bengaluru (formerly Bangalore). All the personal names used in this chapter are pseudonyms. The individuals concerned provided oral permission for the use of pseudonyms or initials in relaying information through interviews and participant observation.

2. In the 1964–1966 period and continuing into the 1970s the Brahmins competed with each other to develop new ideas such as toilets with running water, walled in shower rooms, stoves on platforms above the floor, and an emphasis on education. The youth were careful to observe sufficient orthopraxy to retain the support of their elders. This was a period of transition when the head of the household voluntarily gave his educated son responsibility for land management while the elder focused on family ritual. "A high school education has become expected of Havik boys of average intelligence. More than a high school education adds to a boy's and his family's prestige; less than a high school education implies a lack of intelligence" (Ullrich 1975: 12). Edward B. Harper commented on the changes in education in 1968 contrasted with his 1950s field work (personal communication).

3. Before land reform began in 1961, members of the Divaru caste, a low-ranking Shudra caste, were primarily tenant farmers.

4. Members of the Scheduled Tribes, formerly known as Untouchables or Hoslurus, referred to themselves as ST in 2017.

5. Since 1965, non-Brahmins have had the right to enter temples that in the past only Brahmins entered. During my initial research visit (1964–1966) only Brahmins and I entered the temple in the Brahmin hamlet. By 2017, I observed members of other castes worshipping in this temple. Béteille (1965) discusses the caste use of temples.

6. He reasoned that professional identity was more important than caste identity. As a result, he married a physician of another caste. This was a second marriage of a Totagadde Havik professional man to a woman of a different caste who worked in the same profession. In the first case, there was family approval from the beginning. In the second case, the son had to persuade his parents to provide their permission.

7. A case in Ullrich (2017: 161) has striking similarities to this multigenerational case study. Both case studies illustrate many common features of cultural change and the impact of education in Totagadde.

8. From Devi's perspective, she married her father's sister's son. From her husband's perspective, he married his mother's brother's daughter. Matrilateral cross cousin marriage was the traditional and preferred Dravidian cross-cousin marriage among Havik Brahmins. Clark-Decés (2014) has a fuller depiction of the Dravidian cross-cousin marriage system and the changes occurring in this system.

9. At that time, a marriage between people of two different Brahmin castes was considered an intercaste marriage. Some families whose children had married outside of the Havik caste before the 1970s ostracized their children, a point their relatives now deny.

10. In the 1960s and among the ritually observant, widows avoided visiting the temple for one year. In 2011, one widow felt others criticized her weekly visits to the temple on Monday, a special day for Shiva, as they indicated her primary reason for visiting the temple was to see friends as well as to worship. For many years before her husband's death, she made weekly visits to the temple on Monday. No one criticized her weekly visits before her husband's death.

11. One American physician colleague praised her acquaintances from India because unlike American parents they encouraged their sons and their daughters equally to obtain a good education.

12. American friends have commented that a dependent visa prohibiting an individual from employment is a loss for the United States. The lack of the option to work presented no problem to this woman whose focus has been on her young children. By the time she is ready to work, she likely will have her green card.

13. Divaru women during their period of menstrual pollution avoided participation in religious ceremonies. This may show respect to the gods without diminishing a woman's self worth. I use superficial Sanskritization to convey the complexity of Divaru emulation of Brahmin behavior as in their jewelry and clothing while retaining their belief in female self-assertion. They have retained aspects of their culture that enhances their status while altering stigmatizing behavior.

14. Havik girls were traditionally married before menarche. Even if their mothers wanted to teach them about housework and cooking, their fathers objected. This pattern of girls having no work obligations in their maternal home continued after marriage. Thus college-educated girls may have little knowledge of housework or cooking, as their parents gave priority to their education and need to study.

15. My interviewing in 1995 focused on cross-cultural psychiatry issues. Although no one else in Totagadde had difficulty with my taping interviews, this was likely a confounding factor. Her sensitivity about her lack of education contributed to her determination to educate her daughters.

16. Brahma is said to write a person's fate on her forehead at the time of birth. This explains good fortune as well as bad fortune—especially when bad things happen to good people or good things happen to undeserving people.

17. Sreya volunteered that she forgot about the memorial service. In my field notes I made no note of her explanation for forgetting. However, Suzanne Hanchett (written communication) suggested the possibility that Sreya feared evil spirits (*devva*) associated with an inauspicious death. Indeed, the room that was the site of the suicide remained unoccupied for the year following the suicide.

18. Another poignant example was a marriage between a Brahmin woman and an educated Divaru man who had eloped. The Totagadde Divaru parents were against the marriage and had nothing to do with their son until he had a child. Then the Divaru parents accepted the couple. Yet when they went to Bengaluru to visit the couple, they refused all invitations that their daughter-in-law's parents extended. The Divaru mother told me she wanted to avoid any negative effects that her low caste might have on her son's marriage. The distance between castes among the educated was narrower than the distance between illiterate, uneducated parents and their educated son. Every time I think of this exchange with the mother and her love for her son, I marvel at the sacrifice these parents have made for their children's happiness.

19. The only other Totagadde children to receive these scholarships are Brahmins. One held the scholarship about thirty years ago. The other was a student in 2017. All three attended different, but similar schools. Admission was on the basis of test scores.

20. Initially, the Pre-University Certificate (PUC) was for two years. Now there are two certificates—the first PUC and the second PUC.

REFERENCES

Béteille, André. 1965. *Caste, Class and Power: Changing Patterns of Stratification in a Tanjore Village*. Berkeley: University of California Press.

Clark-Decés, Isabelle. 2014. *The Right Spouse: Preferential Marriage in Tamil Nadu*. Stanford: Stanford University Press.

Mukhopadhyay, Carol Chapnick, and Susan C. Seymour (eds.). 1994. *Women, Education, and Family Structure in India*. Boulder: Westview Press.

Srinivas, M.N. 1989. *The Cohesive Role of Sanskritization and Other Essays*. Delhi: Oxford University Press.

Ullrich, Helen E. 1975. Competition and Modernization in a South Indian Village. In *Competition and Modernization in South Asia*, ed. H.E. Ullrich, 9–25. New Delhi: Abhinav Publications.

Ullrich, Helen E. 2011. The Impact of Cultural Factors on the Ego Ideal, Depression, Psychosis, and Suicide: A South India Community Study of the Widow. *The Journal of the American Academy of Psychoanalysis and Dynamic Psychiatry* 39 (3): 453–470.

Ullrich, Helen E. 2017. *The Women of Totagadde: Broken Silence*. New York: Palgrave Macmillan, Springer Nature.

CHAPTER 10

Thinking Through Livelihood: How a Peasantry of Princely *Rājpuṭāna* Became Educated and Activist Rural Citizens of Rajasthan, India

R. *Thomas Rosin*

In the savannah of western India among the Aravalli Hills bordering the Thar Desert of central Rajasthan, semi-arid conditions and princely domination set the scene for the emergence of a resourceful peasantry. In a region known as *Marwāṛ* (Region of Death), within the state of Jodhpur, evolved an adaptation of harvesting rainfall to recharge groundwater for irrigation. The collecting of rain runoff into basins (*āgor*), ponds (*nāḍī*), silt ponds (*khaḍin*), and reservoirs (*talāb*s) allows animal husbandry and farming to include a second winter crop of wheat, barley, lentils, and gram. Irrigated farming enables full-year village residence for an increasingly dense population of humans and domesticates.[1] From the village Gangwa I illustrate the synchrony, movement, and coordination required by the four joint family teams of partners to work their demanding, but effective lift technology.

R. T. Rosin (✉)
Emeritus Professor, Department of Anthropology, Sonoma State University, Rohnert Park, CA, USA
e-mail: thomasgailrosin@att.net

© The Author(s) 2019
H. E. Ullrich (ed.), *The Impact of Education in South Asia*, Anthropological Studies of Education,
https://doi.org/10.1007/978-3-319-96607-6_10

This look at informal education, learned through on-the-job training, reminds us of the richness and complexity that may be found in traditional occupations in challenging environments. On-the-job training both in cognition and social organization had a significant impact upon the political development of princely Jodhpur State, and subsequently the emergent democratic polity of Rajasthan Province.

In these pages I document cognitive skills in monitoring, calculating, mnemonics, reckoning, and estimating that are involved in the pursuit of local livelihoods. Collaborative relations of partnership (*sīrī*) include careful accounting and transparency in pursuit of fair play and equity, making long-term working relationships of trust possible. Actively thinking through the challenges of making a living together and in accumulating hydrological benefits for descendants prepared them for hostel living making possible town-based formal education and eventual transformation of a kingdom through land reform.

In Gangwa Village, I joined farmers at their work sites, occasionally participating in their tasks. They were anxious not only to demonstrate their skills, but to teach me what they knew. In each of the three cases presented below local farmers were disappointed that I still had much to learn. Their keenness to make me understand led to recovering a folk system of knowledge heretofore ignored. They wanted their knowledge written up so that government engineers and hydrologists would listen to them. The results of subsequent research, appearing in diverse publications and papers, add incrementally to what I and others have come to know.

In this recovery of a pre-Independence form of adaptation, I illustrate the complexity of their system. While ethno-scientific studies of folk knowledge have flourished for indigenous peoples, notions of peasants toiling in an arid zone, utilizing only locally available sources of water, and exploited under local Lords (*Ṭhākur, Jāgīrdār*), Estate holders (*Ṭhikānedār*), or royal regimes (*darbār*) have delayed systematic study of their cognitive capabilities and bodies of local theory. Folklorist and music impresario Komal Kothari, through his revitalizing and globalizing the region's musical traditions and his enticing conversations (Bharucha 2003), heralded a post-Independence wave of scholars documenting local lore, women's songs, the performance arts, architecture, wall paintings, and more.[2]

I elicit from and interview villagers in the kinds of practical information and problem solving on site, as opposed to how they would talk about problems in a separate interview session. Such intellectual and collaborative capabilities, both in agrarian and pastoral production and in the assessing, taxing, and selling of their products, provide a foundational understanding of how peasant subjects of princely Rājpuṭāna[3] become the educated and activist citizens of Rajasthan, India.

This inquiry into the knowledge and mental operations exercised in local livelihood fits within the broader tale crafted by Hira Singh (1998). Singh opens the royal archives of the Maharajas of Jodhpur and Jaipur for the regions of Marwāṛ and Shekhāwāti to analyze the peasants' petitions to their Maharajas during the turbulent years from 1920 to 1940.

Can peasants become active agents in their own liberation? Such a question returns us to the lively debates of the 1960s (Moore 1966; Wolf 1969; Gough 1968; Hobsbawm 1959; Sen 1982).

In this inquiry into the foundations for the emergence of an educated and activist peasantry, we theorize that informal on-the-job training was preparation for success in formal education. Using historical sources (Sisson 1969, 1972; Singh 1998; Saxena 1971; Choudhry 1968; Surana 1983) and the Jat community's own open access website (https://www.jatland.com/home/Mool_Chand_Siyag. Accessed February 12, 2017), I point toward the shift to formal education among the descendants of share-cropping tenant farmers (kisān). Such education was initiated through the uplift efforts of the Aryan Samāj (Sisson 1972: 77–78; Saxena 1971: 111–115), Hindu and Jain monks, consolidated through schools opened by several successful merchant families, and supported by an array of hostels established by such early Jat leaders as Mool Chand Sihag (also written Siyag) in the 1930s.

Such hostels, providing lodging and fellowship for sons of tenant families seeking formal education contributed to a revolution in aspirations, in farmer associations and in activism. This led to the princely Jodhpur State's reform of land tenures under Jat Justice Kan Singh Panihar— first in Jodhpur State 1949, and then as a model adopted by the newly formed province of democratic Rajasthan. I write in the terms of my own discovery through the explanations of Gangwa villagers who were eager to get me to understand their knowledge as embedded in practice.

1

On my first night in the village Gangwa in early 1964, distant work chants echoing across the fields, each followed by an unmistakable crashing surge of water, rouses me from sleep. I rise at dawn to meet the teams that had worked through that moonless darkness to give an extra watering to their crops. I watch as a massive leather bag (*charas*) rises dripping out of the well shaft (*kuān*). This pouch is stitched on a metal ring. The farmer leading his team (*sīnchārā*) stands on the four-foot stone platform surrounding the well shaft opening. He grabs the ring and chants to his partner.

Sixty feet away down a double ramp, his partner is seated upon the draw line behind his yoked bullock (*zori*). Upon chanted command, this partner bounces several times on the line, lifting and lowering the leather bag. As the dripping bag lifts and lowers at the wellhead, the *sīnchārā* swings its load from a vertical movement into a horizontal oscil-lation away from the shaft toward the edge of the platform where it will be spilled and channeled to the field. Just as the three-hundred-pound leather water bag swings out, the pin attaching it to the bullocks' yoke must be pulled. A lapse in synchrony and the *sīnchārā* guiding the swing-ing bag can be thrown off balance, tottering precariously at the platform's edge—the *charas* weighs three times his weight. Chants echo across the fields, mingling with chants from other irrigation teams. Such is my expe-rience in 1964, then in 1965, 1971, 1979–1980, and 1982–1983.

During my early years of field work I kept records on every working well, joined crews deepening 60 feet well shafts, and roamed the coun-tryside with farmers after the rains to estimate (*kuntno*) the effect of surface impoundments of rainwater. We theorized the extent of aquifer recharge in order to estimate the next season's groundwater reserves for lift irrigation. I listened to plans for improving the recovery of rainfall and expanding the fertilized area (*māl*) primed for irrigation.

The centrality of two-crop cultivation and husbandry for inter-regional livestock markets is the basis for settled, year-round village life in this arid zone in the densely settled Aravalli Hills (Rosin 1968, 1978: 467–468). This allows a degree of self-sustainability upon which the set-tled community depends. Where the technology for irrigation is most effective,[4] lifting a volume of groundwater sufficient to bring a winter crop to maturity, we discover elaborate forms of social organization. These involve the full labors of patrilineally extended joint families, often working with other joint families in a common enterprise. Their in-laws are near at hand to aid in deepening wells, harvesting crops, improving soils, and building water catchment embankments. This cultivation of an irrigated crop depends upon the transformation of the landscape and watershed over successive generations (Rosin 1993).

While most members of such multi-caste villages plant a rain-fed, single monsoon (Hindi: *kharīf*, Marwāṛi: *siyālū*) crop of millet, sorgum, and melons, they augment their livelihood through crafts essential to irrigated farming. These include carpentry, leather working, pottery, or protection of the crop from the village bull and wildlife. The shepherd community leaves the village seasonally to graze its flocks. The laboring community works in local well excavation or in marble mines and construction in towns and cities. From several castes come entertainers or eulogizers performing for land-owning elites. Other castes remove impurities or inauspiciousness from the village households, corrals, and streets.

Cultivating an irrigated crop in winter, as initially witnessed for two full seasons, involves a range of thoughtful observations, reflections, and decisions among partners. All depend upon their prior estimates of likely groundwater reserves. These are based upon monitoring rainfall, its collection in various impoundments, and estimating the likely soakage recharging one's own well.

Reckoning is comprehensive and reflexive. Should they have planted at all? How much acreage? Farmers discussed cutting off water to some of their crop, letting it go dry and turn to chaff, reserving water to bring only some of the crop to maturity. Others with ample water supply were wondering why they had not sown more land to make optimal use of land and water available. As I arrived at the parcel Laluji Ram and partners worked, I wondered whether they were still learning from experience. Did they compare their prior anticipations at the time of planting against actual outcomes? Estimating well water quantity and quality was important to planning and planting the optimal amount of acreage.

As a first step, I asked a close farming friend, "Lalu Ramji, do you know approximately how many times you watered last year's crop?" My use of the word, "approximately" (*qarib qarib*) angered him. "We know exactly," he replied, "how much water we give our crop. After all this time, did you not know how we count each load of water lifted from our wells?" He then led me by the hand down to the bottom of the double ramps dipping nearly 20 feet below, to the turning spot for the bullock pair. There in the earthen wall two small pockets were dug holding, as he expressed it, four twenty pebbles (*chār bīsī kānkaṛiyā*). While he chose to talk in terms of "four twenties," and number of rotations of team members, he readily could convert these into countable whole numbers.

Laluji explained the method in detail. Keeping track and counting the number of turns taken was known as counting the pebbles (*kānkaṛī giṇṇo*). Eighty pebbles are used to keep accounts: One of the two teams of man and bullock drawing water (*khāmī*) moves the pebbles from one pocket to the other until filled. Then his fellow *khāmī* returns them. Each pebble moved over and then back again represents four loads of water delivered.

In a four-partner well, two teams (*khāmī*) drive a pair of bullocks, working simultaneously. As one team descends pulling the rope raising the water-filled *charas* in the well, the other team ascends to take the next load. After completing "*chār bisī*" turns, the shift is over and the two sets of paired bullock are rested and fed, replaced by the other two team's bullock. The fourth partner directing the flow (*pāntyā*) to the crop takes over as a *khāmī*.

Jat farmers were facile in counting in natural numbers. Laluji prefers to speak of shifts: three shifts in a day amount to nine hundred and sixty deliveries, marking the end of a work day. The work chant to bounce the draw line and to pull the pin, the chant of synchrony among partners, was echoed nine hundred and sixty times a day throughout the village fields.

Working through the night, another two shifts might be accomplished for a rapidly maturing crop. Regarding the amount in each delivery, he told me 3–4 maunds (4 maunds = 160 kilos = 352 pounds), depending upon pouch size. "We had 7 cycles of watering last season, with 2 night sessions," he said, as he squeezed moisture from the thick calluses of his palm.

A full day's shift of 960 deliveries of water, with a 4 maund bag, equals 315,977 USA pounds of water lifted from a 60 to a 100-foot-deep well shaft. Each full daylight of 3 shifts brings up 169 USA tons of water! Only a mature pair of animals could manage 160 lifts in a shift. The strength and capacity for labor of a bullock would be evaluated in terms of "four twenties" (*chār bisī*).

Lalu Ramji did monitor and recall the total volume of ground water delivered to his acreage over different seasons. These comparisons of actual outcomes against imagined or planned outcomes I would call reckonings, leading to critical reflections on how to achieve optimal use of groundwater, seed, and acreage. Lalu Ramji easily converts *chār bisī* into 80 pebbles (*ussī kānkaṛiyā*) or 320 (*tīn sau bīs*) deliveries. Laluji knew the boundaries of the fields he rented or owned by the earthen berms or embankments designed to collect air- and water-borne silts and manure. He knew the acreage (*bighās*) seeded. He remembered the harvested crop over successive seasons in units of 40 kilo (*ek maund*) sacks reported to the Village Revenue Officer (*Paṭwārī*).

As these cycles of delivering well water progressed, they were projected in a regular modular pattern. But in fact, work was often disrupted. When cultivating winter crops, well water would diminish, irrigation would slow or cease, making all partners wait out the hours, or days, needed for the well to recharge. But the pebbles marking their progress to complete a shift of watering remained locked in place, marking physically and visually where they left off. They had to remember, however, to which pocket the pebbles were moving.

During my first winter season Mangilal Khalera invited me to his field to see the division of harvest. Quilts were spread in 5 spots, and a large pottery pot was filled from the grain pile. As the pot was refilled and distributed, he and others chanted together the number of successive deliveries. The chaff was piled in cart loads, so each partner benefitted equally. In a similarly transparent fashion they counted each partner's cartloads of manure and silts delivered to the shared well and fields. Mangilal demonstrated how partners cooperated in this fair division of grain and chaff as well as draught and human labor.

Mangilal was known for working young bullocks. They drew half the full load (*ādha chār bisī*) and then were replaced in mid-cycle with another pair of juveniles. He was attentive to the various inter-regional cattle and camel fairs that brought buyers from the Gangetic Plains or Malwa Plateau into these interior lands of the Jodhpur Kingdom to buy prized Nagauri bullock. Such fairs brought tenant farmers together, a time to share pleasure, plans, and news from the farthest reaches. They could discuss the nascent movements of protest (*āndolan*), the formation of farmer assemblies (*kisān sabhā*), or other organizations sanctified at the Parbatsar Fair dedicated to Tejājī, a folk hero and saint to the farming community.

But how would sellers and buyers communicate when dialect, languages, and lifestyle were so different? Jat farmers worked in local currency. Children were sent to the shop with a handful of coinage. The *rūpiyā* coin was large, deceasing in size to the ½ *rūpiyā*, smaller yet to the 4th, then to the single *ānā*. Coins manipulated in hand, each familiar by spoken name, children knew the *rūpiyā* consisted of 16 parts, or *ānās*, a conception of currency going back to ancient times. The clustering of *ānās* into groups of 4, created an intermediate level of 4ths, or *pau* (Marwāṛi: *pāv*).

An animal that could pull a full load, or could race at top speed, would be called *soleh ānā*, meaning 16 annas, or 16/16ths, in a system

Kothari calls *ānāwari* (Bharucha 2003: 79). Dividing a whole into its parts permits evaluation of quality. Highest quality received a whole 16 *ānā*; lesser might be given 12.

2

Here again in the field, I discovered competencies in computation through an encounter that challenged a person's sense of personal worth. Rup Singhji and I had visited a goldsmith, trained in *Mahājani*, who could make complex computations using memorized tables, much as we in the west memorize multiplication tables. For a weight of gold, 3 and ¾ *tolā*, the goldsmith scribbled on paper the sum I would owe. The value of gold per *tolā* in 1970 was 6 and ¾ *rūpiyā*. While I could not make that computation in my head, Rup Singhji heard the figure, and challenged the goldsmith, "I will check your figures and get back to you." Knowing Rup Singhji was not literate, and couldn't write figures on paper, I queried him. "You put him in his place Rupji, but really, will you check his figures?" "Of course," he said, and across the next 11 days in the rainy drizzle, I listened to and documented his arduous calculations. In viewing Rup Singhji's incentive to check the goldsmith's calculations, we are witnessing the non-literate relating to the literate—exactly the kind of challenge that would drive the unschooled to mastery and innovation.

Having sat beside Rup Singhji those wet days long ago, let me now argue his suitability as a key example of computing skills presented in "Gold Medallions" (Rosin 1973). Rup Singhji's situation provides contextual insights into the community about which you are reading. Furthermore, since I place my work alongside Hira Singh, a sociologist who must keep his complex analysis at the local level to broad categories—farmer (*kisān*), Lord (*Thākur*), or Estate holder (*Thikānedār*), I welcome this chance to show in the person of Rup Singhji the observed complexities found in a typical village.

Rup Singhji is a Rajput with title to land; he is not of the tenant class. Yet his allegiance is closely woven with the Jat cultivators, as many small land holders who are self-cultivators share the interests of the tenant class. While factionalism splits Rup Singhji's caste; his ritual ties to a Jat activist prove stronger than blood or caste. The details follow.

Rup Singhji and his lineage were titled *bhomiyā*, with an inalienable grant of land, (*bhom*). They lived in a neighborhood known as the *Rāvaḷo*.

His Rajput lineage was separate from the dominant Rajput *Jāgīrdār* residing in the village fort, who once claimed title to half the village lands worked by share-cropping tenants. In contrast, members of the Rajput *Rāvalo* were often self-cultivators, hiring laborers, and working their own crops. They served in rotation as assistant to the Manager (*Halwadār*), who resided in the village to oversee the interest of the grand absentee Estate holder, the *Thikānedār* of Kuchamen City, who held title to the other half of the village lands. Accordingly, Rup Singhji's lineage had the political leverage and stature to stand against the dominant Rajput lineage, while as self-cultivating farmers they felt solidarity with the Jat tenant farmers. The factional opposition between the two Rajput linages in the village proves more important than their shared caste identity.

Most importantly, Rup Singhji's family and lineage were directly affiliated with the most important farmer Jat activist, Permaramji, who had settled in the outskirts of Gangwa village into which his sister had married. He came to lead the fight for land reform. Rup Singhji's own mother had become ritual sister (*dharam bāī*) to Permaramji, by tying his wrist with a *rakshi* band on the ritual occasion of *Rakshibandhan* in the month of *Shrāwān*.

Rup Singhji regarded Permaramji as his mother's brother, *maro māmoji*. Rupji's earliest years had been spent living in the natal village of his mother, with his mother's birth-given brother's family. The warmth and mutual support shared with a maternal uncle, a mother's brother, were very much part of his experience. Rup Singhj was ready to protect physically Permaramji, as he did with a staff (*lāthī*) on several occasions, once in a threat to the dominant *thākur* of the fort. The activist Permaramji defended Rup Singhji's lineage's inalienable *bhom* rights, even against neighboring Jat farmers of Dukhliya Village who challenged their conferment of title.

Rup Singhji, making twice daily deliveries to teashops and homes in the nearby marble industrial town of Makrana, became a milk wholesaler for his ritual uncle. His task of wholesaling milk on credit for Permaramji and other suppliers required feats of memory and computation, as well as interpersonal maneuvers and subversions, to extract a profit from his wholesale dealings. Yet he had an uncanny ability to remember accurately elaborate details about his twice daily deliveries of milk to 2 score of clients, collecting payments and reimbursing farmers twice a month.

Most impressively, he was affiliated so closely with the agitating Jat caste, that he joined them when they were charged in court for disrupting a local election. When the Jats discovered Permaram's name was not on the ballot, they threw the ballot box into a sixty foot well. Unwilling to bow before the previous Chief Accountant (*Kāmdār*) of the Ṭhikānedār, Rup Singhji alone among the *Rāvalo* Rajputs joined a dozen Jat defendants in their monthly summons to court for 7 years, until finally acquitted. Rup Singhji's sympathies with and absolute loyalty to Permaramji were far more important to Rupji than his birth-given position. Conversely, the *Rāvalo* Rajput's lineage's class interests converge with the tenant class, and were protected by the Jat activist leader.

Some of Rup Singhji's mathematical abilities, we conjecture, were grounded in childhood. Little children sent to the village shop are taught to watch the shopkeeper sharply. He pours grain, sugar, or tea into a pan until it balances the marked and standardized weights on the other pan of the balance. The child must monitor the process carefully to determine whether the scale is honest with the right combination of standard weights. The scale, 2 pans hanging on a balancing beam, is a powerful measuring tool, transparent and, examinable by both parties. Midway on the balancing beam a bar tapers to a point. When perfectly balanced, or when the pans are empty, the bar should point straight down for all to see. Farmers watch carefully for a tradesman's finger tipping the scale to feign a balance, concealing an inequality between the loads in the pans. I have heard accusations about finger tipping or impeding the free movement of the scale to distort a correct weighing.

Multiplication is an observed skill. The scales allow doubling, quadrupling, and even an eightfold increase. Since the balancing scale measured equal amounts, these can then be poured into a single pan, doubling the amount. That doubled standard itself can then be balanced against an equal amount. From childhood, individuals learn by observing doubling and quadrupling. Counting whole numbers appears a common capability among the Jat farmers. But addition takes computation. One number can be added onto another by "counting the finger joints" (*ginna angnī ka perva*). For Rup Singhji, each hand has 15 joints (*perva*), with a nod of the thumb to register the third joint: 15 joints per hand; 30 joints for 2 hands. To add 2 numbers, he counts the first number onto his joints, marking how many hands, and at which joint to stop. Then he takes the second number, counting from it out loud to the first joint, and proceeds to count joints until the final marked hand and joint is reached. That spoken number is his sum. This trio of numbers he memorizes, ready to use in another problem. In a similar fashion, he moves backwards on his joints to subtract.

In the west, with a number system on the base 10, we learn graphically to add the unit column, then the tens column, and finally the hundredth column, to handle such operations as addition and multiplication. If we re-examine "Gold Medallions," step by step, (Rosin 1973: 5–6), we see how Rup Singh treats whole numbers, fractions of a fourth, or *pau*, and *ānās* as separate registries, or "scales of differing magnitude," computing each separately, then converting to the next higher registry.

Turning to his problem: 6¾ times 3¾ tolas. He can treat the integers, 6, as on one registry, and the fourths (*pau*), of which there are 3, as a separate registry. We must triple each, getting the full value for each of three tolas. (But remember there is another 3 *pau* (or ¾) that must also be taken of the 6 and the 3 *pau*, since the full number of *tolās* is 3 and ¾, and we have computed only 3 of them.)

Puzzling over how to multiply that extra ¾th, Rup Singh has a simpler strategy. He recognized that to find ¾ of a number, you halve that number, then halve that half—then add together the two sums, the half and the quarter. His master strategy intuitively grasped the distributive law in mathematics.

He would apply this to each separate registry: units, fourths, sixteenths, then combined their sums correctly at the end. Hence, our argument about a natural number system on the base 4.

Using pen and paper, upon the numbers base ten, I confirm his answer. He got it right. (Answer: 25.31 *rūpiyā*; in 1970 @ 1 US$1=about 7 *rūpiyā*.)

His abilities rest on the convergence of several distinct traditions:

a. The practice of teams of 4 partners sharing all inputs and rewards, associated with the *poṭalyā charas* technology engaging 4 families at a single well (Rosin 1994: 35–37).

b. A set of special terms increasing by fourths to denote a fourth, a half, threefourths, a whole, a whole and a fourth, a whole and a half, a whole and threefourths, two, two and a fourth, two and a half, etc. (respectively in Hindi *pau, sadha, pauna ek, ek, savā ek, dedh, paune do, do, savā do, dhāy*) (Rosin 1984: 44).

c. The observation of measuring on the balancing scale makes doubling and quadrupling an operation real as a visual experience.

d. The uses of 16 *ānās* to the *rūpiyā* to denote "*solah ānā*" as full quality, with lesser proportions indicated by the number of *ānās* among that whole of 16.

e. Finally, the very manner of calculating complex multiplication involving fractions, on 3 different scales of magnitude, as demonstrated in Rosin's "Gold Medallions" (1984: 44–46).[5] All these traditions converge to support a natural number system on the base 4.[6]

Rup Singhji's skills were totally unexpected. Through his computations, Rup Singhji demonstrated that he is a man of learning, able to generate his own discoveries and add to his repertoire for problem solving, unlike the rote memorization practiced in the village school.

3

Years later Umaid Singhji and Dholaramji Jat called me out to their well. First they challenged me, "Roshniji, in these years you have come here, what have you done for this village? (*Roshniji, e baras ke mayne the aṭhe hamāre ganv men ā giyo, lekin kyā sevā hamāre ganv ke vāste ker diyo?*)" The water in their well had become more abundant, but increasingly saline. They complained about the dam downslope in the hollow of a neighboring village that was collecting water over a salt formation. "That dam was broken before, and will be broken again. (*Bī bandho pahale tor diyo, or dujī bār tuṛaelā.*)" They complained that well-educated engineers (Sengupta 2007) came to the village but never talked to villagers to find out what they recommended or knew about water. "Learn about this; write about it. Get them to listen. Do our village such service. (*ī ke bad sīkho, likh ker do, bī admī ne sunṇo karāvījio; ganv ke vāste eṛo seva ker dījio.*)" Umaid and Dholaram launched our study on rainwater harvesting and its relationship to groundwater recharge for shaft well irrigation (Rosin 2008: 51–54). I was one among a number of researchers, practitioners, and NGOs recognizing the traditional folk system of rainfall harvesting for aquifer recharge (Rosin 1993: 73–77, 83–86).

The rains were a joyous time, with villagers dispersing out to roam the countryside both for pleasure and also for reconnaissance. Together, we inspected the various rainfall harvesting facilities. The *Pimpolāy Bandho* was a broad expanse of relatively flat land that impounded water (*johṛo*), collecting rain runoff from the thousand-foot ridge nearby. The *Pimpolāy*, they said, feeds the outer irrigated fields (Outer *Chhopaṛ māḷ kā*) (Rosin 1995a, Fig. 3: 20). Its front water gate and earthen berm had eroded, a matter of distress for farmers. The villagers showed me a number of ponds (*nāḍī*) valued for their soakage, whose silts were carted out to fertilize the fields. Near such berm embankments, well water levels were strikingly high, near overflowing, at only 7 and 14 feet from the surface. Away from the berm, water levels decreased to the 40 s. We measured water levels and well depths for 32 wells in the village (Rosin 1993, Fig. 4: 68), uncovering a northeastern flow pattern in the abundance of well water recharge (ibid.: 67–69).

I researched and published during a period of intense extension of irrigated farming through deepening old and excavating new wells. The number of working wells increased from 34 to 76. Each well invited an empirical probing and theorizing about what did and did not work. What strata of limestone bearing rock and pebbles herald the trickle of water? What new strata of hard rock hide more promising strata below? From which direction does the groundwater flow? What other wells share its water's taste, and thus its common source? Which surface impoundment contributes to groundwater flows to which wells? The percolation of groundwater was important, for such flows flush out salts from the aquifer.

The quest for improving water facilities rested upon, and perhaps explains, the large work force mobilized and managed by Jat farmers. To trace the putative relationship visualized among surface collection and groundwater wells, my partner Wread drafted linen maps showing water impoundment, earthen works and wells that could be spread out on the lanes and fields for discussion with farmers. Villagers proposed ways of refurbishing and expanding catchment areas (*āgor*), check dams on ravines and flow gates on silt ponds (Rosin 1993: 56–73). Using information on the founding of the village, the order of arrival of different castes, the placement of funerary sites, and of stepwells (*baovṛī*) we could reconstruct a probable sequence in the development of water facilities (ibid.: 59–66).

During a month of my absence, farmers working different fields (*chhopaṛ*) got together to draft a petition to the district's highest officer, the Collector of Nagaur, for rebuilding the *Pimpolāy*. They asked me to join them, which I did. Armed with maps and published papers we argued our case to the District Collector (Rosin 2008: 53–54). Initially he resisted, convinced that this was all my idea. But when persuaded that the farmers had initiated the request, he finally approved. Within a year the *Pimpolāy Baṇḍho* was rebuilt. Finally, a success by farmers in educating a top government official!

At that time, Jat farmers were alarmed, talking to neighbors about protecting the flood plain leading to the village reservoir. The government had given residential (*abādī*) grants to Gujjar shepherds and Baowri laborers to build homes and corrals on its flood plain. Now, upon a season of good rains when the plain flooded, these shepherds and laborers threatened to make an opening in the earthen berm to the ravine to release water and avoid flooding of their homesteads. But breakage would diminish the quantity of impounded water. Farmers feared such sabotage in the night. These competing interests separated farmers from shepherds and laborers.

Few farmers thought the river bed (*nālā*) with its rushing waters in flash flood was a source of recharge. But infra-red LANDSAT satellite imagery taken during the dry months of January and February when uncultivated lands lay bare, shows the prevalence of irrigated farming all along such streams (Rosin 1994: 56, Footnote 6).

The indigenous system, which favors water seepage to recharge the aquifer and the use of silt to enrich fields, attempts to avoid long-term surface storage and open canal transport to minimize evaporation and salinization (Rosin 1993: 77–82). Transport to the fields is visualized as percolation through subterranean aquifers. This wave of practice and scholarship convinced officials, water engineers, and hydrologists to combine the two viewpoints into an innovation they called "*conjunctive use*" (Moench 1995).

In summary, irrigated farming with groundwater involves mental construction of interrelations of a complex order, demanding the means not only to see connections, but to monitor and recall analogic units such as 80 pebbles representing volume, and thinking with those units. The farmers of Marwār were explorative in tapping new water sources and empirical in observing consequence. They were theoretical in visualizing nature's interrelationships. These are cognitive and imaginative capabilities of a high order, creating a legacy in learning and thinking predisposing their progeny for success in formal education.

The evidence I have presented about the complexity of their adaptation, to the rigors of climate and the vigor of feudal domination, documents the cognitive skills utilizing an analogic system of markers and mnemonic recorders, and mathematics on the base four. Collaborative relations of trust assured ready transmission of their skills in observation, measurement, and computation. We have a peasantry that, though once dominated by a ruling class of land-entitled priests, warriors, and moneylenders, managed a complex agrarian enterprise with its valuable extensions into animal husbandry and inter-regional livestock markets.

4

Hira Singh grounds his analysis in farmer's access to resources through occupancy rights to agricultural lands (Singh 1998: 100–108), and to commons of pasturage, and forests (ibid.: 118–121), but not to their developing these resources through livelihood practices and aspiration to enhance water, silts, and soils, as pursued in this paper. Such information I would add to Hira Singh's holistic analysis of the farmers and their readiness to petition their Maharaja (*darbār*). He documents shifts in the content, tone, and goals in peasant petitions to their regal Lords over a 20-year period. This windfall in royal archival research on the most political active peasants among the princely states in Rājpuṭāna is from the very areas of my own and Pauline Kolenda's longitudinal research.[7]

What began as a movement of social and internal reform raised the Jats' awareness of their own history and stature. Jats learned about their success as a dominant caste under direct British rule to the north, as well as about the Bharatpur Kingdom to the south where Jat lords ruled over Rajput tenants. Traveling monks of the Arya Samaj[8] and gatherings at festivals and inter-regional livestock fairs played an important role in bringing news of *satyāgrahā* campaigns and reforms occurring in British India (Sisson 1972: 76–78).[9] Such discoveries intensified their aspirations for status equal to Rajputs. Challenging the dominant order, Jats staged religious, cultural, and life cycle rites without paying cesses (*lāg-bhāg*), and wore gold or silver adornments without asking permission. They wore shoes before the village fort. A groom could now ride a horse at his wedding or attempt to ride an elephant as part of religious pageantry—all of which had been forbidden to Jats by Rajput lords. Jats withstood the Rajput violence and murder perpetrated upon them (Mathur 1982: 159–160). They felt that their subordination, historically resulting from invading Rajputs, must now to be reversed.

As Jat resistance intensified and their illegal organizations proliferated, the organizations remained non-violent.[10] Their rebellion against Rajput dominance advanced to a refusal to give free labor (*begār*), pay taxes (*lāg-bhāg*) or exorbitant rents (*bānṭo*) in kind. Their network of caste councils (*jāti panchāyat*) could sanction Jats who refused to join their growing resistance. For 3 decades the Jodhpur State had outlawed civil, student, and peasant organizations, obstructing demonstrations, public events, and outcries for reform. The end of their story, however, is revolutionary, climaxed by the Maharaja Umaid himself.

One of the first organizations the Maharaja granted legality was crafted by Jat Mool Chand Sihag. At the grand Parbatsar Cattle and Camel Fair August 22, 1938, Sihag formed the Marwāṛ Jat Farmers Reform Society (*Marwāṛ Jāt Ḍrishk Sudhark Sabhā*). The Maharaja not only granted it legal status in 1941, but upon the second day of its second anniversary celebration in Jodhpur, the Maharaja Umaid Singh himself appeared and announces he would implement a policy of land reform (JatLand.com 2017) and responsible government (Singh 1998: 188–191). He will carry through reform of land tiles executed through settlement officers documenting every hamlet and village. He would end feudal titles and replace them with a single ownership title. At a time when Maharaja Umaid Singh along with his son Hanwant Singh as successor were unwilling to give up their kingdom to the Indian Union (Mathur 1982: 162, 175), they vowed to change its internal order.

Settlement officers would be sent through the domains of *Jāgīrdārs* and *Ṭhikānedārs* to gather documentation and testimony into a *Misl Bandobast* (Rosin 1987: 49–80) upon which reforms would be based. The settlement officers arrived in Gangwa in 1954 leaving a copy with the local revenue officer. This was less than a decade prior to my first arrival to conduct research in Gangwa.

Based upon the collected *Misl Bandobasts*, Jodhpur State officials set out the legal framework for contesting the singular and primary right of *khatedāri*, to inherit, transfer, or sell, based upon evidence of self-cultivation (*khudkāsht*). Lord, Estate holder, and tenant farmer alike were given an opportunity to contest title. Three years of cultivation by a tenant were deemed sufficient to claim title through the Revenue Courts. For a decade or two after reform these local contests took place, *khatedāri* rights sometimes were awarded to landlords, other times to share-cropping tenants.[11]

Many ex-landlords were neither attentive nor cognizant of their ex-tenant's capabilities. Upon reform and the receiving of self-cultivation *khudkāsht* lands for their own management, many ex-landlords proved incapable of the task. Ex-landlords were rightly fearful of leasing out fields to knowledgeable farmers who might later claim the land in a revenue court as *khudkāsht,* awardable after three successive years of cultivation. Such land was often put on the market to be bought by successful farmers or moneyed interests from outside the village.

Not all agricultural laborers were reflective about hydrology. Their interest depended on their aspirations, acuity of observation and attentiveness to the conversations of those who managed irrigation. Some laborers were highly knowledgeable, selected by ex-landlords to move into managerial roles.

For Marwāṛ and Shekhāwāti Pauline Kolenda and I can add to Singh's analysis of characteristics empowering peasants as activists and petitioners—Kolenda, from the Jat hamlet (*dhāṇī*) near Jaipur; I, from the twenty-four-caste (*jāti*) village Gangwa in Nagaur. We document the collaboration among partners (*sīrī*), joined as independent extended households, or as relatives, irrigating fields from a single shared well. Such joint families increased internal solidarity through sibling- and collateral-set marriages (Kolenda 1978; Rosin 1968: 159; 1995b) which brought a set of related women as wives into the joint household of related men.[12]

Furthermore, affinal allies were close at hand in neighboring villages through a tradition of egalitarian in-laws (Male: *byāī sagāī*; Female: *byānjī*) where neither wife-givers, nor wife-receivers were dominant. The elder generations dominated over younger ones. These terms of address were spoken reciprocally. As terms of reference they were transitive joining together not only one's own direct in-laws, but those of one's brothers, or sons. Also included were one's sisters or daughter's, as well as one's father's, father's brothers, mother's and mother's sisters (Rosin 1987: 152–53). When deepening a well to improve recharge, in-laws from neighboring villages could bring labor and draft animals to double the pace of draining, making possible the use of dynamite to extract rock from the bottom of a well shaft. These characteristics of irrigated farming we argue explain the degree of peasant mobilization in Nagaur. Are they found as well in equally activist Shekhāwāti? Sisson (1969, 1971) provides a most useful comparison between the two districts in their respective kingdoms.

This grander story, however, pivots on three legendary Jats in Jodhpur State who gained entrance into the royal administration: Mool Chand Sihag, the enabler of formal education; Buldev Ram Mirdha, the enforcer of royal edit, and Kan Sangh Parihar, the crafter of legislation. I have chosen to review the Jat community's own telling, as found on their website (JatLand.com 2017). Historic and scholarly publications often do not mention the legendary Sihag.

Mool Chand Sihag helped create the first town hostel to enable Jat youth to attend formal schooling in Jodhpur in 1927. He then funded a second in Nagaur in 1930 in his own home, and yet another in Barmer in 1934. There follows Merta City, Didwana, Maroth, and Parbatsar— the pace ever accelerating across Marwāṛ and Shekhāwāti.

Training in cognitive skills and participation in their family's farming practice prepared youths from tenant families for formal education. The content and pedagogy of that formal schooling in towns remains yet unknown to us, but Sihag gives us a clue. At nine he entered a Jain temple and retreat, where monastic discipline shaped his character. Near its front gate was a school where

> teachings were based on traditional mathematical tables through Hindi language…He read almost all available Hindi books, apart from solving mathematical quizzes and memorizing some Sanskrit shlokas with their meanings. (JatLand.com 2017)

After educating himself in English with the help of a railway guard, he chose to inspire village children to pursue an education by teaching Mathematics, Hindi, and English.

Learning Hindi and English was also the route taken by Buldev Ram Mirdha, as he prepared himself to enter the royal administration as postman. Mirdha joined the royal police in 1914, rising to Deputy Inspector General, serving more than 33 years before retiring in 1947. In the course of his career, his officers prevented street demonstrations, disrupted meetings, and thwarted conferences by such disallowed, illegal organizations as the Prayal Mandal and Lok Parishad. They exiled the leaders Jai Narayan and Saraf of Lok Parishad. They and their newspaper *Tarun Rajasthan* were forced to quit the kingdom to find safety in Ajmer-Merwara under British rule. Upon one of their many illegal returns to the Jodhpur State, they were arrested and held in solitary confinement for months. They were tried, convicted, and sentenced to prison for 4 and 5 years respectively, but were released after 2½ years on the day the Gandhi-Irwin Truce was celebrated across India. Buldev Ram Mirdha was, indeed, a law and order man for the Jodhpur Kingdom. He did not believe in agitation, disruptions, or public disorder. But he proved devoted to the work of Mool Chand Sihag. Quietly he had been recruiting the best of Sihag's student-wards, capable in Hindi and English, into the Royal Administration.

Among the students recruited was Kan Sangh Parihar, at 23 the first lawyer from the Jat community of Marwār. In 1936, he joined the bar at Jodhpur, and 2 years later established his own practice in Nagaur District. In 1949 Parihar entered the Marwār State Judicial Service as Hakim (Administrator). Subsequently, he was appointed Legal Remembrancer in Marwār's State Law Department at Jodhpur. There he drafted the Marwār Tenancy Act and the Marwār Land Revenue Act that intended to end the regime of landlords over landless share-cropping tenants. He was eventually appointed Chief Justice of the High Court of Rajasthan. In 1949 the Jodhpur State was amalgamated into the modern province of Rajasthan under pressure from the newly Independent Republic of India. It was Kan Sangh Parihar as Chief Justice who validated these 2 acts as the law of the land.

What began among Jat farmers as a movement of social up-lift, had advanced to a new sense of community pride and empowerment. With education followed a citizens' rebellion against free labor (*begār*), cesses (*lāg-bhāg*), and exorbitant rents in crop (*hasl*) or cash. This culminated in a revolution, as the Maharaja vowed to end the titles of Lord and Estate holder, heralding the end of an oppressed tenant class.[13]

In summary, a legacy of learning and cooperation incrementally improved water resources for human use that Mayank Kumar in *Monsoon Ecologies* traces back to the early medieval centuries as the development of "artificial irrigation," enhancing the possibilities for permanent human settlement in an increasingly arid zone (Kumar 2013: 149–160). As argued in "Locality and Frontier" (Rosin 1994: 49–52), these capabilities in collaborative work were turned from the natural to the political environment that was becoming increasingly onerous as feudal landlords increased their extraction of rents, cesses and free labor. For 30 years farmer assemblies (*kisān sabhā*) deeply committed but decentralized sprang up throughout the two regions, as documented by Sisson (1969: 946–963; 1972: 73–96) researching Rajasthan in the 1960s.

Transplanting the sons of peasant farmers to the hostels of towns supporting formal education was the next step in shifting local discontent and resistance into a consolidating rebellion uniting localities. Sisson stresses the comradeship and cohesiveness among Jat students living and studying together in townships that felt alien to them (ibid.: 80). He stresses three sources for the modernizing spirit among Jats, their education, their service in British armed forces in world War I, and their training in colonial India as lawyers (ibid.: 81). Hostel living and studying supported the most promising of students to learn language and law enabling the most successful of them to enter the royal administration. Co-housing in hostels forged alliances useful later as Congress Party incorporated activist Jats into electoral politics in the democratic province of Rajasthan.

Upon his retirement in 1947 from the Royal Police, Buldev Ram Mirdha had formed the Marwāṛ Kisan Sabhā, centralizing and providing an urban link for the diverse assemblies forged in the countryside of Jodhpur State. This Superintendent of Police proved to be a silent worker, steadily bringing, one by one, the best educated among the Jat student-wards of Sihag into the regal administration. What an irony that such daring transformative acts were perpetrated by a man with a life-long passion for law and order! (Sisson 1972: 79–82) His efforts were supported by Parihar, who crafted the laws the Maharaja ultimately approved for his kingdom.

In the dialectic sparking first a social movement, then a citizen's rebellion against feudal extractions emerges a revolution validated by their Maharaja himself. Thirty years of respectful petitions to their Maharajas, joined by rising agitation and rebellion throughout Marwāṛ and Shekhāwāti culminate in a non-violent revolution of *satyāgrahā* (Singh 1998: 148–154). The peasants in their diverse assemblies and networks, joining such long outlawed civil, student, and urban organizations under Narayan Vyas and others, become prime agents in their own liberation. Answering the debates of the 1960s, peasants were active agents, who as members of the vanguard helped demand and craft their future powers as citizens.

Acknowledgements I am indebted to Vito Victor for his sharp critique, Gail Wread for rescuing me on redundancies, Helen Ullrich for her editorial care in keeping us on subject, and the American Institute of Indian Studies, Fulbright Foundation, and National Science Foundation for funding enabling this research.

NOTES

1. M. Sato and B. L. Bhadani (1997: 92–95). Evidence of irrigated farming from the seventeenth century in the Merta District compares with its density and importance in 1960. Utilizing Tessitori's analysis of Muhnot Nainsi's *Marwāṛ-ra-pargana-ri-Vigat*, they find that 6,947–7,782 well sites in Pergana Merta in 1638, averaging 3.63–4.07 wells per square mile, is comparable to Nagaur District in 1960.

2. Revitalizing and globalizing traditional forms of the performance arts, crafts, textiles, architecture and landscaping, and the training and apprenticeships that have sustained such practices, had an impact. In this spirit of preservation and recovery, a flourishing industry of heritage tourism would emerge in Rajasthan (Henderson and Weisgrau 2007). Of the artisans and performers at the Festival of India, sponsored by the Smithsonian in 1985, 19 of the 39 airlifted to Washington, DC. were from Rajasthan.

3. For a reconstruction of the feudal past under kingly, princely, and local lord's domination see *In the Times of Trees and Sorrows; Nature, Power, and Memory in Rajasthan* (Gold and Gujar 2002). Ann Grodzins Gold and Bhoju Ram Gujar eloquently reconstruct through interviews and folk narratives the remembered realities of living in regal Sawar. They recover the past in the kingdom of Sawar, while Rosin recovers the feudal traditions of a single village in Marwar where tenant farmers were under the control of both local Lord (*Jāgīrdār, Ṭhākur*) and noble Estate holder (*Ṭhikānedār*). He analyzes the *Misl Bandobast* settlement document filed with the local Revenue Officer at the time of land reform (Rosin 1987: 49–80).

4. Four technologies for lifting water from a well occurred in Rājpuṭāna. In order of highest efficiency, volume, depth of well, and size of the work force engaged, they are the potted leather bucket (*poṭalyā charas*) requiring a team of several families, the persian water wheel *(araṭh)* limited to high groundwater levels, the nossled leather bucket *(sundiya charas)* allowing a single family or two to awkwardly draw water, and the counter-balanced dipstick (*denkūlī*) often worked for shallow wells by a single person (Rosin 1994: 35–40, 57).

5. Dr. Dwight Berreman, mathematician and physicist at Bell Labs, states "Rosin's paper is the nearest thing to a fully developed system on a base other than 10 (i.e., 4) that I have heard of except that the base 2 and 8 system have recently taken hold among computer programmers" (Rosin 1984: 50).

6. For a brief period after Independence the India Republic 1947–1950 introduced the "pice" at 64 to a *rūpiyā*, alongside the 16 *ānās,* following the logic of a base 4 number system. The "new pice," or "paise" of 100 to the *rūpiyā* soon replaced it, introducing the decimal system into contemporary currency.

7. Our colleague Pauline Kolenda, to whom this volume is dedicated, excelled in the comparative study of family and marriage, both in scholarly review of prior writings, seeking compatibility among definitions and analytic frames, and through field research in south and north India. Utilizing 1960 government census material on the prevalence of joint families in Rajasthan Kolenda (1987) sharpened her analysis of the factors involved. The frequency of joint families within Rajasthan proved the

highest among any province in India, peaking in Nagaur and Shekhawati Districts within the Jodhpur and Jaipur princely states. Her imaginative use of census material allowed her to construct then test her theory on their occurrence (Kolenda 1993).

8. Inspired by Swami Dayananda Saraswati in 1875, *Arya Samāj* societies for social service, education, and public discussion spread throughout the princely states, and northern India. Dayananda had the ear of the Maharajas of Udaipur, Jodhpur, and Jhalawar states, while monks from his order brought such messages to the towns and villages. Affirming Vedic religion, the order awakened ideas of a united India that was opposed to casteism, communalism, and untouchability (Choudhry 1968: 109–111).

9. The nationalist movements launched by Congress Party in British India, such as the Civil Disobedience Campaign of the 1930s and the Quit India Campaign of 1940s, had a delayed effect, stimulating non-violent *satyāgrahā* actions within the princely states (Saxena 1971: 157–267). Until 1938 Congress Party took a hands-off cautious policy toward the princely states (Ramasack 1988: 387–389). Gandhi favored regal stewardship and constitutional monarchy, and trusteeship of the natural wealth, keeping good relations with the princely class in his home region of Kathiawar and with industrialists from Gujarat and Rajasthan. Nehru was more sympathetic to organizational intervention, becoming President of the All India States' People's Conference (AISPC) from 1938 to 1946, visiting Jodhpur, and convening AISPC meetings in Jaipur, and then Udaipur. Both Nehru, Gandhi, and Patel celebrated the up-surge of political activity under local and indigenous leadership (ibid.: 390–393). Rudolph and Rudolph (1984: 187) point out that these organizations of resistance and up-lift were the only elements of civil society to arise during the princely period, becoming key to the political development of subsequent Rajasthan Province.

10. Irrigated farming with its extensions into livestock raising for sale at inter-regional fairs extended the web of tenant farmer solidarity bringing them into recurrent contact and communication with their regional tenant neighbors and to the awakenings of peasant resistance in other princely states and *satyāgrahā* campaigns in British India.

11. Rosin (1981) makes use of Dool Singh's survey (Singh 1964) of some 116 villages in 13 of the 26 districts of Rajasthan. Relative success in reform is presented in 167 charts and tables. Rosin and Henry's tabulation and re-analysis of findings show that the one consistent variable associated with success in awarding title to the cultivator was the prior landlord's residence. *Ṭhikānedārs* residing outside the villages they controlled appear more likely to lose title, than residential *Jāgīrdāri* Lords (Rosin 1981). Behind these figures is the fact that Estate holders would

receive compensation from the government, while the small local Lords could protest by mass demonstrations their exclusion from compensation, but lost the battle (Rudolph and Rudolph 1984: 57–66). They turned to protect those fields over which they might claim status as self-cultivators by evicting their tenants. Among the first acts of the Rajasthan legislature was Protection of Tenants Ordinance 1949 to undo and halt such evictions (Rosin 1987: 95–100).

12. In organizing this section on family types for both the original research and its later publication (Rosin 1968, 1987: 137–163) I benefitted directly from Kolenda's brilliantly concise and orderly, adverbial scheme for classifying (Kolenda 1993).

13. Jat public records (JatLand.com 2017) recognize these milestones in regal recognition of citizen organizations with rights to assemble and demonstrate. Lok Parishad, the Marwāṛ Kisan Sabhā, the Marwāṛ Jat Reform Society are given legal status. Jat activists, as well as urban leaders previously convicted for their political activity, are prevented from running for seats in the Jodhpur Municipal Council, the Constituent Assembly of Jodhpur, or to the Constituent Assembly to design law for a newly Independent Indian Union. Not until Menon of the India Congress Party forges an agreement with Maharaja Hanwant Singh in 1948 (Mathur 1982: 174–177, 188–190) does Vyas enter the "Intern Ministries" of Jodhpur State as Prime Minister completing the revolution to a representational and responsible government.

REFERENCES

Bharucha, Rustom. 2003. *Rajasthan, An Oral History: Conversations with Komal Kothari*. New Delhi: Penguin Books.

Choudhry, P.S. 1968. *Rajasthan Between the Two World Wars*. Agra: Mehra Offset Press.

Gold, Ann Grodzins, and Bhoju Ram Gujar. 2002. *In the Time of Trees and Sorrows: Nature, Power and Memory in Rajasthan*. Durham and London: Duke University Press.

Gough, Kathleen. 1968–1969. Peasant Resistance and Revolt in South India. In *Sociology of Developing Societies South Asia*, eds. H. Alavi and John Harriss, 276–287. New York: Monthly Review Press.

Henderson, Carol E., and Maxine Weisgrau (eds.). 2007. *Raj Rhapsodies: Tourism, Heritage and the Seduction of History*. Aldershot, England and Burlington, VT: Ashgate.

Hobsbawm, E.J. 1959. *Primitive Rebels: Studies in Archaic Forms of Social Movements in the 19th and 20th Centuries*. New York: Norton.

JatLand.com. 2017. Mool Chand Siyag. https://www.jatland.com/home/Mool_Chand_Siyag. Accessed 12 Feb 2017 [Translated by Dayanand Deswal].

Kolenda, Pauline. 1978. Sibling-Set Marriage, Collateral-Set Marriage, and Deflected Alliance Among Annana Jats of Jaipur District, Rajasthan. In *American Studies in the Anthropology of India*, ed. Sylvia Vatuk, 242–277. New Delhi: Manohar Publications and American Institute of Indian Studies.

Kolenda, Pauline. 1993. The Joint-Family Household in Rural Rajasthan: Ecological, Cultural, and Demographic Conditions for Its Occurrence. In *The Idea of Rajasthan: Explorations in Regional Identity*, vol. II, eds. Karine Schomer, et al., 64–131. New Delhi: Manohar Publications and American Institute of Indian Studies.

Kumar, Mayank. 2013. *Monsoon Ecologies: Irrigation, Agriculture and Settlement Patterns in Rajasthan During the Pre-colonial Period*. Delhi: Manohar Publications.

Mathur, Sobhag. 1982. *Struggle for Responsible Government in Marwar*. Jodhpur: Sharda Publishing House.

Moench, Marcus (ed.). 1995. *Groundwater Management: The Supply Dominated Focus of Traditional, NGO and Government Efforts*. Ahmedabad, Gujarat: Vikram Sarabhai Centre for Development Interaction (VIKSAT).

Moore, Barrington, Jr. 1966. *Social Origins of Dictatorship and Democracy: Lord and Peasant in the Making of the Modern World*. Boston: Beacon.

Ramusack, Barbara N. 1988. Congress and the People's Movement in Princely India; Ambivalence in Strategy and Organization. In *Congress and Indian Nationalism; The Pre-independence Phase*, ed. Richard Sisson and Stanley Wolpert, 377–403. Berkeley: University of California Press.

Rosin, R. Thomas. 1968. Changing Land Tenure and Village Polity in Rajasthan, India: An Interactional Perspective. Ph.D. dissertation, University of California, Berkeley.

Rosin, R. Thomas. 1973. Gold Medallions: The Arithmetic Calculations of an Illiterate. In *Council on Anthropology and Education Newsletter*, vol. IV, ed. John Singleton, 1–9. Pittsburgh: University of Pittsburgh, July.

Rosin, R. Thomas. 1978. Peasant Adaptation as Process in Land Reform: A Case Study. In *American Studies in the Anthropology of India*, ed. Sylvia Vatuk, 460–495. New Delhi: Manohar Publications and American Institute of Indian Studies.

Rosin, R. Thomas. 1981. Land Reform in Rajasthan. *Current Anthropology* 22 (1): 75–76.

Rosin, R. Thomas. 1984. Gold Medallions: The Arithmetic Calculations of an Illiterate. *Anthropology and Education Quarterly Special Anniversary Volume* 15 (1): 38–50.

Rosin, R. Thomas. 1987. *Land Reform and Agrarian Change; Study of a Marwar Village from Raj to Swaraj*. Jaipur: Rawat Publications.

Rosin, R. Thomas. 1993. The Tradition of Groundwater Irrigation in Northwestern India. *Human Ecology* 21 (1): 51–86.

Rosin, R. Thomas. 1994. Locality and Frontier: Securing Livelihood in the Aravalli Zone of Central Rajasthan. In *The Idea of Rajasthan; Explorations in Regional Identity*, vol. II, eds. Karine Schomer, et al., 30–63. New Delhi: Manohar and American Institute of Indian Studies.

Rosin, R. Thomas. 1995a. An Ethnographer's Perspective on the Groundwater Crisis: A Longitudinal Case Study of a Rajasthani Village. In *Groundwater Management: The Supply Dominated Focus of Traditional, NGO and Government Efforts*, ed. Marcus Moench, 5–37. Ahmedabad: Vikram Sarabhai Centre for Development Interaction (VIKSAT).

Rosin, R. Thomas. 1995b. Set Marriages and the Joint Family in Rajasthan: An Ethnologic Construction from Census Data. In *Folk, Faith & Feudalism; Rajasthan Studies*, ed. N.K. Singhi and Rajendra Joshi, 205–240. Jaipur: Rawat Publications.

Rosin, R. Thomas. 2008. Back and There Again: Structuring a Career Around Long-Term Research in Rajasthan, India. In *The Tao of Anthropology*, ed. Jack Kelso, 45–61. Gainesville, FL: University Press of Florida.

Rudolph, Susanne Hoeber, and Lloyd I. Rudolph. 1984. *Essays on Rajputana: Reflections on History, Culture and Administration*. New Delhi: Concept Publishing Company.

Sato, Masanori, and B.L. Bhadani. 1997. *Economy and Polity of Rajasthan: Study of Kota and Marwar (17th–19th Centuries)*. Jaipur: Publication Scheme.

Saxena, K.S. 1971. *The Political Movements and Awakening in Rajasthan (1857 to 1947)*. Ram Nagar, New Delhi: Chand & Co.

Sen, Sunil. 1982. *Peasant Movements in India: Mid-Nineteenth and Twentieth Centuries*. Calcutta and New Delhi: K.P. Bagchi & Company.

Sengupta, Nirmal. 2007. Neglected Sources of Irrigation. In *Economic Studies of Indigenous and Traditional Knowledge*, ed. Nirmal Sengupta, 121–146. New Delhi: Academic Foundation.

Singh, Dool. 1964. *Land Reforms in Rajasthan: A Study of Evasion, Implementation and Socio-Economic Effects of Land Reforms*. New Delhi: Research Programmes Committee, Planning Commission, Government of India.

Singh, Hira. 1998. *Colonial Hegemony and Popular Resistance: Princes, Peasants, and Paramount Power*. Walnut Creek, CA, London and New Delhi: Alta Mira and Sage Publications.

Sisson, Richard. 1969. Peasant Movements and Political Mobilization: The Jats of Rajasthan. *Asian Survey* 9: 946–963 (December).

Sisson, Richard. 1972. *The Congress Party in Rajasthan: Political Integration and Institution-Building in an Indian State*. Berkeley: University of California Press.

Surana, Pushpendra. 1983. *Social Movements and Social Structure: A Study in the Princely State of Mewar*. New Delhi: Manohar Publications.

Wolf, Eric. 1969. *Peasant Wars of the Twentieth Century*. New York: Harper.

CHAPTER 11

The Curriculum, and the Hidden Curriculum, in Indian Education, 1985 to the Present

Nita Kumar

In this essay, I focus on various curricular practices of Indian schools. My intention is not to discuss the declared, intended, or tested curriculum, that is, what the state or an examining board declares should be taught, or what is tested as if taught. Rather, curriculum for me is the experienced, taught, and learnt curriculum, or what may be observed by an ethnographer sitting for the whole school day in various classrooms as the sum total of the processes that are going on under the school roof. Then the "hidden curriculum," as the name implies, includes the non-explicit, implicit, unstated things that are also being taught children in school along with the explicitly stated curricular (and so-called extra-curricular) subjects. This hidden curriculum is always present and relies on the structures and processes of schools, including spatial layouts, language use, interrelationships, rituals, and symbols.[1] Because they are varied and span a large spectrum of activities and experiences, and are extremely formative, we may also justifiably call these curricular practices

N. Kumar (✉)
Claremont McKenna College, Claremont, CA, USA
e-mail: nita.kumar@claremontmckenna.edu

© The Author(s) 2019   245
H. E. Ullrich (ed.), *The Impact of Education
in South Asia*, Anthropological Studies of Education,
https://doi.org/10.1007/978-3-319-96607-6_11

"the culture of schools." My intention is to highlight the importance of this culture, thus pointing to its impact, and to briefly mark the change over thirty years and the significance of the change.

The culture of schools does not occur by accident nor is it created by abstract forces. The story I tell would remain incomplete without an interpretation of the teachers' and administrators' roles. I therefore mention throughout this chapter possible explanations for educators' attitudes. However, since educators are also, in turn, the products of larger processes, a complete analysis of their functioning can only be done elsewhere.[2]

The Indian schools I studied were deliberately selected to straddle the variety of schools, in terms of size, age, ownership, administration, medium of teaching, ideology, and as discussed below, relationship to modernity. My research site is the city of Varanasi, an exuberant precolonial place not among the largest cities of Uttar Pradesh, but proud of its historical dynamism and cosmopolitanism. Its latest reason for pride is its selection by Prime Minister Narendra Modi as his constituency. I would claim that this justifies our searching for aspects of change in its recent history, even beyond all the other reasons, such as demographic, technological, and political change in India.

We must begin, I propose, with marking the hierarchy of schools in India. The hierarchy itself is part of the school curricula, insofar as it determines what is being taught, and how, to specific groups of students, and equally what is omitted, and therefore covertly taught. Schools may be divided into five kinds. What is the basis of this hierarchy? To the public the basis is clearly a case of who is included and who is excluded at each level.

The topmost level of school is the Christian missionary school and the "Public" school, meaning elite private school. These are not only for those who can pay their fees, but equally—because the fees are not always very high—for those whose families demonstrably have the appropriate social capital for the school. Those without the money or the social capital are typically excluded from the admission process. The idea is that only social capital can reproduce itself.

Then comes the "imitation" missionary and public school. This second level caters to middle-class and socially mobile parents. The same criteria apply as for the topmost level schools but in a diluted form. The dilution consists of the acknowledgment that with profound effort, parents may develop the social capital.

The vernacular, Indian-language school occupies the third rung of the ladder. The vernacular schools are open to all community members, but are so oversubscribed that admission depends on networks of contact and connection. The guardians of these schools are interested in education as socialization and skill development, and do not focus on the life-changing opportunities (or benefits) that education should bring about in their wards.

The next rung of the ladder is the small, private, so-called English medium school. These are market propositions: they are willing to take anyone who conforms to their expectations (buy this, wear that). Their ethics are a market ethics—they are searching for the language, images, systems that will enhance their appeal to consumers, but unlike the elite schools, deliberately define their consumers as lacking in both social capital and the knowledge of what it consists, which is partly what they offer to teach.

At the bottom is the Municipal and District Board School, in the city and village, respectively. The Municipal and Board Schools are for those children whose parents cannot afford to send them to private schools. The understanding, equally, is that parents who could afford private schools are ignorant of the value and the awareness of a developing world that would have enabled them to discern the superiority of the private schools over the public schools.

There are exceptions to the ranking: the occasional Municipal school outshines many private ones, the odd missionary school has the reputation of being poorly managed and is shunned. The small private schools at rung two occasionally grow into the large, imitation public schools at rung four.

Even though this simple economic-social alignment of schools and students, and the philosophy behind it, is transparent and consensual, I would like to emphasize one particular aspect of rank that will help my analysis become clearer. This is the family–school relationship, or how far the family and the school trust and respect each other, and try to work together. The trust and respect could well be on the surface, as a professional attitude or a convenient one. Or it could be "genuine." In this ranking, too, we find that the Municipal schools rank the lowest, followed by the small private "English medium" ones. The vernacular ones are stronger in their family–school relationship, thus above them. The schools with the closest family–school relationships are the elite missionary and public schools, followed by the imitation ones. Needless to say, when we say "school," we mean the teachers, administrators and, to a large extent, the support staff as well.

THE MUNICIPAL OR DISTRICT BOARD SCHOOL

Starting from the bottom, the institution which makes the weakest link between the family and the school is the Municipal or Mahapalika School, which is the government school in urban areas, and the District Board or village school in rural areas. These are of three levels: Primary (class 1–5), Junior High (class 6–8), and High School or Secondary School (class 9 and 10).[3]

The buildings of primary schools in both city and village are usually independent buildings with space around. They range from basic box-like structures, whitewashed over brick, with a small verandah, to older structures from colonial times, with archways and deeper verandahs, to which more rooms have somewhat haphazardly been added. The white-washing, when fresh and outlined with paint, makes the school look pleasant. When not fresh, the place looks neglected. The spaces outside, whether a paved entrance way, a courtyard, or a small playing area, are always untended, maybe littered, maybe in the process of being cleaned or constructed. In the village the school has a playing field, sometimes substantial, and grounds all around for many possible activities. This is almost always unleveled and no sports arenas are marked out in them. The trees are rarely very healthy and there are no flower beds or bushes on any side. Clearly, no one in the school practices a philosophy of working with their hands, nor are there efficient professional gardeners or cleaners on regular duty. But equally clearly, everything spatial testifies to the *desire* for a modern school. There is no talk of these schools being of the type of the old-fashioned *pathshala* or village school, either as reality or—the way they are better known—as caricature (as in the movie *Devdas*, 1955). The closest to a "*pathshala* discourse" is in an occasional chapter of a class 1 or 2 Hindi textbook, called "*Hamari pathshala* (Our School)" with a picture of a boxed building surrounded by old-style spreading trees, brick-bordered pathways, flowerbeds with rows of blossoms, and children and teachers working harmoniously in the garden.

Inside the buildings, the schools have tables and chairs for the teachers, simple and serviceable. They have registers for attendance and softboards for notices. They have graded classes, exams, meetings and syllabi—the technologies of a modern school. The Indian Municipal or District Board School is not supposed to be held outdoors under a tree. The students are not supposed to learn their alphabets in the dust or on slates that they wash out. No aspect of the "indigenous" or "alternative" is legitimized in this school. It has the patronage of the modern state and its President and Prime Minister's portraits hang on the office wall. Its teachers are paid handsomely and have all the benefits of government employees. As an arm of the state, it celebrates India's Independence Day and Republic Day with enthusiasm.

But the modern features of the school such as building, outdoor spaces, furniture, teaching materials, or syllabi, are in disarray, and this disarray is what speaks of a weak relationship with modernity. The Municipal and District Board School presents an image of itself that seems to echo a stereotype of "a school for the poor." Smaller children typically sit cross-legged in rows on the floor on one and a half feet wide lengths of jute matting. The school has no shelves or spaces for the children's things, including their cloth or plastic bags for their books which they keep by their sides. As an observer, I may not have thought anything of it but "this is how they do it," and proceeded to rationalize it. But I am told clearly by the Principal and teachers, and the *dai* or maid, that the children are not *expected* to be able to sit on anything but the floor, or to spend on books or materials that may need shelves. They are supposedly *not able* to. The discourse is through and through one of necessity and naturalness, not one of choice and agency. It is proposed as one mutually shared by the observer and the educators.

Now, private schools also may have seating on the floor in the youngest classes. In these private schools, the strategy of floor sitting is obviously a planned one, with wider mats, with low desks to work on, or with shelves along the wall, with an overall sense of rightness. The private school administrators talk of the *choices* they made, and stress both a preferred arrangement and order, and confidence in their autonomy. This autonomy can supposedly be shaken by interference from ignorant guardians or managers, but private schools report such interference with a smile, and not the bitterness with which the government's micro-control is reported by government school administrators.

Guardians' "interference" is, ironically, greater in private than in government schools. Government schools seem to continue in their familiar style, whereas in those private schools that I had visited in the 1980s that had floor seating, the system had been reformed out of existence by the 2010s. Central Hindu School's rationale for replacing floor sitting with heavy furniture was that "guardians *nahin mante hain* (guardians do not accept it)." Ganesh Shishu Sadan's owner has had Montessori training that she was very proud of, and could have explained the floor

seating with reference to its advantages for children, but decided to follow the same course of catering to the less knowledgeable guardians.
Some madrasas, such as Jamia Islamiya, would have claimed a continuity
with the home culture of the children and their opposition to Western
culture. But they, too, quietly switched to heavy desks and chairs, and
all these schools—Theosophical, Montessori, and Barelwi in their ideology—are now proud of this keeping pace with "modernity." It is largely
in comparison to these changes, and from the fact of its own steadfast
continuity, that the Municipal School considers itself inferior: "*Our*
guardians do not even know enough to demand furniture.*"

If this is the hidden curriculum, the explicit curriculum is also problematic. If you ask the teachers what they are teaching, they will tell you
that they follow the State Board curriculum with inexpensive textbooks
in each subject. The teachers are all trained, first with a Bachelor of
Education degree, then with workshops on teaching methods conducted
by the government and by NGOs but in every case they make a point of
not displaying their knowledge of pedagogy in the classroom. As with
space, it is as if the students did not deserve the pedagogical acumen that
teachers have. The teaching consists of the teacher's dictating or putting
up on the blackboard the equivalent of the work for the class level, such
as Math problems or Hindi grammar, and sitting back, or socializing,
while students copy whatever is written and do whatever is required with
it. The students have tattered notebooks and write less than an average
of a few lines a day. Oral work consists of the teacher mouthing a proposition or an answer to a question and the students repeating it to memorize it. If they learn the minimum imaginable in each subject, this is not
only because of the problems usually mentioned, such as teachers' indif-
ference or inefficiency and the illiteracy in children's families, but because
of the poorly designed curriculum and the absence of management systems. Teachers are not required to have a planning register, to do any
weekly planning, nor to demonstrate the use of any teaching methods
but dictation, verbal explanation, or writing on the blackboard. They
take no responsibility for answering students' questions, resolving their
problems, or simply providing careful explanations. Their work does not
include looking after every child. They do not claim to be doing any of
this, no one expects it and no one oversees it. To actually use their training and skills toward better teaching is regarded as "a waste of time,"
and also as kind of lowering of one's status as a superior professional.
Teachers are hardly the only category of educated people in India who

thus mark a distance from the masses. Politicians and civil "servants" are resolute in demonstrating that they are the masters and not the servants of the public. Teachers merely reflect the larger chasm in India between the educated and unschooled, and the larger discourse of all Indians as not possibly equal, with some specifically labeled "backward."

There is a waste of time and energy in the classrooms that teaches children that adults do not care for them, that school is boring, and that the subjects are meaningless. Math consists of tables learnt by heart; Hindi, of letters, words, and sentences copied from the blackboard. No other subjects have scheduled time. Almost no student can answer questions on Indian history or geography even approximately appropriate to their level. Children learn that for them, education means "semi-education." They know that they are inferior to properly educated people, to children in other kinds of schools. Their school teaches them that they belong in this semi-educated category. Schools and studying come to seem the ultimate boring activities in their young lives. I will go so far as to say that if they are late in the morning, leave early, stay away, or ultimately drop out, it is because there is pressure from the school to do so. The school has made itself so uninteresting that children prefer to miss the free food, bear the verbal and perhaps physical abuses for their absences, than to attend the boring classes.

Children clearly learn that adults are hypocritical. Their teachers show one thing on paper or in principle and do a different thing in practice. All children must have sat through inspections and visits. In these, teachers cite different numbers to the numbers attending. They describe their timetable, their curricula, their teaching methods, and the content of each classroom as different to what is going on in practice. More regularly, children overhear the teachers talk among themselves about how to show things, which add up to a picture of double-facedness. Children grasp clearly that their teachers are not to be trusted.

The overt and the hidden curriculum in these schools comes together in a disturbing fashion. The children are almost all from working-class or farming families and almost all from homes without a high level of education, sometimes even literacy. Teachers and administrators look down upon their students and refer to them as being of *neech qaum, chhoti jat, pichhre hue varg, us tapke* (lower class, lower caste, backward sections of society, *that* section). They do this in the hearing of children and often directly to them. Children are made to feel that they cannot learn because their families are uneducated and their home practices are backward. Rather than mentioning specific problems, such as absentee-ism on a certain date, or not paying attention in a certain class, teachers always generalize about the morality of the children's families. Whether every teacher is actually of a different class, caste, or region to the chil-dren or not, they all talk as if they were, and the children's class, caste, or background was indisputably inferior. From a historian's perspective, this ascribing of inferiority to the children is comparable to the racism of colonialism. Colonialism inscribed a superiority coming from education on a class of Indians that curiously became entrenched as an essential dif-ference. No doubt, the habits of caste also made difference easy to prac-tice. But we must remember that caste is not visible and may be easily manipulated, performed, or hidden, unlike education that often becomes knowable as soon as a person opens their mouth.

The distinction made by teachers in Municipal Schools between "us" and "them" is based on class and knowledge, but is not mutable as class and knowledge can be. There is no perceived oneness of the two par-ties, educators, and guardians, by virtue of their sharing the same nation, the same constitution, or the same history. It follows that there is no real effort by the school toward change. The efforts toward change are always defeated by the prior knowledge of how children of certain fam-ilies and backgrounds cannot change. There is a *noblesse oblige* to keep on working, but a conviction that the two parties of the drama are doomed to remain separate and never meet, much as with Forster's "East and West." The school does not treat parents as clients who need to be gratified and does not provide them with what they seek. As an arm of the state, the school is antagonistic to the community and family, to the point that they can ever do anything right. In its alienating and intoler-ant atmosphere, the system stigmatizes parents and children in advance. The school *makes* them fail by starting with the assumption, "These fam-ilies cannot produce educated children." Then it dedicates itself to prov-ing this preconception. Its formula is a simple one: to counterpose the qualities of "culture" such as time-discipline, thrift, cleanliness, and lit-eracy, with those of "backwardness" such as poverty, illiteracy, and seem-ingly unstructured lifestyles; to demand the former set of qualities; and then to fail the family for not possessing them. The problem is not eco-nomic, but inherently a political and discursive one.

Studying British schools, Paul Willis (1981) argued that working-class children re-created their working-class identities through their own agency. Unlike them, the working-class and farmers' children in India have their working-class identities created for them systematically by their Municipal and District Board schools.

THE SMALL 'ENGLISH MEDIUM' OR 'CONVENT' SCHOOL

At the next rung of the ladder is the private 'English medium' school that has an English name, or 'saint' or 'convent' or 'academy' in its name. It is not in fact any of the things the name suggests: a missionary, public school, or English medium school. It uses these words as a market ploy, trusting on the ignorance of parents about what these terms mean, and how to evaluate schools. None of these schools are open to scrutiny. Though always run in a house, or part of a house, the exterior is done up to simulate "English medium education." This means thick paint and bright colors, with cartoon characters, often Disney's, and the English name splashed prominently, evocative of English language and "culture," and through them, of the world of English learning. What parents can see fulfills expectations: the gates are impressive, the signboard impeccable with English lettering and child-friendly pictures; the entrance looks "disciplined," with carefully tended flower pots, a row of chairs for visitors, a vase on the office desk, softboards or chalkboards with the timings, a sample of the uniform displayed, and a list of the rules of the school.

But inside, were you to be able to walk around, you would observe small rooms, as in a house. The walking around is disallowed for guardians and discouraged for visitors under various pretexts, the most interesting of which is, "The guardians here are very backward. They will simply spit everywhere." The rooms are stuffed with benches and desks. Because it is a cramped space but also because there is no idea of an alternative way to sit, the benches are always in straight rows facing the teacher. They are carpentered with the biggest children in mind, so smaller children have to sit doubled over or in variously contorted ways. Authority always emanates from the one spot the teacher occupies. With no space for bags or books, children sit with their bags on their laps or on the desk space in front of them, and write *on top of* their bags and books. The light and ventilation of these rooms are mediocre at best, and bad in most cases. There are no displays in classrooms or work on the walls. The blackboard is usually old and worn out.

This local 'English medium' school is stronger than the Municipal schools partly because it is private and has fees, whereas the Municipal school is totally free. To charge fees means to bear some responsibility for results, both in the public view and its own. Children must actually learn something. They must pass exams and get promoted, they must be made smart. This passing and promotion must have some meaning. The school is competing with hundreds of other such schools and must show results. True, teachers are untrained and almost innocently clueless, but the administration must be strong. The tighter the administration, the better the school—in everyone's perception as well as the school's: "Everything depends on the administration." Tightness consists of superficial discipline, such as ensuring that copy books are regularly checked. The checking consists of putting red marks on the students' work, indifferent to the meaning of those marks. Neither the students or their guardians, nor the teachers or the administrators of the small English medium school or convent school fathom the full meaning behind the modernist features they endorse, but they perform them more solemnly than the Municipal school.

The student in a small English medium school or convent school learns that studying is physically painful. The furniture is hard, classroom conditions harsh, routines unflinchingly repetitive, the work uninspiring, and teachers unfriendly and unimaginative. There are no expectations that the student will sit or move around comfortably, or understand or enjoy the subjects being taught. The student grasps that she is expected to complete the work the teacher assigns, to learn by heart what is required, and to answer examination questions as closely as possible to the ways teachers have pre-dictated.

If the Municipal and District Board schools reproduce features of working-class life such as a low level of formal schooling in science, mathematics, and languages, and the lack of training in wider matters of modern, democratic functioning, the private English medium schools do close to the same. Their students are also working class, and sometimes lower-middle-class children, whose parents, together with some working-class ones, are ambitious that their children achieve a social mobility that they themselves did not have. The parents are not educated enough to question the school or to analyze its successes and failures. They act on faith. They sometimes change schools when they perceive that their faith has been betrayed or realize their child "is not learning anything." On the whole the parents are anxious, but not hopeful. The school is supposed to produce a miraculous change in the child but they do not necessarily believe in the miracles.

Because the pedagogical strategies of these private schools are so weak, students are under greater pressure to demonstrate results without support. Teachers blame students for not learning what they have not been taught. Parents feel guilty when students are blamed for failing. The majority of the parents resort to tutors to work with their children to complete the schoolwork. In the best of cases, students learn to guess at what they are supposed to do, to cleverly fulfill teachers' expectations, to receive reprimand and abuse, to lie low, and to live their own social lives within their own peer groups, separately from adults.

Though these schools face tough competition from each other and have to sell themselves effectively to parents through various devices, there is enough of a market in India given its vast children's population, to make running schools a viable commercial proposition. A schooling market discourse exists in India that states that if you invest sufficiently at the outset in the building, furniture, and teachers, in a few years you would be making a reasonable, then maybe even a fat, profit. Public schools, that is elite private schools, are established partly on this assumption. However, the market savviness which is needed, such as publicity and the daily discipline of efficient management, eludes many school owners. This leads to a downward spiral: poor management, poor schooling, poor or no earnings, poor reputation, and even worse education.

THE VERNACULAR SCHOOL

The middle, or third rung of the ladder from both below and from the top, is comprised of the Hindi medium school, and the madrasa or Urdu medium school, in UP. In other states these are schools in the state language. Such schools were called vernacular schools in the colonial period, and since the name means "local" and "in the people's language," I am using it. These are typically affiliated to the State Education Board. They are private schools, though many are aided by the Government which keeps their fees low. Such a school has a larger building and staff than the Municipal and private English medium school. The vernacular school is community based, founded, administered, and staffed by people from the constituencies it represents, which are typically based on region, language, and religious sect. Thus in all Indian cities, including my own research site, there are vernacular schools founded over the last 150 years by regional-linguistic groups such as Bengalis and

Gujaratis, by Islamic sects such as Ahl-e-Hadis, Deobandi, and Barelwi, and secular schools founded by nationalist reformers for whom the nation was the community. Often this means that the school was a product of philanthropy and the building was donated.

This presents one kind of problem. A school like Amiya Ranjan Banerjee Higher Secondary School, housed in an old, ornate, early twentieth-century aristocratic home with deep verandas and shady, high ceilinged rooms is representative of the role of philanthropy in old urban centers in India. Such buildings are donated with nationalist fervor, and accepted with grace and gratitude. As expansion becomes inevitable, new classrooms are created with tin or asbestos siding, on the roofs, all around in the compound and spawning all over corridors and verandas. This includes an unimaginable range. There is the T.R. Adams Memorial School founded by an Englishman's widow and immensely popular because of its suggested resemblance to a "convent." There is Maulana Azad Public School started by its Old Boys' Association as a "reply" to Christian and Hindu schools. In the case of both old and new buildings, all semblance of the original plan of the building gets lost as classes meet in the verandas, in the courtyard, in front of offices, and literally in nooks and crannies—and, in the case of residential buildings, in bathrooms and garages. Historically, any acquired space may be used for any stated purpose, and failure or success in achieving the purpose—in this instance, education—is not attributable to the space.

To the question "What does the school teach?" the answer for both English medium and Vernacular schools can be given in a nutshell: "The syllabus." Or, to be precise, the teachers do not *teach* the syllabus; in their vocabulary they *cover* the syllabus. It is always an externally determined span that they are given to complete—hence "cover"—from the beginning to the end. Often, in spite of dividing up the ten chapters, let us say, mentioned in the syllabus into the number of teaching days, they cannot in fact complete the chapters because unforeseen holidays result in fewer teaching days. In such cases, the children are advised to "cover" the chapters at home. Because the chapters are mentioned in class, they are ticked off as being "covered." All the chapters "covered" are what "come" at the subsequent exams.

The syllabus for each subject, then, is the book prescribed for the subject and the syllabus for the class is the total of the books that the school has prescribed for all the subjects in that class. Sometimes the syllabus is typed up by the school as a separate list of topics. These topics are the chapters in the textbooks. So, if a teacher were to appear in class every day and open to a page in her textbook and mark out a portion from the page and tell her students, "This is what you must learn," she will have factually done her work. She needs to definitely open the textbook and point out the portion to be studied. She does not need to do anything else. *There are in fact no words in school vocabularies for any other action with regard to the syllabus than "cover."*

The syllabus explicitly does not include: oral answers by children to facilitate fluency in speech; multiple answers to questions; story writing to teach creative writing; imaginative narratives to encourage the use of the imagination; discussions to stimulate curiosity and instill confidence in public speech; and projects that take off from the chapters enabling them to make connections to and in the world around them. *Not a single teacher* in Banaras, with exactly two exceptions in Central Hindu Girls' School, was able to sustain a conversation about what the syllabus was and what it could be. And even these two, who had clear thoughts on what they could hypothetically teach, paradoxically added: "We cannot do it though. We cannot *change the syllabus.*"

The syllabus is the textbooks but the textbooks are also used minimally and not to their full potential. The very first *Workbook* in the Modern English series by Oxford University Press, Delhi, has a page with a composite scene of a child, a man, some animals, a tree, some leaves and fruits, the sky, the sun, and some objects such as an umbrella. The page has instructions to the teacher. On top are brief ones asking that the picture be colored and labeled. At the bottom is a longer set of instructions. Teachers are asked to engage children in a conversation, to ask them what the dog is doing, what the child is feeling, what the man might be saying. The teacher is asked to carry on further and discuss with the children if they like playing with animals? If they have seen birds on a tree? If their own grandfather uses a stick? Where could the scene be set?

Now, while all teachers will echo that the textbooks are the syllabus, and that they are duty bound to complete the syllabus, the teachers do not in fact bother with the teachers' instructions in the book. Why they do not is an interesting question. Answers include: one, following the instructions is simply too much work and requires effort. The responses are neither precise nor measurable, but could lead into any direction since the other party to this activity is an unpredictable child (or unpredictable children). So it is definitely not worth the unforeseeable amount of labor. In response to questions about their teaching strategies, most teachers immediately shift to talking about children's receptiveness. "We cannot plan anything because the children are not going to follow." "Why ever not?" (question from the interviewer)" "They are too energetic." "They have a destructive mentality." The exact qualities of the child that are supposed to be addressed as part of the teacher's job are the ones teachers cite, with naïve non-professionalism, as the forbidding traits of students that preclude the teachers in their direct, orderly work.

Two, the instructions are for "others," such as for elite schools and metropolitan children. The proof of something being exclusively for the elite is simply that "We don't do that." Why they don't is explained in turn with reference to the nature of the children. The families of the children are blamed for being too backward to let the children follow and participate *were* the teachers to take up any special activities in class. In one case, a teacher who prided himself on his innovativeness took up a project described in the textbook which required students to bring in some garbage from home. The majority did not. He complained, "These children are not really interested in their studies. No one brought in the garbage I asked them to. They just do not take any interest, and neither do their parents." A dearth of garbage! The impatient desire of the teacher to label his children and their families 'backward' for not following him along his creative project-oriented approach! Now the teacher, for every subsequent Social Studies project he did *not* undertake, had the ready explanation, "These children will not cooperate."

Finally the most common strategy is to nod in acceptance at the beginning of the meeting and then to quietly refrain from doing any of the work suggested in the teachers' instructions part of the books. Their alibi, if asked, is amazing in its perfect circularity: "We could not do it because the syllabus has to be finished."

Even more than the timetable, the syllabus is something akin to a god. When asked as to who had made it, none of the teachers could say except for 'The Board' or 'The government' or in some cases 'NCERT.'[4] When they were told they were wrong and the textbooks had been made by private people and private publishers, they were incredulous. They could not make the connection between a syllabus akin to a god, and the vision of someone ordinary sitting and writing a book, one of many authors. The godhood of the syllabus gets transmitted to the children. If there is any attempt by an innovative teacher to discuss, or engage in projects with the children, the odd child might ask, "When are we going to cover the syllabus?" and many children, who had not asked, might look up and nod as if they had been thinking that too. And guardians of course, live in the happy dream that if their children are busy *covering* the syllabus, all must be all right with them.

The eerie thing is that almost a century back, exactly the same situation reigned. McKee, author of *New Schools for Young India*, published in 1930, writes, "The daily time table and a syllabus for the work of each class and for each subject of study are usually prepared by the head teacher but are approved by the Government inspector. The time table is rigidly adhered to and the syllabus is often worked out by merely stating the pages of the textbook to be completed in a given time.... The methods used...still place the main emphasis upon securing such command of the material in the textbook as can be quickly and accurately given back to the teacher on demand. Examinations require this type of information and it often meets the requirement of inspectors.... Discipline is strict and often repressive. Generally, the quiet, orderly classroom, in which affairs happen more by mechanical, organized routine, receives recommendation" (1930: 64–65).

In conclusion, the vernacular school ranks higher for me because its reforming ambitions toward its society are ambitious on paper—each school's founding philosophy declares reform to be the goal—but modest in practice. It is critical of the family and community but totally rooted in it. All its policies, such as those regarding school dress, school hours, holidays, and activities, tend to be in line with community wishes and priorities. Its teaching, being in the mother tongue of the students, tends to be friendly and palatable. While studying there, neither the student nor his family get into a frenzy regarding all the future, competitive results that will result from his studies. But the student begins to feel deprived of choice. The feeling of being trapped grows in him, and turns into a permanent one, sometimes continuing into the next generation, thus effectively ensuring *their* entrapment.

THE IMITATION MISSIONARY AND THE PUBLIC SCHOOLS

Finally, the two topmost rungs of the ladder are occupied, respectively, by the imitation and the authentic, English medium, Christian missionary, or Public School. The authentic ones may be found only in the metropolises, large cities, and specially chosen locales such as hill stations. They produce a kind of modernity described by scholars such as

Sanjay Srivastava (1998) largely by distancing themselves from the rest of the population which they construct as responsible for the backwardness of the nation, a population supposed to be ignorant, illiterate, superstitious, communal, hierarchical, and so on. There are usually no examples of the highest ranked schools in small towns and cities, though that statement may be disputed by the imitation schools.

The imitation missionary and public schools are numerous and have names that suggest the models they emulate—Kashi Public School, St. Francis' Convent School, Glorious Academy, Little Flower House— and also the distance they want to maintain—Patanjali Vidyalaya, Aryan Global School. They are English medium like the missionary schools, but not Christian, and want, without saying as much, to follow in Annie Besant's footsteps of synthesizing "the best in Indian culture" with "Western science and the English language" (Kumar 1996). But with their untrained teachers and absence of philosophy on the questions of children and pedagogy, they are successfully deluged by the very surroundings that their "kind" of school (missionary, reformist) has historically been set up to counteract.

The physical plant of these schools is made to impress. The school is a product that competes for elite consumption with modern furniture, foods, and cosmetics. To be impressive the school is always massive and symmetrical in a familiar way. There are no small-scale, child-dimensional, innovatively designed schools in the top range. The idea would not sell, and in any case goes against the grain of their mission. The sign board is huge and the boundary walls are solid. The school is forbidding. There are rows of buses outside if the school provides transport, and private cars blocking the surrounding spaces at times of arrival and departure if the school does not. The air around, the very bricks and mortar, the landscaping and plants, every attendant staff member, and the rules for visitors, all resound with the proposition, "this is elite/exclusive/ privileged/select. You may enter only with permission, which is granted selectively." This works both to confirm the fact of their status for the families whose children attend the school, and equally, to dissuade others, specifically, ordinary, lower-class citizens, from even trying to enter such a school.

Top schools charge whatever fees are necessary to cover the costs. Academic School in Lucknow, for instance, has curtains and air conditioning in most classrooms, and impeccably uniformed support staff, so that the experience of the child is as close to the privileged home environment as possible. Along with that, the child must be subjected to discipline, required to perform, and held accountable for success. An interesting combination of curricular practices is worked out whereby the child is both client and protégé. When the play, *The Merchant of Venice*, was brought to the Academic School managers required the children to stay half an hour past the dismissal time. Believing they knew best, the school managers considered this play as necessary for the child's over-all growth. Then as the play exceeded the planned time by a few minutes, the managers became restless. They did not want to come across as 'wrong' by exceeding the time, as cars rolled up over the driveway to pick up their wards. The school managers' demeanor changed from "the school knows best" to "you must please the customer."

Although well organized and designed to impress, imitation missionary and public schools are always crowded. They vary in the store they set on impressing the customer and depending on the business acumen of their managers. But in all cases it is a performance. Vernacular schools have an identity based on the history of their founding, rootedness in the community and ties to the region and the nation. Imitation elite schools are not cited by anyone, including themselves, as having rootedness or tradition. Their identity comes from their market savviness, such as in their logo and their self-presentation. None of the devices they use, such as a room for media use, or a special sports outfit one day of the week, is based on appreciation for children's needs or a theory of learning. As the Principal of Shining Academy told me in response to my question about the huge success of his young, but large and growing, school, "I did my home-work. I studied the market."

THE AUTHENTIC MISSIONARY AND PUBLIC SCHOOLS

Christian missionary schools have a history going back to the early nineteenth century even before the establishment of state schools in the colonial period. From the beginning the Christian missionary schools have provided a model of good education in India. Their enviable structures of financial support, committed administrators, ongoing and unchallenged public reputation are the result of their painstaking dedication and belief in education from their initial years. With the exception of historians, few are cognizant of the longitudinal development of these missionary schools. As the number of missionaries, at least foreign ones, has declined, elite private schools, "public" schools after the British nomenclature, have shared, taken over, or supplemented the role of the missionary schools.

The campus of these schools, inside and outside, is perfectly clean and orderly. The buildings are spacious and spread out, often on scores or even hundreds of acres. There is an air to the school and its inhabitants of tradition and graciousness, of not trying too hard, of being to the manor born. The school makes a clear statement of efficiency, control, and of difference to the outside world where disorder and filth reigns. Students are made aware of this difference only indirectly. No part of the curriculum teaches students about social class, the history of difference, or exploitation and social injustice, or attempted solutions of reform, or mass resistance and revolt. Only with the vaguest of talk about 'them' and 'their' is the clean world of the school juxtaposed with the other world out there somewhere, and with assorted "social service" ventures.

There are always social service ventures, usually casual and random, but also through a specific curriculum unit called "SUPW" or "Socially Useful Productive Work." This unit, together with the social service activities, and the subject of Social Studies themselves, comprise the lost opportunity to teach elite children an identity of nationhood, where they could feel that they belong to the same nation as less privileged people. SUPW has devolved in almost all cases to nominal service such as a visit to a functioning charitable institution, and often to simple extra-curricular activities such as batik or crafts. Social service is organized in a club called, maybe, Gandhi Club, or teaching opportunities in a school for poor children called, maybe, Rainbow School. In neither case are elite children guided in how to think of the tasks they undertake: how to, in technical terms, actually teach or undertake projects with the underprivileged. They may have the best of intentions but, in the absence of orientation and preparation, the challenge is unsurpassable. The "others" remain mystifyingly different and distant. The "self" remains untouched and undisturbed. I willingly concede that the challenge of overcoming this distancing has shown itself to be staggering, even in the work of organizations such as "Teach for America" in the USA.[5]

As adults who went to elite schools attest, life for elite students could come to be more and more like a game to be viewed with bemusement. One becomes a global citizen before becoming a national citizen. Sasthi Brata (2008) writes

I prefer to stay above and beyond the slow meandering crowd of mediocrities around me. I have carried the feeling of hauteur on which we were generously fed at school well into my adult life. Yet the stance is as much a pose, a kind of protection against the vital onslaught of mere vulgarities.... I find it difficult to be meek and tolerant of my fellow beings. The result is often the false assurance of a clown.

To be intolerant of one's fellow beings is also to regard practices of caste, religion, and community solidarity as problems of others, describable as bigotry, ignorance, and superstition. "In the moral and intellectual world in which she was raised, an individual's caste and religion were completely irrelevant," we hear of a modern intellectual (Guha cited in Mehrotra 2008: 115). From the mid-nineteenth century onward the elite school has established a dichotomy between the English/Western and the indigenous/Indian. This is so stark and abstract that no one directly applies or practices this dichotomy. Yet this discourse serves to enfeeble attempts to conceptualize teaching in better ways and to defeat the more sensitive instincts and choices of people. In practice, almost all elite people in India believe in co-existing plural worlds, and exhibit plural identities that are both "modern" and "traditional." The discourse, however, keeps resounding around them and by them, that you are, can be, and must be one thing or the other. It is simply impossible that Dharma Kumar's world actually excluded "caste and religion," and we should think hard about why we must boast that it did.

Mr. Saxena is the principal of Kendriya Vidyalaya, a school run by the Central Government that is obliged to treat all children equally, regardless of class. In his talk with me, he disclosed with envy that successful schools, private and elite, admitted only those who had English-speaking parents, thus guaranteeing success in their educational efforts. His school could not be selective. Therefore he believed it was doomed to failure. Every educator and most lay people regarded the selective—that is, non-inclusive and discriminatory—schools as the model of an ideal school. The model, however, includes a model of the family as much as a model of the school. No one could describe, and in fact no one seems to be interested in, how the school conducts its classroom practices—except that it is authoritarian and makes strict demands on the family. Everyone is in awe of the fact that the family has to submit to all these demands, and if the family cannot cope, it has to get as much extra help from tutors as needed. It is the family–school relationship which seals the fate of such schools' exclusivity. A new discursive cycle is created. Because these top-ranking schools depend so heavily on the labor of the family, the family's contribution of their labor becomes the norm. The majority of families in India simply *cannot* thus labor. They lack the intellectual or the economic means to provide this labor. They are thus pre-defined, even before the child or the guardians attempt education, as failures in a spectrum from the utter failures at the bottom to the near-failures in the middle. The state, educators, public opinion, and the market all classify the children of these families and these families as different degrees of failures.

These elite schools are crucial to any study of education because they produce the leaders of India and are directly responsible for what is wrong with Indian education. One could be so bold as to say that the reform of these elite schools would improve education for the masses.

There is a curious disjuncture and curious coming together of these two kinds of schools that together form the top rungs of the ladder and the three that form the bottom rungs. The way they all come together is through adherence to what is also called an "idealist curriculum." Education should consist of time-tested classics. Education should pre-pare students for adult life, both with actual skills, and with the culture of wanting to learn and develop. Teachers and students are different: the former are mature and knowledgeable; the latter immature but with a desire to learn (Gutek 2004). This is an old-style formal school model with set courses of study, high expectations of authoritarian discipline, and didactic teacher-centered pedagogy.

In the absence of a "progressivist revolution" in education in India, all schools are still innocent of progressivist discourse and practice, with the exception of some international schools and the rare elite or NGO schools modeled on international ones. A "progressive curriculum" would be a child-centered, activity-based one in which much of the impelling force that led to both the discipline and the learning, came from the students. As opposed to the idealist curriculum, a progressive curriculum is not bound by classics or canons, is open to questioning and revision, and presumes that political questioning shall always guide it. The ironical thing is that once in a while one glimpses a more inter-active, even arts-centered effort to teach in the progressive mode not in the "best" elite schools, but in a Municipal or an NGO school specifi-cally designated as "for the poor." But even while theater directors and arts teachers are considered to have special skills or abilities to reach out to children, and "creative methods" to be unmatched in overcoming the boredom and resistance to learning, elite schools believe that these teachers and methods suit underprivileged children and not their own.

Of a unified set of all Indian schools, the better-regarded, top ones are those that are the most formal and efficient in sticking to the agenda, with tighter discipline and higher authoritarian standards. The worse-functioning, lower-scale schools are the ones who cannot perform as well, albeit the agenda is the same. In this unifying agenda, there is a significant disjuncture between the top two and the bottom three kinds of schools also, one that makes or breaks the student's career. This consists of the different degrees to which families are involved in students' education. As scholars have pointed out (Lancy 2008), it was the emergence of universal schooling as the *sine qua non* of childhood that opened up the divide between the haves and the have-nots. The demands of formal schooling led families, especially mothers, to shoulder the burden for the children. All over the world, and certainly in India, educational policy and structure has evolved toward a model where children are rewarded whose families "own the cultural routines that are effective" (Lancy 2008: 307). Other students either do badly, or they fail, as we have seen in the case of the Municipal schools, the small English medium schools and the Vernacular school.

We must not credit the excellence of the students from elite schools to their curriculum. The curriculum of the schools which was the subject of my research—Loreto in Lucknow and Calcutta, La Martiniere Girls' in Calcutta, Delhi Public School in Varanasi, and Krishnamurthy Foundation of India in Varanasi—, would not merit mention in a world-wide discussion of progressive curriculum. The schools achieve their success because the families have already supplied, and continue to supply, their wards with both a core and even models of intellectual, social, economic, psychological, and discursive resources. The importance of the family has been unrecognized in modern Indian education. The family arranges activities and provides resources supplementary to the hyper-classical and disciplined education in the school to produce a seemingly progressive, liberal arts education. Elite children look as if they came from really rich educational backgrounds, but in reality they come from rich or hard-working, self-denying families that supplement the schools' work. Their children's education has been an aggregate of the work of the school and the family.

THE TECHNOLOGY AND THE POLITICS

To comment on the recent changes in Indian education, we should separate our discussion into two related areas. In technology, which means all the techniques, resources and processes for instruction used in schools, including spatial configurations, teaching techniques, and symbols, there has been only surface change. A change in the concept of the school building to make it less authoritarian and more child-centered has not occurred; only a surface painting and brightening of the building has been proposed. As Kamod Sharma, the Principal of a Municipal School in Mussoorie put it, "Make it colourful. *Jo dikhega vo bikega* (the more striking it is, the more it will sell)." Classrooms are "smartened" including with the introduction of more computers, laptops, and overhead projectors. Gullible guardians feel that their children are definitely on the road to progress, but this is just a variant of the older idea that the syllabus is covered because the textbook has been thumbed through. No matter how we look at it, no paradigmatic shift has occurred in pedagogical technology. The curriculum of Indian schools remains the same over the thirty or so years of my research.

The other technology, that of mobile phones and the internet, at first sight promises to be an equalizer since the availability of information, privacy, connectivity, and so on, does not automatically rise with income between the lower middle, middle, and upper classes. My hypothesis, which definitely deserves further research, is that technology itself improves neither the life prospects nor the self-image of success. No technological device or process has replaced the decisive factor of a strong educational foundation in reading, writing, and Math that guarantees access to higher studies, then to jobs and social mobility. The gap in this educational base between the different rungs of the hierarchy of schools has only widened so that the image of Municipal and small private schools is even poorer than thirty years ago, and that of elite schools even grander.

The politics of the Indian educational system has become more deeply problematic. From its inception, it has been based on a harsh hierarchy of social and cultural-symbolic reproduction which has remained unchanged. Indeed, there is not a crack in this reproductive cycle. There is greater cynicism and more technical finesse in ways to keep out unwanted aspirants. The aspiring classes who want social mobility and glimpse its possibilities through education are kept forever aspiring. Their belief in progress—always in the form of "Our lives are better than our parents' lives"—is really no more than an illusion limited to statistical improvement in technology and lifestyle over time. There is no paradigmatic shift toward greater equality or democracy. On the contrary, the distance between the rich and the poor, the high and the low in terms of social capital, has expanded, and the discourse of "us" and "them" within schooling has likewise become more entrenched. In this, teachers are of course complicit, but only complicit and not solely responsible. The apparent expansion of democracy in India, through consumerism and the performance of modernity, produces a threat to privilege. Educated classes, including teachers, respond to this clear, if unnamed, threat by quietly making sure that the gap between them and the illiterate remains real, both through language and action.

The RTE, or the Right to Education Act, 2009, could also, similarly, be seen to be a potential equalizer, in that randomly selected students from working class families who could never afford to pay the fees of elite schools are now in a position to study in these schools because of the government's imposition on such schools to hold a few seats for these students. I am sure that some students are able to avail of this possibility. My research revealed, however, that all the elite schools I was studying used the devious method of running a parallel school for the underprivileged. They met the government's new requirement through subterfuge. They simply siphoned off some resources to fulfill the letter of the law and not its spirit. The working-class children and the middle- and upper-class children are still resolutely separate today and the same logic is still articulated by educators as for the past thirty years, "*Of course* these children cannot study together." To give Principal Sharma the last word in his combined but perfectly descriptive Hindi-English, "*Hamari ummiden kuchh zyada ho gayi hain* (Our expectations have become somewhat excessive)—that all children should be the same. All cannot be equal." But I would rather keep the last word for myself, in my educator-leader mode. I would like to suggest three methods, out of a few possible, that would enable us to break out of the reproductive cycle of hierarchy.

All three of these ways overlap and scaffold each other. One, teachers have to learn through lectures, discussions, research, and writing, about their place in the larger scheme of things. The teacher in India was not always weak, as practically she is today. The teacher was also the victim of changes in the colonial period, changes which could be reversed. The teacher's problem today is not a cultural or ideological one as much as it is historical and political. This pedagogic approach must be smart and interactive, unlike in teachers' B.Ed. training, which is an exercise in learning to pass tests.

Two, the teachers must be given concrete strategies, resources, and solutions regarding the difficulties of teaching first generation learners. Instead of dismissing difficult students, they would then feel empowered to deal with them in productive ways. And three, the teachers must be made to work with their bodies through specific games and exercises, as in theatre and dance, that would make them experience—that is, feel convinced—that they have the power to change themselves, their surroundings, their relationships, their status, and their work.

NOTES

1. Among many authors on the subject, Anyon (1980), Bowles and Gintis (1976), Gordon (1982), Jachim (1987), Martin (1976), Vallance (1982). The hidden curriculum has been extensively discussed in Western educational literature from the 1970s, but curiously, not so much in the context of India.

2. Chapter 3 in my forthcoming *Educating the Child: The Family–School Relationship in India* deals solely with teachers.

3. Over thirty plus years, I have observed such schools in East and West UP, in Rajasthan, and in Uttarakhand, and visited some in Gujarat and West Bengal. My most recent data is from Uttarakhand and eastern UP. In my observations, I have sometimes generalized and sometimes mentioned particular instances, and have focused mostly on Primary and Junior High Schools.

4. The NCERT, as popularly known, stands for the National Council of Educational research and Training, a decades-old autonomous body set up by the government to, somewhat ambiguously, produce textbooks, conduct research and training on various aspects of education, and generally monitor quality in Indian education together with an effort at equity between social classes.

5. There is a vast literature on the failure of American schools to bridge the class and the race divide. I will mention only two favorite books, Noguera (2008) and Zimmerman (2002).

REFERENCES

Anyon, Jean. 1980. Social Class and the Hidden Curriculum of Work. *The Journal of Education* 162 (1): 67–92.

Bowles, Samuel, and Herbert Gintis. [1976] 2011. *Schooling in Capitalist America: Educational Reforms and the Contradictions of Economic Life.* Chicago: Haymarket Books, reprint.

Brata, Sasthi. 2008. My God Died Young. In *Recess: The Penguin Book of Schooldays*, ed. Palash Krishna Mehrotra, 156–161. New Delhi: Penguin Books.

Devdas. Film. 1955. Produced by Bimal Roy.

Gordon, D. 1982. The Concept of the Hidden Curriculum. *Journal of the Philosophy of Education* 16 (2): 187–198.

Gutek, Gerald L. 2004. *Philosophical and Ideological Voices in Education.* Boston, NY: Pearson.

Jachim, Nancy. 1987. The Hidden Curriculum. *A Review of General Semantics* 44 (1): 83–85.

Kumar, Nita. 1996. Religion and Ritual in Indian Schools: Banaras from the 1880s to the 1940s. In *The Transmission of Knowledge in South Asia*, ed. Nigel Crook, 135–154. Delhi: Oxford University Press.

Lancy, David F. 2008. *The Anthropology of Childhood: Cherubs, Chattels, Changelings.* Cambridge: Cambridge University Press.

McKee, William J. 1930. *New Schools for Young India: A Survey of Educational, Economic, and Social Conditions in India with Special Reference to More Effective Education.* Chapel Hill: The University of North Carolina Press.

Martin, J.R. 1976. What Should We Do with a Hidden Curriculum When We Find One? *Critical Inquiry* 6 (2): 135–152.

Mehrotra, Palash Krishna (ed.). 2008. *Recess: The Penguin Book of Schooldays.* New Delhi: Penguin Books.

Noguera, Pedro A. 2008. *The Trouble with Black Boys...and Other Reflections on Race, Equity and the Future of Public Education.* San Francisco: Jossey-Bass.

Srivastava, Sanjay. 1998. *Constructing Post-Colonial India: National Character and the Doon School.* London and New York: Routledge.

Vallance, Elizabeth. 1982. The Hidden Curriculum and Qualitative Inquiry as States of Mind. *Journal of Education* 162 (1): 138–151.

Willis, Paul. 1981. *Learning to Labour: How Working Class Kids Get Working Class Jobs.* New York: Columbia University Press.

Zimmerman, Jonathan. 2002. *Whose America? Culture Wars in the Public Schools.* Cambridge, MA: Harvard University Press.

CHAPTER 12

A Little Learning: Women, Men, and Schools in Rural Sri Lanka

Deborah Winslow

INTRODUCTION

Literacy rates in Sri Lanka have long been impressive: 67% at Independence in 1948 (UNICEF 2010: 193) and 92% in a 2016 UNICEF report (UNICEF 2016). Furthermore, the gap between rates for males and females has narrowed steadily. In 1881, the differential was 26.7% (Dept. of Census and Statistics 1997: 108), while UNICEF found 3% overall and zero for youth under 24 (UNICEF 2016). Early gains were the fruit of British colonial policy, which, in theory, sought "to provide an elementary vernacular education for every child" (Wickremeratne 1970: 87). This ideal was more fully realized after the introduction of universal adult suffrage in 1931 and the right to a free education soon thereafter. A subsequent flurry of new school construction in the early and mid-twentieth century made education much more widely available, particularly in rural areas.

This chapter examines the relationship between gender and the early spread of schools in rural Sri Lanka. Using data from my longitudinal

D. Winslow (✉)
National Science Foundation, Washington, DC, USA

© The Author(s) 2019
H. E. Ullrich (ed.), *The Impact of Education in South Asia*, Anthropological Studies of Education,
https://doi.org/10.1007/978-3-319-96607-6_12

271

study of a Sinhalese potter village in the Kurunegala District, I focus on the period from 1900 to 1960. National statistics nicely document Sri Lanka's steady educational progress but they cannot reveal how the process played out at the community level. Schools could not be built everywhere at once. The resulting patchiness of access meant that in Sinhalese villages, where one spouse (usually, the bride) often relocates after marriage to the other spouse's village, there was a period when one partner in a marriage had the opportunity to attend school while the other did not. Interestingly, given the South Asian context, it appears that it did not matter if the result was a bride having more education than her husband. As noted by one writer, "Parents and the community in general have a positive attitude to the education of girls" (Jayaweera 1985: 50). However, my data show that in the early years a "positive attitude" was insufficient to assure that girls and boys were equally educated.

Writers on education in Sri Lanka often have pointed to a gender gap in literacy (Sri Lanka 1997: 108). Others have lamented the poor quality and short duration of rural education generally (see, for example, Diaz 1995: 52). Here, my concern is not with the deficiencies of rural schools compared to urban ones, or vernacular-language government schools compared to English-medium elite institutions. Those are important and much considered topics (see, for example, Jayasuriya 1976: 535ff.), which certainly have had consequences for rural communities. But my focus here is more fundamental: how and when did the most basic schooling, which produces at least elementary skills in literacy and numeracy, first come into a rural community? And how did women's access compare to that of men? Observers of rural Sri Lanka have been ambivalent about the relative status of women and men (Stirrat 1988: 89–96). But in this community of Potters, where women work alongside their husbands, women's worth has never been in question (Winslow 1994). Schooling is part of that story.

EDUCATION IN EARLY TWENTIETH CENTURY SRI LANKA

In his well-known review of the census of 1911, Edward Brandis Denham, the Superintendent of the Census, observed, "One of the most remarkable features of the decade (1901–1911) has been the rush into education" (Denham 1912: 399). A practical man who later became Governor of Jamaica, Denham attributed this rush in part to the building of schools. Remarkably, in the Kurunegala District, where my study village is located, the number of schools increased almost 90% in just ten years, from 106 in 1901 to 198 in 1911 (Denham 1912: 405).[1] Correspondingly, the average distance between schools was reduced by more than a quarter, from 5.71 miles to 4.18 miles (Denham 1912: 405).[2]

Like many of his contemporaries, Denham had a strong interest in women's education.[3] He took pride in the fact that even at this early date, "Ceylon [is] ... far in advance of India; there are nearly four times as many male literates and ten times as many female literates in Ceylon as in India" (Denham 1912: 423). In his analysis of the 1911 census data, Denham described a growing demand for women's schools and the narrowing gap between male and female literacy rates, which he helpfully broke down by religion. The previous census of 1901 had found that Buddhist males had a literacy rate of 59.7%, which was 14 points higher than the 45.6 rate for females. One decade later, the gap had narrowed to 9.3%: the male rate had increased from 3 to 61.7% and the female rate showed an impressive 15% increase to 52.4% (Denham 1912: 429, Table O).

Denham's relatively happy view of education in Sri Lanka in the first decade of the twentieth century is not shared by all scholars. J.A. Jayasuriya, formerly Professor of Education at the University of Ceylon, Peradeniya, and a distinguished authority on British-period educational policy, drew a quite different picture of the same period. Where Denham underscored improvements, Jayasuriya enumerated a glass-half-empty litany of failings: underfunded government schools; continued dominance of denominational grant-in-aid (that is, government subsidized) schools; limited Sinhala and Tamil curricula; unenforced compulsory attendance laws; and "class bias" that supported better education for the elite English-speaking urban minority than for the rural Tamil or Sinhala-speaking majority (Jayasuriya 1976: 405–408).

After 1920, however, even Jayasuriya found signs of improvement in British support for education, although it was never, he wrote, "sufficiently distinguished in its contribution to the life and well-being of the people as to warrant bouquets of thanks" (Jayasuriya 1976: 543). The Education Ordinance of 1920 shored up funding for public education by moving the responsibility from local authorities to the central government (Jayasuriya 1976: 535). After franchise became universal in 1931, the now enlarged and more representative electorate was able to force the government to accede to the popular demand for free education from kindergarten through university. However, the system's old dualisms persisted throughout the colonial period. Rural schools continued to offer only a basic core curriculum with little thought for preparing rural students for education beyond the primary level; and other than a few teaching training schools, opportunities for vocational education were limited, as well (Jayasuriya 1976: 535–536; Jayaweera 1973: 466, 472–473).

Nonetheless, schools continued to be built and literacy rates continued to rise, as documented by subsequent censuses. By Independence in 1948, there was a school every 8 square miles, compared to approximately one every 14 square miles in Denham's time (Central Bank of Sri Lanka 1998: 68). The 1946 census, the final one carried out before Independence, did not disaggregate education data by religion and ethnicity, so we cannot make a direct comparison to Denham's figures. Nonetheless, it did report overall literacy rates, merging all religions and ethnicities. For the Kurunegala District, these figures show a 21.7% improvement for males (from 60.3 to 72.5%) and an astonishing 233% improvement for females (from 12 to 39.9%) between 1921 and 1946 (Ranasinha 1950: 189).[4] Thus Denham's 1911 account, which portrayed widespread local enthusiasm for education as schools spread through the countryside, is a useful backdrop for understanding the early years of schooling in the Kurunegala District village, Walangama.[5]

WALANGAMA

Walangama is a Sinhalese Buddhist community located in the middle of the Kurunegala District. Most Walangama residents are of Potter caste (*Kumbal* or *Badahäla*)[6] and pottery production and sales have long been key elements of the village economy. Non-Potters, but never the Potters themselves, may consider Potters to be a lower caste (Ryan 1993 [1953]: 94). But because Sinhalese villages are typically single-caste, caste-based interactions are few and notions of hierarchy tend to be vague. "Caste without a caste system," is how one historian described it (Peebles 1995: 45). In general, scholars regard the Sinhalese Buddhist caste system as less onerous than the Indian Hindu version (e.g., Ryan 1993 [1953]: 21). It is not, for example, associated with notions of pollution (*killa*) nor does a traditional caste occupation limit ownership of productive resources such as agricultural land. Some caste discrimination does exist, but it plays only a small part in my story.

The west-central region where Walangama is located is a transitional area between Sri Lanka's wet and dry zones. Rainfall is too variable for irrigated rice agriculture to be reliable as a sole subsistence strategy. When I first knew Walangama in the mid-1970s, most households supported themselves by combining pottery making, vegetable gardening, growing dry grains in swiddens, and, if they had access to land, wet rice farming.[7] This multi-pronged approach had old roots. In the 1880s, the acting government agent of the region, G.S. Williams, visited a Potter community near Walangama while touring the devastated region during an extended drought. Williams had been offering villagers "relief work," opportunities for participating in public works projects in return for food, but the potters he visited were not interested. They told him that they could "...live by their pottery," which complemented the stores of rice from their fields and millet from their swiddens (Williams 1885: 110A).

However, by Independence in 1948, this flexible system for making a living was at a breaking point. Walangama had recovered from the devastating malaria epidemics of the 1930s, which, in the Kurunegala region, claimed almost three-fourths of the newborns and many of their mothers. The resulting population increase was not matched by new land for either housing or farming. Then the village lost access to swidden land when the colonial government sold it to Colombo investors for coconut estates (Wickremeratne 1973: 432–438; Winslow 2016: 218). I remember well how older residents described Walangama life in the 1940s: crowded, mud-walled houses that were noisy with too many children; no land to grow food; and pottery sales that were insufficient to fill the economic gaps. Fortunately, the situation improved soon after Independence. In 1949, the local Member of Parliament helped the village to develop a pottery marketing co-operative, which quickly increased both production and sales. Soon thereafter, he assisted them in acquiring adjacent land for housing (Winslow 2003: 56–57). This new balance, which emphasized pottery more than ever, supported the community well through the austere years of the closed import-substitution economy in the 1970s (Winslow 2016: 217–218).

Women appear always to have played a central role in pottery making in Walangama. As pottery increased in importance in the household economy, so did women's contributions. In contrast to most of India, Sinhalese[8] potters in Sri Lanka have no proscriptions that limit women's participation. Hindu women in India generally are forbidden to use the true potters' wheel, considered sacred to the deity Shiva. When menstruating, they must separate out even their hand-formed pots in the kiln (Winslow 1994). But neither restriction applies to Sinhalese Buddhist potter women in Sri Lanka. Both Walangama women and men dig and process clay from abundant local deposits; form pots on potter's wheels; do final shaping with paddle and anvil; and stack and fire the pots in open pit kilns. It was only men and boys who took the long bullock cart trips north to trade pottery for grain in the harvest season but both men and women carried their wares to local weekly markets throughout the year. Furthermore, as this nuclear household-based industry expanded, men and women each had their own co-operative accounts and, thereby, separate incomes. Women attended and spoke out at co-op meetings. They seem always to have had an active, recognized, and important role in household and community.

I do not mean to suggest that there were no gender-based differences in Walangama (Winslow 1994). Gender is certainly as much a social organizing principle there as it is anywhere. But women are not viewed as inferior to men and I have never heard or observed a preference for male over female children; when I asked directly, my village informants denied partiality. But there were areas where men and women behaved differently, such as those having to do with mobility. Work and play seemed to keep women and girls closer to home and, consequently, they had less intimate knowledge of the far reaches of village geography than did men and boys. Other than for group pilgrimages, which left out no one who had the funds, time, and physical capability, women and girls also were less likely than men and boys to travel long distances away from the village although there were some exceptions to this general pattern. For example, a few women pottery traders traveled with their husbands to the far reaches of the island and women were quick to undertake hospital visits or seek out specialist practitioners on their own.

Given that girls and boys are equally welcomed and women and men are equally respected, it is not surprising that as schools spread in the Kurunegala District, both boys and girls attended.

EDUCATION IN WALANGAMA

The first time I thought about the early years of Walangama schooling was in 2013. I was again in the village and visiting Raninachiri, then eighty-three and a widow living with her married daughter. Raninachiri had first moved to Walangama in 1946 as a sixteen-year-old bride, following in the footsteps of her older sister, Punchihami, by marrying

Punchihami's husband's younger brother. Double in-law marriages, where siblings marry siblings, are not uncommon in Walangama, a natural outcome of bilateral cross-cousin marriage, Dravidian kin-terms, and a strong preference for living among kin. Punchihami died in 2003, but I had lived with her in the 1970s and knew her to be illiterate; I had always assumed her sister was, too. Therefore, Raninachiri surprised me when she said that she herself had gone to school for four years, and certainly could read and write. Puzzled, I asked, "But Punchihami? She couldn't, could she?" And Raninachiri explained: "That's right. That school was not built in her time. But I came later."

This brief exchange made me reconsider what I really knew about literacy and Walangama's oldest residents. How much had I assumed just from seeing the X's and thumbprints on the signature lines of old co-op receipts or watching great-grandchildren read aloud to their elders? I recalled that Punchihami's husband, born about 1918, had once been the co-op's manager, so he must have been literate. Then I remembered the old woman who led the prayers at Goddess rituals while reading from a printed text; and a friend's mother, born in 1924, a pottery trader alongside her illiterate husband, telling me she had gone to school for an impressive eight years. Once I put my mind to it, in fact, I could think of several of the oldest Walangama residents, both men and women, who were able to read and write. So I set upon a systematic review of notes from earlier periods of fieldwork to see if I could construct an overall picture. Who was more typical, literate Raninachiri, born in 1930, or Punchihami, born ten years earlier? Who had access to schools when, and who actually went?

My field notes did not have schooling information for everyone but I was able to extract data for 120 women and 137 men out of conversations with 364 people held between 1974 and 2004.[9] This information, broken down by birth decade and by gender, is summarized in the Table 12.1 and Fig. 12.1.

My data, while not sufficiently complete to support calculation of meaningful overall literacy rates, reveal some clear and interesting patterns. Most obviously, we see the expected growth over time in schooling for both men and women. Despite being lower caste rural farmers and artisans, the Potters apparently shared in the early enthusiasm for going to school that characterized the district as a whole. However, if we look more closely we can see that the rise is not uniform. There is, first, a dip, in parallel for males and females, in the second decade of the series,

Table 12.1   Years of schooling, by decade of birth and gender

Birth decade	Schooling known, female (N)	Schooling known, male (N)	Average schooling female (yrs.)	Average schooling, male (yrs.)
1901–1910	3	3	1.3	3.7
1911–1920	11	11	0.8	2.5
1921–1930	15	14	2.2	3.2
1931–1940	14	19	2.8	4.5
1941–1950	24	28	6.2	6.8
1951–1960	53	62	8.2	7.4

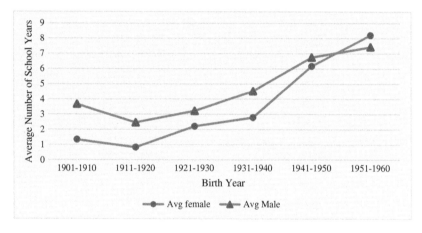

Fig. 12.1   Average years of schooling by decade and gender

the period 1911–1920. Children born during that time would have been of school-going age during the late 1920s and the 1930s, a time when the region was characterized by "drought, crop failure, and a devastating malaria epidemic ... in the wake of the Great Depression" (Meegama 2012: 268). We can assume that these conditions set school attendance back, but only temporarily. After 1920, each successive decade sees the average years of schooling go up. After 1930, however, there is a second anomaly: the rise for women is steeper than for men until, for my interviewees born in the period 1951–1960, women overtake and pass men in years of school attendance.

Table 12.2 Mode, median, and range of years of schooling, by decade and gender

Birth decade	Mode (yrs.)		Median (yrs.)		Range (yrs.)	
	F	M	F	M	F	M
1901–1910	0	2	0	2	4	7
1911–1920	0	4 and 5	0	3	6	8
1921–1930	0	5	0	4	8	8
1931–1940	0	5	4	5	9	13
1941–1950	0	5	6	7	13	11
1951–1960	11	8	8	8	15	16

Although the averages show interesting trends, like all averages they also conceal internal variation. To get at the hidden variability, we turn to the mode, median, and range of years of schooling (Table 12.2).

A *mode* is the number that occurs most frequently in a set of numbers. The number of years of schooling that occurred most frequently for women in each decade is zero, right up until the final decade when it jumps to eleven years. Despite the rising average, a *typical* girl had no schooling at all. But the *median* and *range* add more detail to this picture and do so in interesting ways. From the median, we can see that by the 1930s, a typical girl in this group might not have been in school at all but half of the girls were going to school for four years or more, just one year less than the median for boys. So from the beginning, there was considerable variability in school attendance for girls, and it was more so than for boys. The figures for *range*[10] emphasize this point by telling us the difference between the girls with the most education and the girls with the least. Even in the earliest decade, the range was four years and by the 1950s, it was fifteen years as a few village girls went on to take national advanced-level exams.

This look at internal variability provides two important insights. The first is that even as schools were becoming more widespread and schooling was on the rise, many Potter children, particularly girls, were not attending at all. On the other hand, the medians and ranges reveal that there also were some girls who were in school from the earliest decades and often for comparatively long periods of time. This second point makes it hard to sustain an argument that schooling for girls was not valued. So why were the patterns for the women and men so different?

Also, Walangama did not have a school until the 1950s, so where did this early schooling take place? The answers to these questions turn out to be linked.

The men in my sample, almost all of whom were born in Walangama, were educated in a variety of places. Some told me that they were taught by monks, either informally or in *pansala* (monastery) schools. Others walked to towns several miles away where they had to sit at the back or just outside of multi-caste classrooms. One man, whose family was for a while Catholic, boarded in a convent school. But these options were not available to girls: they could not be taught by monks and were not expected to walk even the three miles to the nearest town school much less live away from home. So women born before 1941 who went to school were like Raninachiri. They grew up in villages that had schools and only settled in Walangama later as brides. Interestingly, they all came from a cluster of four small pottery-producing communities[11] that happened to lie near commercial junctions, where some of the first schools in this region were located.

One result of the patchy availability of schools in the early years was that there was frequently educational inequality between spouses; interestingly, it seems to have gone both ways. Some Walangama men who did not attend school married women who did. Conversely, women who had grown up in Walangama or who came from villages equally remote and without schools might marry men who had at least some schooling. These discrepancies are summarized in the following bar graph (Fig. 12.2).

For each decade, the bar is divided into three portions. The bottom portion represents couples where the wife's years of schooling exceeded her husband's; the middle portion, couples where husband and wife had equal years of schooling; and the top portion, couples where the husband's years of schooling exceeded his wife's. In the first three decades, husbands' years of schooling were always greater; in the 1931–1940 decade, the three measures are about equal; and in the last two decades, women increasingly have more education than their husbands. It was in the 1940s that a school opened in a village right next to Walangama, and that is when we see the first big uptick in women's schooling. This is true both for the overall averages (Fig. 12.1) and for wives' education relative to that of their husbands' (Fig. 12.2). The second uptick occurs for girls who grew up in Walangama after it got its own school in the 1950s.

I have been told various versions of the Walangama school's history but the gist of it seems to be that a group of village leaders approached

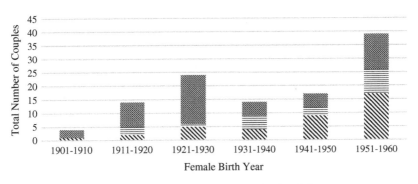

Fig. 12.2 Which spouse has more years of schooling?

representatives of the Education Ministry to request a school. They were told that if they started one on their own, as permitted by the ordinances, then the government could step in and take it over "to educate the village children," as my most knowledgeable source, Vijayasooriya, puts it. So they did. At the beginning, it was a modest affair. Vijayasooriya's older brother, who had some education but no certification or training as a teacher, started instructing young children in a room in his house. Meanwhile, Vijayasooriya went off to do a teacher's training course. When he returned, Vijayasooriya said he hesitated to step in because he had become a stalwart of the Sri Lanka Freedom Party (SLFP) while the village predominantly supported the United National Party. "I let two others do the teaching," he recalled. But two years later, the government was dominated by Vijayasooriya's party, the SLFP. It did take the school over and on October 1, 1959, Vijayasooriya joined as a government employee. Land was acquired and a proper school building was put up soon afterwards.

Walangama's school was very much a school not just in the village but also of it. Vijayasooriya described himself as a strict schoolmaster and, later, school principal. "When children failed to show up, I didn't mark them absent, I went round to their house with a cane and they ran to school!" He remembered that one woman had covered her boys with a mat. He lifted the mat and the boys ran to school. He said that parents tried to keep older children back to look after the younger ones. "It was boys they kept back, not girls. The girls were too afraid to skip school!" Villagers seem always to have been enthusiastic school supporters, doing fund raising, showing up for special events, and helping out where needed. Today, the school is ranked second in the district for student performance on national exams.

Once they had easy access, girls did indeed go to school. I heard no stories from women about not being allowed. But both women and men told me tales of school careers shortened by poverty. One man, who had been pulled out early, said he was one of eleven children and his parents struggled to educate them all. Like others, he remembered having to do all his work on a slate because they could not afford books or paper. Both men and women also spoke of their schooling being interrupted by family trauma such as parental illness, death, divorce, or a financial downturn that meant older children were needed to work and contribute to the support of younger siblings. A man who never married spoke with pride of leaving school early so he could earn money to keep his sister in school through university. For others, childhood illnesses interfered with going as far in school as they would have liked: deafness from an ear infection; cognitive impairment from Japanese encephalitis; a bad limp from polio. But there was nothing in these stories that spoke of one gender being favored over the other.

CONCLUSION

Sri Lanka is an outlier in South Asia. It not only has the highest overall literacy rates for both males and females, it also has the lowest birth rate, the lowest infant and maternal mortality rates, and the highest per capita income. As summarized by a recent World Bank Report, "Sri Lanka has made significant progress in human development. Social indicators rank among the highest in South Asia and compare favorably with those in middle-income countries" (World Bank 2017). Nonetheless, some social scientists who have done fine-grained studies of rural Sinhalese communities in Sri Lanka have reported that there continues to be an expectation of female domestic subordination, whether because of tradition (e.g., Gamburd 2008: Chapter 5; Stirrat 1988: 89) or colonial discrimination (Risseeuw 1988: Chapters 1–3). At the same time, these studies also detail considerable female power and autonomy.

The information I gleaned from my field notes might be deployed to argue that in the early decades of the twentieth century, the education of Sinhalese Buddhist boys was favored over the education of Sinhalese Buddhist girls. But, as I have explained, these data also support the view that education was sought equally for both. Innovations are more likely to face resistance when they threaten "entrenched patterns of social relations" (Centola 2018: 15). There were no entrenched social relations that worked against the education of little Sinhalese girls. I suggest that this early culture of gender evenhandedness in education set the stage for the equality observed today.

Nonetheless, little Walangama boys, like little boys in most places (Mitra et al. 2014: 3414), did have greater freedom to wander beyond the protective borders of the village itself than did girls. This one factor, rather than ideas about either the desirability or the possibility of girls' education, is sufficient to explain the marked differences in average years of schooling for women and men in the earliest decades of my data. Even now the people I talked with seemed to regard little boys of five, six, or even seven years as better able than little girls to take care of themselves, to endure long walks, and, more generally, to be safe. There were then, as there are today, objective dangers: pythons, lightning strikes, and poisonous snakes are perpetual hazards. There may also have been anxieties about strangers since the town school was located at a commercial junction and I was told one story about a boy who died as a result of being mugged while walking home from this school. But once Walangama girls had a school nearby and especially after there was one in the community itself, girls were quick to take advantage and their families did not stand in their way. Today, even inequality in mobility is fading. As older Walangama children are successful in the competition for places in better town schools, girls are as likely as their brothers to be boarding the buses to take them there.

Acknowledgements The author was employed by the National Science Foundation (NSF) when writing this chapter. The NSF also supported part of the research through a senior research award (BCS-9246632) and a Long Term Professional Development Leave (2013). Additional funding came from the United States–Sri Lanka Fulbright Commission (2013), the American Institute for Sri Lankan Studies (2004), and the University of New Hampshire. Any opinion, findings, or conclusions expressed here are those of the author and do not necessarily reflect the views of the NSF or any of my other funders. I also am grateful to the School for Advanced Research, which has provided space and support during several summers of data analysis, and to Fatima J. Touma for her assistance in preparing the figures. Finally, I extend warm thanks to Dr. Helen Ullrich, the editor of this volume, whose tireless efforts have made it possible.

NOTES

1. These are schools that receive government support, which include both local schools run by the government (usually for education through vernacular languages) and private schools, often run by religious institutions that receive government subvention.

2. Denham calculated the distance between schools with the artificial assumption that schools were equally distributed over the district territory. He argued that even though this is clearly not the case, the results allow useful comparisons over time and between provinces (Denham 1912: 404–405).

3. An interesting example of British interest in women's education is Samuel Langdon's novel for young adults, *Punchi Nona: A Story of Female Education and Village Life in Ceylon* (1884). Langdon was a Methodist missionary who, along with his wife, was one of the founders of Kandy Girls High School in 1879, which is still considered to be one of the country's best schools (Harris 2006: 101).

4. These overall figures include Muslim and Hindus, which is why they are lower than the rates cited earlier. The earlier rates included only Buddhists.

5. Walangama, which literally means Pottery Village, is my pseudonym for this community.

6. *Badahäla* is the traditional Sinhala name for the Potter caste. *Kumbal*, the Potters' preferred term, may have its origin as a loan word from Tamil.

7. As the village population grew and the agricultural land base did not, pottery making has increased in importance (Winslow 2009). Today, with a population of around 1000 people, about two-thirds of Walangama households depend primarily on pottery (Winslow 2016).

8. The Sri Lankan population comprises multiple ethnic and religious groups. The majority Sinhalese, who are primarily Buddhist, comprise 74.9%; Tamils, primarily Hindu, comprise 15.4%; and Muslims, who also speak Tamil, comprise 9.2% (Sri Lanka 2012: 68).

9. In 1975–1976 and in 1992, I conducted extended informal and semi-structured interviews in over 90% of all households. In 2004, my sample was opportunistic and much smaller, reaching perhaps a quarter of all households.

10. I am using the word range in the technical sense of the differences between the highest and the lowest number.

11. These are Bäddegama, Rukmale, Yahalagedera, and Nungamuva.

REFERENCES

Centola, Damon. 2018. *How Behavior Spreads: The Science of Complex Contagions.* Princeton: Princeton University Press.

Central Bank of Sri Lanka. 1998. *Economic Progress of Independent Sri Lanka.* Colombo: Central Bank of Sri Lanka.

Denham, E.B. 1912. *Ceylon at the Census of 1911: The Review of the Results of the Census of 1911.* Colombo: H. C. Cottle, Government Printer.

Diaz, Hugo. 1995. *Sri Lanka Poverty Assessment.* World Bank Report No. 13431-CE, Country Management Unit-A, South Asia Region.

Gamburd, Michele Ruth. 2008. *Breaking the Ashes: The Culture of Illicit Liquor in Sri Lanka.* Ithaca: Cornell University Press.

Harris, Elizabeth J. 2006. *Theravada Buddhism and the British Encounter: Religious, Missionary, and Colonial Experience in Nineteenth Century Sri Lanka.* London: Routledge.

Jayasuriya, J.E. 1976. *Educational Policies and Progress During British Rule in Ceylon (Sri Lanka).* Colombo: Associated Educational Publishers.

Jayaweera, Swarna. 1973. Education Policy in the Early Twentieth Century. In *University of Ceylon History of Ceylon*, vol. 3, ed. K.M. de Silva, 461–475. Colombo: Colombo Apothecaries and Peradeniya: University of Ceylon.

Jayaweera, Swarna. 1985. Women and Education. In *UN Decade for Women: Progress and Achievements of Women in Sri Lanka*, 47–68. Colombo: Centre for Women's Research.

Langdon, Samuel. 1884. *Punchi Nona, a Story of Female Education and Village Life in Ceylon.* London: T. Woolmer.

Meegama, S.A. 2012. *Famine, Fevers and Fear: The State and Disease in British Colonial Sri Lanka.* Dehiwela: Sridevi.

Mitra, Raktim, Guy E.J. Faulkner, Ron N. Buliung, and Michelle R. Stone. 2014. Do Parental Perceptions of the Neighborhood Environment Influence Children's Independent Mobility? Evidence from Toronto, Canada. *Urban Studies* 51 (16): 3401–3419.

Peebles, Patrick. 1995. *Social Change in Nineteenth Century Ceylon.* New Delhi: Navrang.

Ranasinha, A.G. 1950. *Census of Ceylon 1946: Vol. I, Part I: General Report.* Colombo: The Ceylon Government Press.

Risseeuw, Carla. 1988. *The Fish Don't Talk About the Water: Gender Transformation, Power, and Resistance Among Women in Sri Lanka.* Leiden: E. J. Brill.

Ryan, Bryce. 1993 [1953]. *Caste in Modern Ceylon: The Sinhalese System in Transition.* New Delhi: Navrang.

Sri Lanka, Department of Census and Statistics. 1997. *Changing Role of Women in Sri Lanka*. Colombo: Ministry of Finance and Planning.

Sri Lanka, Department of Census and Statistics. 2012. *Census of Population and Housing 2011: Basic Population Information by Districts and Divisional Secretary Divisions*. Colombo: Ministry of Finance and Planning.

Stirrat, R.L. 1988. *On the Beach: Fishermen, Fishwives, and Fishtraders in Post-colonial Lanka*. Delhi: Hindustan Publishing Corporation.

United Nations Children's Emergency Fund (UNICEF). 2010. Education for All: Global Monitoring Report. http://www.unesco.org/education/GMR2006/full/chapt8_eng.pdf. Accessed 22 Jan 2017.

United Nations Children's Emergency Fund (UNICEF). 2016. State of the World's Children. Statistical Tables. https://www.unicef.org/infobycountry/sri_lanka_statistics.html. Accessed 22 Jan 2017.

Wickremeratne, L.A. 1970. 1865 and the Changes in Education Policies. *Modern Ceylon Studies* 1 (1): 84–93.

Wickremeratne, L.A. 1973. Economic Development in the Plantation Sector, c 1900–1947. In *University of Ceylon History of Ceylon*, vol. 3, ed. K.M. de Silva, 428–445. Colombo: Colombo Apothecaries and Peradeniya: University of Ceylon.

Williams, G.S. 1885. *Administrative Report for the Northwestern Province 1885*. Colombo: Government Press.

Winslow, Deborah. 1994. Status and Context: Sri Lankan Potter Women Reconsidered After Fieldwork in India. *Comparative Studies in Society and History* 36: 2–36.

Winslow, Deborah. 2003. Potters' Progress: Hybridity and Accumulative Change in Rural Sri Lanka. *The Journal of Asian Studies* 62 (1): 43–70.

Winslow, Deborah. 2009. The Village Clay: Recursive Innovations and Community Self-Fashioning Among Sinhalese Potters. *Journal of the Royal Anthropological Institute* (N.S.) 15: 254–275.

Winslow, Deborah. 2016. Living Life Forward: Technology, Time, and Society in a Sri Lankan Potter Community. *Economic Anthropology* 3 (2): 216–227.

World Bank. 2017. The World Bank in Sri Lanka. http://www.worldbank.org/en/country/srilanka/overview. Accessed 28 Jan 2018.

CHAPTER 13

Discussion and Conclusion—Reflections on the Impact of Education in South Asia: From Sri Lanka to Nepal

Helen E. Ullrich

Two themes occur throughout the chapters: gender roles and the impact of culture on the educational system. Intertwined with these themes are poverty, school availability, socioeconomic position, caste and religion, and western versus traditional education. The chapters at the beginning of this volume focus on the value of education. The middle chapters focus on the ways in which the educational system preserves the traditional hierarchy with Christianity as a way to become casteless. The closing chapters draw attention to both the value and the deficits of the educational system. These chapters show strengths of practical education as well as those of Western education. The tragedy of the Indian educational system is that too often the assumption is that poor or low caste individuals lack the ability or the interest in learning.

H. E. Ullrich
Tulane University
Medical School, New Orleans, LA, USA

© The Author(s) 2019
H. E. Ullrich (ed.), *The Impact of Education
in South Asia*, Anthropological Studies of Education,
https://doi.org/10.1007/978-3-319-96607-6_13

287

Case studies illustrate how individuals have negotiated and brought change to the culture and to the educational system. LeVine, Seymour, Mukhopadhyay, Ullrich, and Gold, C. Gujar, G. Gujar, and M. Gujar all depict the evolution toward increased female autonomy, educational options, and marital choice. These chapters illustrate the extent to which change in gender roles has resulted in women's increased education. Now the rewards for the educated woman are greater than the risks. Fifty years ago the risks were greater than the rewards. Even further back women were assaulted for venturing alone (Ullrich 1977: 96–97) and are still at risk for assault. In their initial studies LeVine, Seymour, and Mukhopadhyay portray education as a detriment to a woman's marital options and reputation. More recently it has become an asset.

The longitudinal studies of LeVine, Mukhopadhyay, Seymour, Ullrich, Gold, and Winslow all have depicted the impact of culture on education in their communities. Mukhopadhyay, Ullrich, and Seymour present the challenges which education poses for patrifocal cultures, as well as changes in increased opportunities for women. In contrast, the sisterly threesome— C. Gujar, G. Gujar, and M. Gujar—show appreciation for their father's support and arrangements at a time when patrifocal ideals and modesty concerns limited most of their female classmates' educations. Their portrayal, as does those of the other longitudinal studies, indicates the challenges to obtain an education when there is limited school availability.

The chapters that focus on Dalits poignantly portray the negative aspects of the government educational system. Caste discrimination most harshly affects people of Scheduled Castes and Scheduled Tribes. Paik and Vasavi relate the challenges and the overt/covert discrimination experienced in the neighboring states of Maharashtra and Karnataka. Paik in her interviews with Matang women reveals the discrimination they endured to obtain an education and professional achievement. Positive role models have been significant, even essential, in their career trajectories.

Vasavi in her case study of a Dalit's waiting interminably for interviews and an appointment as headmaster illustrates his determination for a job in the government educational system. This provides a stark example of the broken government educational system. The irony is that rather than facilitating Dalit education and professional progress, the reserved positions have fueled others' resentment. Reserved positions for members of the SC and ST maintain social discrimination by highlighting students' caste identity. Dalits who earn first classes (85% and above) in their examinations remain in the "reserved seat" category, giving their caste status more importance than their accomplishments. In contrast, non-SC/ST students may proudly state they have "Merit seats" in recognition of their high academic scores.

Burkhart in his paper on schooling and identity focuses on the caste-lessness of Christians. Although many may have converted from lower castes and Dalits, others are from high castes. Christianity then provides an alternate sense of identity along with a tradition of excellent education. While this chapter focuses on Christian identity, it also indicates concerns for equitable treatment and a belief in equal status regardless of family origin or gender identity.

Winslow and Ullrich through case studies portray the positive aspects and increased value of education. Sri Lanka is essentially a literate country in contrast to Totagadde, Karnataka where illiteracy among the lower caste elders remains common. Kumar in her chapter on the hidden and overt curricula reveals the many layers of educational institutions and their respective quality. The education available for those in poverty implies that the practical education, which Rosin describes, may be more appropriate to their lives. Moreover it may be more rigorous and useful than attending school where the teachers are often absent or punitive. The treatment that C. Gujar, G. Gujar, and M. Gujar endured in their schooling would have discouraged less determined students and those with parents less supportive of education.

The authors have used a variety of methods in their research. Carol Mukhopadhyay has extensive statistical studies of women experiencing education at the Indian Institutes of Technology, as well as personal interviews. Susan Seymour compares different caste groups in the Old Town and New Town populations of Bhubaneswar through extensive observation, participant observation, and in-depth interviews. Deborah Winslow in her statistical analysis disproved her initial hypothesis that Potter women were slightly more highly educated than their husbands. The availability of schools was the determining factor in Sri Lanka, unlike LeVine's, Mukhopadhyay's, Ullrich's, and Seymour's studies which showed difficulty or fear of difficulty in arranging marriages for educated women. These authors in their case studies and overall perspectives on education in India, Sri Lanka, and Nepal have presented characteristics of global education, as well as information which educators will find useful in improving the education of the three countries.

The educational similarities and experiences in the different regions is perhaps more surprising than the differences. The types of education vary from traditional knowledge taught by an oral tradition to priestly knowledge to Western tradition. With the exception of Thomas Rosin's chapter, the focus in this book is on the Western type of education. Nita Kumar demonstrates the various types of schools from excellent to pathetically poor.

Before Western education and literacy, there were intelligent individuals in all social strata, as well as ignorant, stupid individuals. In some areas the castes were so segregated that the members of one caste had no idea of the beliefs and practices of other castes. In the 1970s when I did research on the Totagadde caste dialects, a group of Havik Brahmin women asked to accompany me to one of the non-Brahmin hamlets where they received generous hospitality. One Brahmin woman, curious about the Scheduled Caste hamlet, needed a reason to view that hamlet. Even though her family owned no cows, she used a search for a missing cow as justification for going to the SC hamlet. My linguistic research in the non-Brahmin, SC and ST hamlets stimulated Havik women's curiosity about the non-Brahmin Totagadde hamlets. They never questioned me, but wanted to expand their own worlds.

The non-Brahmins' reputation among Brahmins for being lazy lasted until land reform. The Divaru, a low-ranking non-Brahmin caste, quickly revealed the Brahmin stereotype to be a fallacy. In managing their own land with caste cooperation, hard work, and intelligence, they rapidly earned respect and found prosperity. Tom Rosin and Nita Kumar both argue that informal education may have more practical value than the rote learning often required in government schools. Tom Rosin's chapter on Rajasthani farmers, emphasizing their practical knowledge as a precursor to Western education and activism, presents the skills of the traditional farmer in mathematics knowledge as a guarantee for the fair distribution of services and goods. Their formally educated sons, in turn, used their knowledge to seek democracy for Rajasthan.

Although education is compulsory in Nepal, India, and Sri Lanka, gender, socioeconomic status, school availability, and caste differentials still separate those receiving an excellent education from those dropping out of the inadequately run government schools. Illiterate generations are nonetheless giving way to increasing numbers of educated men and women. With succeeding generations, the opportunities an educated person enjoys have stimulated the encouragement of further education with the result that changes in the social structure include a rise in the age of marriage and an impact on health and nutrition.

The positive value which Gold's three co-authors portrayed in writing about their personal experiences shocked her, as she was aware of the inadequacies of their education and the difficulties they had obtaining the jobs for which they had trained. Their focus was on their achievements and self-confidence, which they attributed to education. Despite failing to realize their occupational goals, they value their education. They have educations equivalent to men's, believe themselves to be as capable as their husbands, and are earning equivalent salaries. This forms a sharp contrast with the US state of Louisiana, whose current governor's wife, Donna Edwards, pointed out recently that, "Women in Louisiana earn just 66% of what men earn. For women of color, the numbers are even worse, 49% for African American women and 52% for Hispanic women..." (*New Orleans Advocate* 8A: 8, Wednesday November 15, 2017).

The significance of the Indian family in decisions about a girl's future is a theme throughout many of the chapters. In focusing on girls' pursuit of science and engineering degrees, Mukhopadhyay's assumption is that individuals' internal cultural models for decision-making unite culture, the family, and cognition. Family support or lack of family support meshes nicely with Gujar women, Old Town and New Town women, as well as Totagadde women. In the 1980s one Totagadde mother urged her daughter to study IT in college. The daughter refused and instead pursued a B.Com. By 2011, many Totagadde women were in the IT field. Those women not only had supportive parents, but also supportive grandparents. In contrast, other families educated their daughters, but regarded the workplace as unsuitable for women. Some parents, especially mothers, were critical of their married daughters who found employment. Others were proud that their daughters found profitable and interesting jobs. As in Gold, C. Gujar, G. Gujar, and M. Gujar, the husbands were proud of their employed wives. In 2011, one suitor's mother's brother was trying to persuade a Totagadde girl's father's younger brother to convince the girl, who was studying for an advanced IT degree, to consider marriage. The father's brother firmly indicated that the girl planned to finish her education and have appropriate employment before marrying, a plan which she followed. This further indicates Mukhopadhyay's importance of the family in facilitating a girl's goals.

Mukhopadhyay writes of the higher quality education given sons in contrast to daughters. This resonates with my observations, as well as those of Seymour's, Levine's, Gold, C. Gujar, G. Gujar, and M. Gujar's chapters but contrasts with Winslow's chapter on Sri Lankan education. Her discussion of examinations to enter some public (private) schools also reflects my experience with the current Totagadde generation (grandchildren) who married software engineers employed in Bangalore.

Although Ullrich portrays a more positive view of education in Totagadde, Karnataka, members of the Scheduled Tribes there have experienced similar discrimination as Dalits elsewhere. Loans for their children's educations and for establishing their own businesses are primary reasons that members of an ST female microlending group borrow money. This group has also educational purposes and is a support group for its members. The group feared one member whose young daughter tested into a government English-medium boarding school, which provided her with room, board, clothing, books, and all expenses of education, would miss her daughter so much that she would remove her from the boarding school. They emphasized to the mother the importance of education for her daughter's future. The daughter has continued in school, and in 2017 had already earned her first Pre-University Certificate (PUC) (11th grade certificate) and was studying for her second PUC (12th grade certificate).

Traditions of prepubertal marriage once severely limited educational opportunities for women. The availability of a college education, which provides women with the qualifications for employment, has contributed to the end of prepubertal marriages. The principle challenges formerly faced by an educated woman were the difficulty or fear of difficulty in arranging her marriage. Whether in Nepal, Bhubaneswar, a Karnataka village, or at Indian Institutes of Technology, finding a groom for an educated daughter was a challenge. Yet when educated men started demanding a dowry for uneducated, but not educated, women in the Karnataka village, Totagadde, and a mother-in-law boasted that her daughter-in-law was more highly educated than her son, parents realized that education enhanced a woman's marriage prospects. When suitors began seeking educated women, parents gave priority to education. This occurred in Bhubaneswar, Karnataka, Rajasthan, Sri Lanka, Nepal—in other words throughout the areas studied.

The freedom from family chores Mukhopadhyay describes is typical of urban Karnataka dwellers, as well as Totagadde Brahmins, Scheduled Tribes, and Divarus. If at all possible, members of all Totagadde castes give priority to schooling and employment over family chores. This applies to sons and daughters, as parents strictly protect their children's study time. Grandparents vary. Some give priority to grandsons and expect granddaughters to be at their beck and call.

Finding time to study while obtaining an education was a challenge for women in North India. Their domestic duties took precedence over their studies. Employed educated Rajasthani Gujar women received self-confidence and prestige from their jobs, but their domestic chores took priority over their studies and professional responsibilities. This formed a sharp contrast with Havik Brahmin women who rarely had domestic duties before their marriage. This pattern of learning household skills after marriage originated with those married before puberty and generally extended to women studying in college. Their education has priority over any domestic responsibilities. Among Havik Brahmins, including even those in poverty, job or education takes precedence over housework. The reasoning is that they will learn how to do housework after marriage. Taught by their mothers-in-law, they would learn the cooking and housework suitable to their husbands' households. In 2017, the mothers of Totagadde non-Brahmin and Scheduled Tribe women in boarding schools and college give priority to their daughters' education. Just as brides who married before puberty learned about housework after marriage, so do brides marrying after a bachelor's degree or a master's degree. One very angry Havik bride in an extended family was expected to do all the housework and cooking in deference to her sister-in-law's employment. After a short period of time, the extended family split into two nuclear families. However, in non-Brahmin Totagadde households the amount of housework the family expects varies from none to abuse. In the case of illness in a Havik Brahmin household, a girl may stop her education to help at home. This also applies to Brahmin boys who have quit college to help an ill grandmother or a father who has had a stroke. The difference is that the family may hide family illness from a son for fear he will give up his education in filial devotion, while expecting a daughter to come home.

The availability of school has made a major difference in education in India, Nepal, and Sri Lanka. Initially many women needed chaperones to travel to other villages or within the same city. Without public transportation or a school within walking distance, women had little access to education. This explains how women in one village with bus service to town could commute to college while nearby towns had no transportation to send their students to college. With the establishment of bus service, girls were more likely to attend nearby colleges while boys were more likely to attend more rigorous institutions at a distance. Whenever possible, the Rajasthani and Karnataka female students traveled by bus in groups to college. Both groups of brave women feared and endured harassment. When Havik girls traveled by bus to school, they came prepared with pins with which to stick harassers. The women reasoned that boys or men who complained about being stuck would develop a reputation as harassers and lose respect. Hence they would remain silent and desist from harassing women. Conventions of modesty prevented Rajasthani girls from traveling by bicycle or motorcycle. This contrasts with the first Totagadde educated employed woman who bought her own motor scooter for commuting to work while living at home.

When one had relatives in a city, both girls and boys stayed with these relatives during their education. In some cases such as the Gujars, a father or family rented an apartment or house where a parent could stay while their children attended college. Some relatives came to Totagadde to stay while attending the local government school or commuting to the nearby town for college. Even those who would have preferred that their relatives' children went elsewhere hosted them. One never knew when reciprocity would allow one's own children to reside with relatives while studying in a distant town. This arrangement has enhanced close kinship ties, especially for women whose parents were reluctant to have them live in hostels. However, hostels with strict visiting rules provided parents with the security to allow their daughters to reside there while in college or at work. In the Totagadde area, female students in 2017 chose hostel life over residing with kinfolk.

Some families, both rural and urban, hired autorickshaws to convey their daughters to school. Later the same private schools had vans to convey the students to and from school. The relocation of families to urban areas, the sending of children to reside with relatives employed in urban areas, and the creation of hostels where families believed their daughters were safe all illustrate the greater accessibility of schools in urban areas. From Nepal to Sri Lanka, in Rajasthan and Karnataka, schools proliferated. Private (Indian public) schools both of the regional language and English-medium created more options to the original missionary or convent schools and the government schools.

In spite of the Indian constitution, which outlawed caste, affiliation with a caste has a significant impact on the quality of education students receive. Although I have heard Potter children praised for their intellectual brilliance, Dalits have rarely been the recipient of encouragement from others. Paik's insightful portrayal through Dalit interviews provides a valuable dimension showing the success of those with positive role models and encouragement in "public" (private) schools contrasting with the boredom in the government school system. Teachers too often assume that Dalits lack motivation and support from their parents. If only the teachers realized the value of encouragement and belief in their students' potential, there would be a more robust educational system.

The gender differential appears as a South Asian phenomenon. Longitudinal studies reveal unexpected changes as the value of education for women has increased with regard to earning potential and marriage arrangements. Fifty years ago and even more recently, finding a more highly educated groom proved difficult for an educated woman. Education as an asset occurred gradually and in increments. Totagadde women, as an example, who married before puberty, were often illiterate. Husbands or their school-going children taught their wives or mothers to read. This is still occurring among Dalits with illiterate mothers being taught to write their names by their children in college. Then women married slightly later, before puberty but after a primary school education. When college education became important for marriage arrangements, parents sent their daughters to college. Proud parents and grandparents have told me of their granddaughters' jobs in foreign countries—both before and after their marriages. But the gender gap in education may also be related to poverty and caste. School availability has resulted in less of a gender gap as revealed in Deborah Winslow's chapter on Sri Lanka.

Poverty is also a factor limiting the quality and quantity of education. Nita Kumar's chapter, in describing the different types of schools in India, rates the public (private in the United States) and elite missionary schools as those providing the most rigorous education. On the other extreme the government schools, which teach the poorest individuals of all castes, provide the least rigorous education. Many of these teachers appear to believe that their students lack the intelligence to learn and so provide uninspiring classes with the result that many students quit. As LeVine indicates, caste often parallels economic status with those from castes of higher economic status receiving the superior education.

The chapters of this book eloquently illustrate the types and qualities of schools in India. Kumar focuses on the "hidden curriculum," the implicit manner in which teachers encourage or discourage students.

Paik, through ethnographic research and interviews, provides a poignant view of the school failure to recognize Dalit intelligence with tragic unrealized potential. She contrasts this with successful Dalit professional women, one of whom had a father who provided her with a positive role model and a private (public) school education. Vasavi's case study further illustrates the professional challenges which a Dalit experiences. In fact, her view is that reserved seats have increased Dalit discrimination.

Paik and Vasavi poignantly describe the discrimination which the female Dalit experiences. LeVine shows that women in Nepal were subject to discrimination; as does Ullrich, for Karnataka; Gold et al., for Gujars in Rajasthan; Mukhopadhyay, for students at the prestigious IIT; and Seymour for those in Odisha. The situation has changed for the women of the higher castes and in some cases for educated women of lower castes. Seymour (2002: 110) reports "In 1965–67, *all* eligible girls and boys from middle and upper-status families in both the Old Town and the New Capital attended school. In the Old Town the majority remained in the school through the secondary level (11th Standard) with some continuing on to college and even acquiring postgraduate degrees." Positive as my view of Totagadde seems, Susan Seymour's research shows that education in Bhubaneswar was more readily available. Once a woman has achieved her education, Ann Gold et al. noted her three co-authors had developed self-confidence and a realization that they were equal to their husbands and received the same salary for the same job. Deborah Winslow indicates that in Sri Lanka school availability and not gender has been the limiting factor for obtaining an education. Indeed, in her research Sri Lanka has gender parity in which women's education is on par with men's. Moreover, Burkhart notes that among the adult Lutherans in his Polar, Tamilnadu study, more women than men stopped school after elementary school; however the same number dropped out of high school with almost as many women as men completing high school. Of four individual who went beyond high school, three were men and only one was a woman. Although Christians converted from many castes, the casteless nature of Christianity may have provided greater self-confidence and a belief in success.

Queries for future research might focus on the challenges of getting an education and seeking employment. Caste, poverty, school availability, gender inequality may persist throughout life as they do in the United States. Another possibility is that education and professional skills result in an achievement-based society, where caste, poverty, and gender inequality become secondary to a class-based society. The implications for an improved government school system in India, in which the teachers utilize their skills to provide an optimum learning situation rather than perpetuating the vast difference in education for the poor and the wealthy, are critical. Moreover, a good government school system might draw students of all castes and socioeconomic levels.

REFERENCES

New Orleans Advocate 8A: 8, Wednesday November 15, 2017.

Seymour, Susan. 2002. Family and Gender Systems in Transition: A Thirty-Five-Year Perspective. In *Everyday Life in South Asia*, eds. Diane P. Mines and Sarah Lamb. Bloomington: Indiana University Press.

Ullrich, Helen E. 1977. Caste Differences Between Brahmin and Non-Brahmin Women in a South Indian Village. In *Sexual Stratification: A Cross-Cultural View*, ed. Alice Schlegel, 94–108. New York: Columbia University Press.

INDEX

A
Affirmative action, 138, 145, 147, 158, 211
Ambedkar, B.R., 113, 116, 123, 125, 131, 133, 138, 157

B
Berreman, Dwight, 239
Bhadani, B.L., 238
Bharucha, Rustom, 220, 226
Bourdieu, Pierre, 124, 132, 133
Brahmani, 112, 123–125, 130
Brahmanical hegemony, 112, 123
British colonialism, Sri Lanka
Education Ordinance of 1920, 273
education policy, 3
support for female education, 190
Burkhart, Geoffrey L., 3, 167, 181, 183, 184, 289, 296

C
Caste

caste differentiation, 290
caste discrimination, 116, 122, 123, 126, 127, 130, 274, 288
"castelessness", 170, 289
caste oppression, 111
caste specific, 112, 125
cultural politics of caste, 165, 177
Divaru, 189, 190, 200–202, 209, 210, 212, 214, 216–218, 290
dominant caste, 120, 123, 127, 233
elite caste, 13, 125
Gujars, 87, 97, 98, 109, 294, 296
high caste status; Brahman, 19, 123–126, 129; Brahmin, 4, 8, 22, 24, 25, 32, 38, 42, 44, 47, 51, 54, 86, 123, 138, 147, 148, 190, 191, 194–196, 200, 202, 204, 206, 209–211, 214–218, 290, 293; Havik Brahmin, 189, 190, 193, 196, 200, 202, 204, 212, 214, 216, 290, 293
humiliation, 126, 178
Jat, 86, 221, 224–228, 231–235, 237, 238, 241

© The Editor(s) (if applicable) and The Author(s) 2019
H. E. Ullrich (ed.), *The Impact of Education in South Asia*, Anthropological Studies of Education,
https://doi.org/10.1007/978-3-319-96607-6

CPSIA information can be obtained
at www.ICGtesting.com
Printed in the USA
LVHW072148070119
603100LV00016B/150/P